June 7–8, 2012
Toronto, Ontario, Canada

Association for Computing Machinery

Advancing Computing as a Science & Profession

NOSSDAV '12

Proceedings of the 2012 ACM Workshop on

Network and Operating System Support for Digital Audio and Video

Sponsored by:
ACM SIGMM

In cooperation with:
ACM SIGCOMM & ACM SIGOPS

Association for Computing Machinery

Advancing Computing as a Science & Profession

The Association for Computing Machinery
2 Penn Plaza, Suite 701
New York, New York 10121-0701

Copyright © 2012 by the Association for Computing Machinery, Inc. (ACM). Permission to make digital or hard copies of portions of this work for personal or classroom use is granted without fee provided that copies are not made or distributed for profit or commercial advantage and that copies bear this notice and the full citation on the first page. Copyright for components of this work owned by others than ACM must be honored. Abstracting with credit is permitted. To copy otherwise, to republish, to post on servers or to redistribute to lists, requires prior specific permission and/or a fee. Request permission to republish from: permissions@acm.org or Fax +1 (212) 869-0481.

For other copying of articles that carry a code at the bottom of the first or last page, copying is permitted provided that the per-copy fee indicated in the code is paid through www.copyright.com.

Notice to Past Authors of ACM-Published Articles
ACM intends to create a complete electronic archive of all articles and/or other material previously published by ACM. If you have written a work that has been previously published by ACM in any journal or conference proceedings prior to 1978, or any SIG Newsletter at any time, and you do NOT want this work to appear in the ACM Digital Library, please inform permissions@acm.org, stating the title of the work, the author(s), and where and when published.

ISBN: 978-1-4503-1430-5 (Digital)

ISBN: 978-1-4503-1730-6 (Print)

Additional copies may be ordered prepaid from:

ACM Order Department
PO Box 30777
New York, NY 10087-0777, USA

Phone: 1-800-342-6626 (USA and Canada)
+1-212-626-0500 (Global)
Fax: +1-212-944-1318
E-mail: acmhelp@acm.org
Hours of Operation: 8:30 am – 4:30 pm ET

Printed in the USA

Welcome to NOSSDAV 2012!

It is with pleasure that we welcome you to Toronto, Canada, for the 22nd edition of the ACM Workshop on Network and Operating Systems Support for Digital Audio and Video (NOSSDAV) from June 7-8, 2012. Similar to previous editions, the workshop covers topics in network and system support for multimedia, such as cloud and peer-to-peer system architectures, media streaming, distribution and storage support, multimedia communications and system security, multi-core and many-core architecture support, networked GPUs, graphics and virtual environments, networked games and real-time immersive systems, operating systems, middleware and network support for multimedia, Web 2.0 systems and social networks, as well as wireless networks and embedded systems for multimedia applications.

In addition to reporting on the latest academic research in the field, NOSSDAV is also known for its fruitful discussions and for educating researchers about the views and needs of the industry, which have influenced the direction of many researchers who have attended the workshop in the past. This tradition of the mix of academic and industry views continues with NOSSDAV 2012, where we welcome our keynote speakers Dr. Ali C. Begen from Cisco Systems and Prof. Wu-chi Feng from Portland State University, who will keep us up-to-date with both the quickly changing reality of networked multimedia industry, as well as the latest developments in academic research in the field, respectively. NOSSDAV 2012 also provides a mixed industry-academia panel for discussions of the hottest research topics in network and system support for multimedia.

NOSSDAV 2012 received 47 submissions from around the globe. As is common for high quality workshops, each paper was first reviewed by at least three reviews independently, and then the reviewers discussed the paper together and under the moderation of TPC chairs. Based on the results of both the reviewers' scores and the discussions, the papers were then ranked by the TPC chairs, and after careful considerations we accepted 17 papers for inclusion in the final NOSSDAV 2012 proceedings. We are very pleased with the overall quality of the final program, and we hope that researchers and practitioners in the field will benefit from and enjoy it as well.

We take this opportunity to thank our program committee who did an outstanding job with their timely and high quality reviews, allowing us to offer you the final program. We also thank the ACM and the ACM SIGMM for their sponsorship, as well as ACM SIGOPS and ACM SIGCOMM for their cooperation. Last but certainly not least, we thank the authors and attendees of NOSSDAV 2012 and wish them an enjoyable and fruitful workshop.

Sincerely,

Baochun Li, University of Toronto, Canada
Shervin Shirmohammadi, University of Ottawa, Canada
Program Co-Chairs

Table of Contents

NOSSDAV 2012 Welcome Message iii
Baochun Li *(University of Toronto)*, Shervin Shirmohamadi *(University of Ottawa)*

NOSSDAV 2012 Organization List vii

NOSSDAV 2012 Sponsors and Supporters viii

Keynote Speech

- **TV Everywhere** 1
  Ali C. Begen *(Cisco)*

Session 1: HTTP Streaming

- **Why are State-of-the-Art Flash-Based Multi-Tiered Storage Systems Performing Poorly for HTTP Video Streaming?** 3
  Moonkyung Ryu, Hyojun Kim, Umakishore Ramachandran *(Georgia Institute of Technology)*

- **What Happens When HTTP Adaptive Streaming Players Compete for Bandwidth?** 9
  Saamer Akhshabi, Lakshmi Anantakrishnan *(Georgia Institute of Technology)*, Ali C. Begen *(Cisco Syatems)*, Constantine Dovrolis *(Georgia Institute of Technology)*

- **To Chunk or Not to Chunk: Implications for HTTP Streaming Video Server Performance** 15
  Jim Summers, Tim Brecht *(University of Waterloo)*, Derek Eager *(University of Saskatchewan)*, Bernard Wong *(University of Waterloo)*

- **Interactions Between HTTP Adaptive Streaming and TCP** 21
  Jairo Esteban, Steven A. Benno, Andre Beck, Yang Guo, Volker Hilt, Ivica Rimac *(Alcatel-Lucent)*

Session 2: Cloud and Middleware Support

- **Quiver: A Middleware for Distributed Gaming** 27
  Giuseppe Reina *(Technicolor)*, Ernst Biersack *(Eurecom)*, Christophe Diot *(Technicolor)*

- **Cloud Transcoder: Bridging the Format and Resolution Gap Between Internet Videos and Mobile Devices** 33
  Zhenhua Li *(Peking University)*, Yan Huang, Gang Liu, Fuchen Wang *(Tencent Research)*, Zhi-Li Zhang *(University of Minnesota - Twin Cities)*, Yafei Dai *(Peking University)*

- **A Content Replication Scheme for Wireless Mesh Networks** 39
  Zakwan Al-Arnaout, Qiang Fu, Marcus Frean *(Victoria University of Wellington)*

Session 3: Multiview and Panoramic Video

- **Evaluation of Distribution of Panoramic Video Sequences in the eXplorative Television Project** 45
  Peter Quax, Panagiotis Issaris, Wouter Vanmontfort, Wim Lamotte *(Hasselt University)*

- **Collaborative View Synthesis for Interactive Multi-View Video Streaming** 51
  Fei Chen, Jiangchuan Liu *(Simon Fraser University)*, Edith Cheuk-Han Ngai *(Uppsala University)*, Yuan Zhao *(Simon Fraser University)*

Keynote Speech

- **Streaming Media Evolution: Where to Now?** 57
  Wu-chi Feng *(Portland State University)*

Session 4: Streaming

- **On Tile Assignment for Region-of-Interest Video Streaming in a Wireless LAN** 59
  Ravindra Guntur, Wei Tsang Ooi *(National University of Singapore)*

- **Minimizing Server Throughput for Low-Delay Live Streaming in Content Delivery Networks** 65
  Fen Zhou *(Telecom Bretagne)*, Shakeel Ahmad *(De Montfort University)*,
  Eliya Buyukkaya *(Telecom Bretagne)*, Raouf Hamzaoui *(De Montfort University)*,
  Gwendal Simon *(Telecom Bretagne)*

- **SmartTransfer: Transferring Your Mobile Multimedia Contents at the "Right" Time** 71
  Yichuan Wang, Xin Liu *(University of California, Davis)*,
  Angela Nicoara *(Deutsche Telekom Innovation Laboratories)*,
  Ting-An Lin, Cheng-Hsin Hsu *(National Tsing Hua University)*

Session 5: Content Sharing

- **Content and Geographical Locality in User-Generated Content Sharing Systems** 77
  Kévin Huguenin *(École Polytechnique Fédérale de Lausanne)*,
  Anne-Marie Kermarrec, Konstantinos Kloudas *(INRIA Rennes - Bretagne Atlantique)*,
  François Taïani *(Lancaster University)*

- **Video Sharing in Online Social Networks: Measurement and Analysis** 83
  Haitao Li, Haiyang Wang, Jiangchuan Liu *(Simon Fraser Unversity)*, Ke Xu *(Tsinghua University)*

Session 6: Video Compression

- **Sensor-Assisted Camera Motion Analysis and Motion Estimation Improvement for H.264/AVC Video Encoding** 89
  Guanfeng Wang, Haiyang Ma, Beomjoo Seo, Roger Zimmermann *(National University of Singapore)*

- **CAME: Cloud-Assisted Motion Estimation for Mobile Video Compression and Transmission** 95
  Yuan Zhao, Lei Zhang, Xiaoqiang Ma, Jiangchuan Liu *(Simon Fraser University)*, Hongbo Jiang *(Huazhong University of Science and Technology)*

- **Understanding the Impact of Inter-Lens and Temporal Stereoscopic Video Compression** 101
  Wu-chi Feng, Feng Liu *(Portland State University)*

Author Index 107

NOSSDAV'12 Organization

Program Co-Chairs: Baochun Li, University of Toronto, Canada
Shervin Shirmohammadi, University of Ottawa, Canada

Program Committee: Maha Abdallah, LIP6, France
Dewan T. Ahmed, King Saud University, Saudi Arabia
Kevin Almeroth, University of California, Santa Barbara, USA
Ali C. Begen, Cisco Systems, USA
Ernst Biersack, Institute Eurecom, France
Doreen Bohnstedt, TU Darmstadt, Germany
Surendar Chandra, FXPAL, USA
Kuan-Ta Chen, Academia Sinica, Taiwan
Songqing Chen, George Mason University, USA
Mark Claypool, Worcester Polytechnic Institute, USA
Wu-chang Feng, Portland State University, USA
Wu-chi Feng, Portland State University, USA
Carsten Griwodz, University of Oslo, Norway
Yang Guo, Bell Labs/Alcatel-Lucent, USA
Pal Halvorsen, University of Oslo, Norway
Behnoosh Hariri, Google Research, USA
Mohamed Hefeeda, Simon Fraser University, Canada
Shun-Yun Hu, Academia Sinica, Taiwan
Cheng Huang, Microsoft Research, USA
Jin Li, Microsoft Research, USA
Kang Li, University of Georgia, USA
Jiangchuan Liu, Simon Fraser University, Canada
Yong Liu, Polytechnic Institute of New York University, USA
Andreas Mauthe, Lancaster University, UK
Ketan Mayer-Patel, University of North Carolina at Chapel Hill, USA
Klara Nahrstedt, University of Illinois at Urbana-Champaign, USA
Wei Tsang Ooi, National University of Singapore, Singapore
Sanjay Rao, Purdue University, USA
Reza Rejaie, University of Oregon, USA
Jose Saldana, University of Zaragoza, Spain
Henning Schulzrinne, Columbia University, USA
Karsten Schwan, Georgia Institute of Technology, USA
Ishan Vaishnavi, Docomo Labs, USA
Mea Wang, University of Calgary, Canada
Chuan Wu, University of Hong Kong, Hong Kong
Roger Zimmermann, National University of Singapore, Singapore
Michael Zink, University of Massachusetts, Amherst, USA

NOSSDAV'12 Sponsor & Supporters

Sponsor:

In cooperation with:

SIGOPS
ACM SIG on Operating Systems

TV Everywhere

Ali C. Begen
Cisco
Toronto, ON Canada
abegen@cisco.com

Abstract

As more and more PC and handheld like devices get connected, consumers are migrating to the Web to watch their favorite shows and movies. Increasingly, the Web is coming to digital TV, which incorporates movie downloads and streaming. Similarly, consumers also want their TV content on alternative devices. What does this mean for service and content providers? What do they have to do to not lose their subscribers and revenue streams? This talk overviews the TV Everywhere technologies available for integrating the emerging over-the-top content into a managed network and making premium content accessible for unmanaged devices. The talk also provides a few real-world use cases.

Categories & Subject Descriptors:

C.2 [COMPUTER-COMMUNICATION NETWORKS]: General

Keywords: Adaptive streaming; over-the-top video; TV everywhere; content delivery.

Bio

Ali C. Begen is with the Video and Content Platforms Research and Advanced Development Group at Cisco. His interests include networked entertainment, Internet multimedia, transport protocols and content distribution. Ali is currently working on architectures for next-generation video transport and distribution over IP networks, and he is an active contributor in the IETF in these areas.

Ali holds a Ph.D. degree in electrical and computer engineering from Georgia Tech. He received the Best Student-paper Award at IEEE ICIP 2003, and the Most-cited Paper Award from Elsevier Signal Processing: Image Communication in 2008. He is a member of the IEEE and ACM. His public Web site is http://ali.begen.net.

Why are State-of-the-art Flash-based Multi-tiered Storage Systems Performing Poorly for HTTP Video Streaming?

Moonkyung Ryu
College of Computing
Georgia Institute of Technology
Atlanta, GA, USA
mkryu@gatech.edu

Hyojun Kim
College of Computing
Georgia Institute of Technology
Atlanta, GA, USA
hyojun.kim@cc.gatech.edu

Umakishore Ramachandran
College of Computing
Georgia Institute of Technology
Atlanta, GA, USA
rama@cc.gatech.edu

ABSTRACT

MLC flash memory is a promising technology for building a high-performance and cost-effective video streaming system when it is used as an intermediate level cache in a multi-tiered storage hierarchy. Therefore, we were quite surprised when through extensive measurements we found that two state-of-the-art flash-based multi-tiered storage systems (namely, flashcache and ZFS) have quite disappointing performance for HTTP video streaming using the DASH protocol. We have conducted a thorough analysis to understand the reasons for the poor performance of these two systems. In a nutshell, unless attention is paid to the unique performance characteristics of flash memory-based SSDs, we could end up with suboptimal or even poor performance as we discovered through experimentation with these two systems. Based on the analysis, we present design guidelines for building a cost-effective high-performance HTTP video streaming server.

Categories and Subject Descriptors

C.4 [**Computer Systems Organization**]: Performance of Systems

General Terms

Experimentation, Measurement, Performance

Keywords

Flash Memory, Solid-State Drive, Video-on-Demand, HTTP Video Streaming, Content Distribution Network

1. INTRODUCTION

There is proliferation of video on the Internet. Hulu [7], a web service that streams premium contents such as news, TV series, and shows, and Netflix [9], the largest subscription service for DVD rental and streaming video over the web, are huge successes.

Dynamic Adaptive Streaming over HTTP (DASH) [8] is a new paradigm of video streaming over the web currently being used by major content distributors, including Netflix. DASH does not depend on specialized video servers. Instead, DASH exploits off-the-shelf web servers. The advantage of this paradigm is that it can easily exploit the widely deployed content distribution network (CDN) infrastructure for the scalable video streaming service, and the firewall and NAT traversal problems can be greatly simplified. On the other hand, its weakness is that there is no QoS mechanism on the server side to guarantee video delivery. It relies on the large resource provisioning (i.e., CPU, RAM, storage capacity, storage and network bandwidth, etc.) that is customary with CDNs. This approach achieves simple system design, scalability, and jitter-free video streaming at the cost of large resource over-provisioning.

The video streaming system requires a number of hard disk drives (HDDs) both for capacity (to store the video library) and for bandwidth (to serve the video library). While the cost per gigabyte of HDDs has decreased significantly, the cost per bits-per-second of HDDs has not. Moreover, an array of HDDs consumes a lot of power (approx. 5-15 watts per drive) and generates a large amount of heat; therefore, more power is required for cooling a data center hosting a large array of disks. The amount of video content and the corresponding number of viewers are increasing explosively on the web. In addition, the DASH approach requires storage bandwidth over-provisioning for reliable video streaming service; therefore, the cost of storage for a large scale service is significant. For these reasons, the storage component of the video streaming system needs a careful re-evaluation to achieve higher throughput for the same dollar investment while lowering the power consumption and cooling costs.

Solid-State Drive (SSD) is a new storage device that is comprised of semiconductor memory chips (e.g., DRAM, Flash Memory, Phase Change Memory) to store and retrieve data rather than using the traditional spinning platters, a motor, and moving heads found in conventional magnetic disks. Among various types of SSDs, flash-based SSDs currently have the maximum penetration into modern computer systems. The advantages of flash-based SSDs are fast random read, low power consumption (approx. 0.1-1.3 watts per drive), and low heat dissipation due to the absence of the mechanical components. On the other hand, its high cost per gigabyte compared to magnetic disks, poor small random write performance, and limited lifetime are major concerns compared to the disks.

Though flash-based SSDs are attractive as an alternative to HDDs for video storage for all the above reasons, the cost per gigabyte for SSD is still significantly higher than HDDs. Moreover, despite the increasing affordability of SSDs, the

---

Permission to make digital or hard copies of all or part of this work for personal or classroom use is granted without fee provided that copies are not made or distributed for profit or commercial advantage and that copies bear this notice and the full citation on the first page. To copy otherwise, to republish, to post on servers or to redistribute to lists, requires prior specific permission and/or a fee.
NOSSDAV'12, June 7–8, 2012, Toronto, Ontario, Canada.
Copyright 2012 ACM 978-1-4503-1430-5/12/06 ...$10.00.

ratio of capacity costs of SSD to HDD is expected to remain fairly constant in the future since the bit density of HDDs is still continuously improving. Therefore, a viable architecture is to use the flash-based SSDs as an intermediate level between RAM and HDDs for caching hot contents. In our prior work [19], we explored the efficacy of such a design. In particular, we showed via simulation that low-end flash devices are ideal to incorporate in the design of such multi-tier video servers to reduce the overall capital expenditure and operating costs while achieving a high throughput.

While enterprise-level multi-tier storage systems (incorporating high-end Single Level Cell (SLC) flash memory-based SSDs) have been around for a while, they are not cost-effective for use as streaming video servers. Recently, commercial products have emerged that have incorporated low-cost Multi Level Cell (MLC) flash memory SSDs. Zettabyte File System (ZFS) [10] and Flashcache [5] are two state-of-the-art solutions that serve as good examples.

Our goal in this paper is to experimentally verify the performance of two commercial solutions that incorporate flash in their storage hierarchy, namely ZFS [10] and Flashcache [5], to serve as HTTP streaming servers embodying the DASH protocol. Based on our prior simulation work [19], our expectation is that these two systems will be ideal vehicles for realizing our vision of low-cost high-performance HTTP servers. However, our experimental results are surprising since neither of these two systems met our performance expectations. The core of the intellectual contribution of this paper is shedding light on the reasons for the poor performance of these two systems for HTTP video streaming. Unless otherwise mentioned, a *cache* refers to a flash memory SSD rather than RAM in this paper.

The unique contributions of our work are as follows:

1. We measure performance of two state-of-the-art flash memory caching systems, which are Zettabyte File System (ZFS) [10] and Flashcache [5]. By running an Apache [1] web server on these two systems, we evaluate the storage performance of the systems for video streaming using the DASH approach.

2. The performance of both these systems is surprisingly disappointing. We undertake an in-depth analysis to understand the reasons for the poor performance of both these systems for the video streaming workload.

3. Armed with the knowledge of the sources of poor performance of these state-of-the-art systems, we propose design guidelines for a high-performance HTTP video streaming server.

The rest of the paper is organized as follows. Section 2 provides the background about flash memory SSD and dynamic adaptive streaming over HTTP. In Section 3, we measure the performance of 3 different storage configurations, HDDs only, ZFS, and Flashcache, for HTTP video streaming using the DASH protocol. Section 4 analyzes the measurement result in detail. Section 5 presents guidelines for a high-performance HTTP video streaming server stemming from our experimental study. Our concluding remarks are presented in Section 6.

2. BACKGROUND

In this section, we briefly review two technologies central to the problem being addressed in this paper: flash-based SSDs and DASH protocol for video streaming.

2.1 Flash-based SSD

Flash memories, including NAND and NOR types, have a common physical restriction, namely, they must be erased before being written [12]. Flash memory can be written or read a single page at a time, but it has to be erased in an *erase block* unit. An erase block consists of a certain number of pages. In NAND flash memory, a page is similar to a HDD sector, and its size is usually 2 to 4 KBytes, while an erase block is typically 128 pages or more.

Flash memory also suffers from a limitation on the number of erase operations possible for each erase block. In SLC NAND flash memory, the expected number of erasures per block is 100,000 but is only 10,000 in two-bit MLC NAND flash memory.

An SSD is simply a set of flash memory chips packaged together with additional circuitry and a special piece of software called the Flash Translation Layer (FTL) [14, 17]. The additional circuitry may include a RAM buffer for storing meta-data associated with the internal organization of the SSD and a write buffer for optimizing the write performance of the SSD.

To avoid erasing and re-writing an entire block for every page modification, an FTL writes data out-of-place, remapping the logical page to a new physical location and marking the old page invalid. This requires maintaining some amount of free blocks into which new pages can be written. These free blocks are maintained by erasing previously written blocks to allow space occupied by invalid pages to be made available for new writes. This process is called *garbage collection*. FTL tries to run this process in the background as much as possible while the foreground I/O requests are idle, but it is not guaranteed, especially when a new clean block is needed instantly to write a new page. Due to random writes emanating from the upper layers of the operating system, a block may have valid pages and invalid pages. Therefore, when the garbage collector reclaims a block, the valid pages of the block need to be copied to another block. Thus, an external write may generate some additional unrelated writes internal to the device, a phenomenon referred to as *write amplification*.

2.2 Dynamic Adaptive Streaming over HTTP

Dynamic Adaptive Streaming over HTTP (DASH) [8] is a new paradigm for video streaming over the web. Rather than rely on the dedicated video servers of yesteryears, DASH exploits off-the-shelf web servers for video streaming. The protocol works as follows: A *video object* can be in two different forms; a single large file or multiple small *segment* files that have the same play-out duration, typically a few seconds long. Further, there may be multiple versions of the same video object, supporting different bitrates and different quality levels. Web servers on the Internet that constitute a CDN store these multiple versions of videos. A player (i.e., a client) can then request different segments at different bitrates depending on the state of the underlying network. If the video object is in the form of a single file, the player requests a segment using the byte ranges protocol of HTTP/1.1 [6]. On the other hand, when the video object is in the form of multiple small segment files, the player requests a segment file download. Notice that it is the player that decides the bitrate to request for any segment. The server treats requests for segments of video files similar to any other normal web request and does not do anything special. This greatly simplifies the server design, and allows the use of existing CDN systems without modification.

3. MEASUREMENT

In this section, we measure the performance of 3 differ-

	SSD A	SSD B
Model	INTEL X25-M G1	OCZ Core V2
Capacity	80 GB	124 GB
4KB Random Read Throughput	15.5 MB/s	14.8 MB/s
4KB Random Write Throughput	3.25 MB/s	0.02 MB/s

Table 1: MLC Flash Memory SSDs that were used for our experiments. Both SSDs have similar performance for small random reads. On the other hand, the different SSDs have significantly different small random write performance.

ent storage configurations of an HTTP streaming server using the DASH protocol: HDDs only, Flashcache, and ZFS. Apache [1] is used as the web server. We implement a workload generator that emulates a large number of concurrent DASH clients. To measure the storage subsystem performance exactly and to avoid network subsystem effects, the Apache web server and the workload generator run on the *same* machine communicating via a loop-back interface. The machine has Xeon 2.26 GHz Quad core processor with 4 GB RAM, and Linux kernel 2.6.32 is installed on it. Unless otherwise noted, *cache* in this paper refers to the flash device used as an intermediate level in the storage hierarchy and not RAM.

3.1 MLC Flash Memory SSDs

Table 1 lists the MLC flash memory SSDs we used for our experiments. Due to space limitations, we present only results with SSD A. However, the results with SSD B are similar.

3.2 DASH Workload

Zipf distribution is generally used in modeling the video access pattern of a video-on-demand (VoD) system, and typically a parameter value between 0.2 and 0.4 is chosen for the distribution [16]. We use 0.271 for the parameter in our study. For a test video sequence, we use *Valkaama* [3] which is available in the public domain. The video object is segmented into 10-second long segments, the total length of the video is about 78 minutes, the size is 1.06 GB, and the average bitrate is 2 Mbps. The video object is composed of 466 segment files. Though each segment has the same play-out time, the size of each segment is different since the video is encoded with a variable bit rate (VBR). In the DASH approach, a video object is encoded in a few different bitrates so that a client can adaptively select a bitrate according to the dynamically changing network state. In our experimental setup, the workload generator that emulates a number of client requests and the web server run on the same machine. Hence the network state is stable and the different bitrate profiles available in the web server for supporting the DASH protocol are not necessary. Moreover, for a controlled experiment and a fair comparison of results, it is better to use a single bitrate profile for the video, as we do in this study. We copy the video, and make 300 individual video objects.

In every t seconds (which is the inverse of the request rate), the workload generator selects a video object according to the zipf distribution. Next, it chooses a segment of the video object according to the uniform distribution; each segment of the video object has the same probability. The reason for using a uniform distribution is as follows. A large scale HTTP video streaming service like Netflix relies on the CDN infrastructure that widely deploys web cache servers near the edge networks. For an effective load balancing, a video segment (or object) is replicated to a number of web cache servers, and a client's request for the segment is directed to a web server holding the segment via request rout-

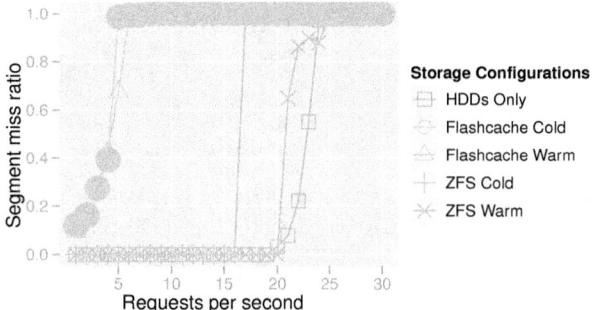

Figure 1: Segment miss ratio as a function of Request Rate.

ing techniques such as DNS routing, HTML rewriting [13], or anycasting [18]. For this reason, there is no guarantee that a client who downloaded a segment i of a video will download a next segment $i+1$ from the same server. The next segment can be served by other web servers that hold a replica. Therefore, it is reasonable to assume a uniform distribution of segment requests to any given web server.

The workload generator sends an HTTP request for the chosen segment to the web server. When the segment is not downloaded to the client within the segment's play-out time (i.e., 10 seconds for our test video), the client counts it as a segment deadline miss. We measure the segment miss ratio against different request rates. *Segment miss ratio* is defined as the ratio of the number of segment deadline misses to the total number of segment requests for a given request rate. Therefore, the *requests per second* is a control parameter, and the segment miss ratio is the measured figure of merit of the storage subsystem.

3.3 HDDs Only

As a base configuration for comparison, we use two 7200 RPM HDDs striped per Linux's software RAID-0 configuration. Software RAID is implemented in Linux using the device mapper, which is a Linux storage stack infrastructure. The ext4 file system [4] is installed on these RAID-0 disks. We measure the segment miss ratio with different request rates, and each measurement is run for an hour. Figure 1 shows for this configuration that the system could serve up to 19 requests per second when the required QoS is 0% segment miss ratio. Since the observed average CPU utilization during the measurements was below 10%, we can conclude that storage is the bottleneck beyond 19 requests per second for this configuration.

3.4 Flashcache

Flashcache [5], developed by facebook, is a write-back persistent block cache designed to accelerate reads and writes from slow storage like HDDs by caching data in faster storage like SSDs. While ZFS is a file system level solution for caching in flash memory, flashcache is a block device level solution, therefore, it is very general and can be utilized at different levels of the software stack (e.g., file systems, applications).

We create a single logical block device by having flashcache use the two 7200 RPM HDDs striped per RAID-0 configuration and SSD A (see Table 1). Out of the total 80 GB available in the SSD, 60 GB are used as flashcache for the experiment. We measure the performance in two different cache states; a cold cache and a warm cache. For the cold cache, we flush the cache at the beginning of each measurement. For the warm cache, we run the workload

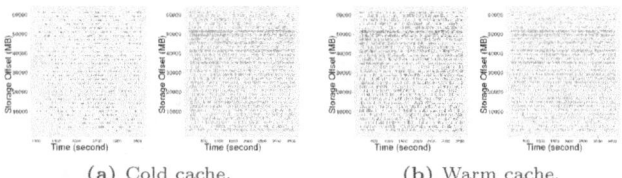
(a) Cold cache.   (b) Warm cache.

Figure 2: Flashcache's Read (Blue) and Write (Red) access pattern on the cache during 1 hour with 1 request per second. The x-axis is time and the y-axis is the storage offset. Both read and write access patterns are severely random.

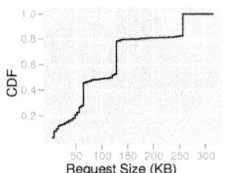 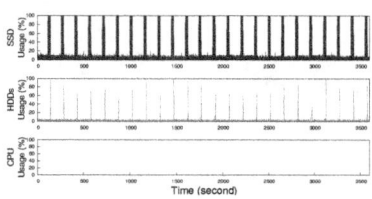

(a) Cumulative Distribution Function (CDF) plotted against the write request sizes sent to the cache over a period of 1 hour.

(b) Resource utilization for SSD, HDD, and CPU (respectively, from top to bottom) as a function of time. SSD (top graph) is 100% busy periodically.

Figure 3: Flashcache's write request size distribution and resource utilization during 1 hour with 1 request per second and cold cache. The median write request size is 116 KB.

generator until the cache filling rate falls below 100 KB/sec. We filled the cache up to 60% (i.e., 36GB) by running the workload generator with 1 request per second for 12 hours. Each measurement is run for an hour. Figure 1 shows that flashcache could not serve even 1 request per second when the required segment miss ratio is 0%. The flashcache performance is the same whether the cache is cold or warmed up.

3.5 ZFS

ZFS [10] is a file system that has an intermediate layer to serve as a read cache between the RAM and the HDDs, called L2ARC. Storage devices that are faster than HDDs are used for L2ARC devices. Though not a requirement, flash memory SSDs can be used as L2ARC devices. ZFS was originally introduced and implemented in the Solaris operating system, but it has been ported to other operating systems such as FreeBSD and Linux. We use ZFS on Linux for this measurement.

ZFS creates a single storage pool using the two 7200 RPM HDDs in RAID-0 configuration together with SSD A to serve as the intermediate read cache layer. Like the flashcache experiment, we use 60 GB of the SSD capacity for the L2ARC cache, and measure the performance in two different cache states; a cold cache and a warm cache. For the cold cache, we flush the cache at the beginning of each measurement. For the warm cache, we have run the workload generator until the cache is filled in full. Each measurement is run for an hour.

Figure 1 shows that ZFS with the cold cache could serve up to 16 requests per second when the required segment miss ratio is 0%. On the other hand, when the cache is warmed up, ZFS could serve up to 20 requests per second. ZFS shows a lot better performance than flashcache, but it is still worse than the base configuration (HDDs-only) when the cache is cold and only slightly better after the cache is warmed up.

4. ANALYSIS

The poor performance of flashcache and ZFS is very surprising since both ZFS and flashcache are designed with flash memory SSDs in mind. In this section, we investigate the reasons for this result.

4.1 Flashcache

Flashcache organizes the flash memory as a set associative cache. The block size, set associativity, and cache size are configurable parameters, specified at cache creation time. The default block size is 8 sectors (i.e., 4 KB), and the default set associativity is 512 (i.e., a given disk block could be in one of 512 members of a given set) Replacement policy is either FIFO or LRU within a set, and FIFO is the default. We use default values for all the parameters in our flashcache measurements.

In what follows, dbn refers to *disk block number*, the logical device block number in sectors. To compute the target set for a given dbn

$$target\ set = (\frac{dbn}{block\ size \times associativity})\ mod\ (number\ of\ sets)$$

Once we have the target set, flashcache does a sequential search of the set (linear probing) to find the desired disk block. Note that a sequential range of disk blocks will all map onto a given set. On the other hand, disk blocks that have a dbn difference greater than the associativity will map onto different sets.

When flashcache gets a read request, it calculates the target set from the dbn of the request. Then, it probes the cache set to find the requested block. If it finds the block in the cache, it returns the block. Otherwise, flashcache reads the block from the disk, copies the block into the appropriate cacheline, and returns the block. A block request that misses in the cache, will first write the block into the cache before returning it to the application. Thus the cache write operation is in the critical path of satisfying an application layer block request that misses in the cache. Therefore, random reads on disks that miss the cache will generate random writes to the cache, and the read could be delayed and miss its deadline if the cache write operation takes a long time to complete.

Figure 2[1] depicts the read and write access patterns on SSD A for flashcache in two different cache states for an hour period with 1 request per second. This graph is plotted based on the trace data collected using *blktrace* [2], which comes with the Linux 2.6 kernel, to trace the I/O activities at the block device level. To remind the reader, read requests to the flash come from the client requesting video segments that are already cached in the flash; the write requests come from the need to copy blocks from the disk to the flash for requests that miss the flash. The upshot is that both the read and write access patterns are random, and the median write request size is 116 KB (See Figure 3(a)). The request size is defined by the I/O request size sent by the block device driver to the physical block device, which we can determine using *blktrace*. Flash memory shows the best write performance when the request size is a multiple of the erase block size, which is 32 MB for SSD A. A write request size of 116 KB is much smaller than the optimal write request size (i.e., 32 MB). The effect of these small random writes is disastrous on the flash memory performance. In particular, since flash

---
[1]The purpose of this figure is to show that both read and write access patterns for cold and warm cache settings are completely random, as is evident from the distribution of the data points in the scatter plot shown in the figure.

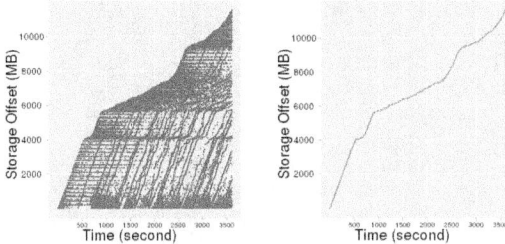
(a) Read access pattern. (b) Write access pattern.

Figure 4: ZFS's Read (Blue) and Write (Red) access pattern on the cache during 1 hour with 16 requests per second and cold cache. The write access pattern is sequential while the read access pattern is random. The median write request size is 128 KB.

memory does not support in-place writes, requires erase-before-write, and also requires the erase size be larger than the page size, the small and random write operations will consume fresh pages in a clean block. Ultimately this will lead to the situation where all available clean blocks are used up, thus kick-starting the garbage collection process. Looking at the top chart in Figure 3(b), which shows the SSD utilization, we can see the utilization peaking up to 100% periodically (around every 140 seconds). It is highly likely that this is due to the garbage collection process. Overall, flashcache generates a very inefficient access pattern for the MLC flash memory SSD. Considering that SSD A is known to handle small random writes much better than the other MLC flash memory SSDs (see Table 1), flashcache generates extremely inefficient write access pattern that even SSD A cannot handle very well.

The read hit ratio of flashcache with a cold cache (Figure 2(a)) is 0.7% while the read hit ratio of flashcache with warm cache (Figure 2(b)) is 25.7%. However, as we have seen in Figure 1, flashcache shows absolutely no difference in performance as measured by the application level segment miss ratio. This can be explained as follows. From the scatter plot for write requests shown in Figure 2(b), we notice that there is a significant volume of write requests to the cache even when the cache is warm. Thus, the application generated reads and system generated writes (a consequence of miss handling) are competing for resources on the SSD device (RAM buffer and CPU). Further, the device processes the requests in order. Thus, if the reads are queued up behind writes, they are likely to miss their deadline even though they hit in the cache since random writes take a long to complete. This is the most likely reason for the poor application level segment miss ratio observed even with a warm cache in Figure 1 for flashcache.

The reasons for the high segment miss ratio for flashcache while dealing with the DASH workload can be summarized as follows:

1. Upon a cache miss, the block read from the disk has to be first written to the cache before being served to the application. The ensuing small and random write pattern results in long latencies.

2. Second, since flashcache does not give priority to reads over writes to the cache, reads which would be hits in the cache get queued up behind ongoing writes.

Serving the requested segments should be the top priority for a video streaming system. Not respecting this criterion is ultimately the failing of flashcache for this workload.

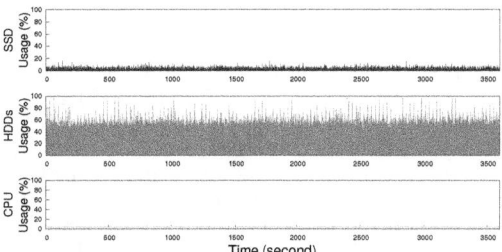
Figure 5: ZFS's resource utilization during 1 hour with 20 requests per second and warm cache. SSD, HDDs, and CPU from top to bottom.

4.2 ZFS

ZFS is smarter than flashcache in handling the flash memory. By analyzing the source code for ZFS L2ARC, we have determined that ZFS basically uses the L2ARC as a FIFO buffer. By definition, the blocks written into the cache are clean (i.e., they are just copies of the disk blocks) and therefore they never have to be written back to the disk. ZFS maintains a *write pointer* to the FIFO buffer that L2ARC represents. Once the write pointer reaches the end of the FIFO buffer it simply wraps around to the beginning overwriting the existing blocks in the cache. In other words, ZFS L2ARC converts the random writes to sequential writes. This is evident from Figure 4(b), where it can be seen that ZFS L2ARC sequentially fills up the cache over time.

We have measured the median write size to be 128 KB from the block traces. Interestingly, we have ascertained by executing a micro-benchmark for SSD A that its sequential write throughput peaks at 128 KB. Figure 5 also corroborates our analysis. The top graph in Figure 5 is the activity observed on the SSD. It can be seen that this activity is very low indicating that the SSD performance is not the bottleneck. Thus overall ZFS L2ARC seems to be optimized in handling the MLC flash memory SSDs. That begs the question as to why ZFS performs much worse than the base configuration (HDDs-only) as shown in Figure 1?

The answer is simply due to the fact that L2ARC is being used as a FIFO buffer. In other words, the replacement policy for the L2ARC cache is FIFO. As we noted treating L2ARC as a FIFO buffer is great for write throughput considering the nature of the flash device. However, this leads to a very poor hit ratio. Unfortunately, it is not possible to empirically verify this hypothesis since Linux port of ZFS does not provide statistics such as L2ARC hit ratio. Therefore, we approximate the hit ratio from the amount of read size requested from the cache and from the disks, which can be obtained by analyzing the block trace. We use following formula to approximate the hit ratio:

$Hit\ Ratio = \frac{Amount\ of\ read\ on\ SSD}{Amount\ of\ read\ on\ SSD + Amount\ of\ read\ on\ disks}$

Using this approximation, L2ARC hit ratio is 4.2% and 11.1% for the cold cache and the warm cache, respectively. The low hit ratio is reflected in the low SSD utilization shown in Figure 5.

We have also applied the above formula to flashcache, and the hit ratio is 0.67% and 23.6% for the cold cache and the warm cache respectively. Compare these numbers to the statistics that flashcache provides. They are 0.7% and 25.7% for the cold cache and the warm cache respectively (Refer to Section 4.1), therefore, we can say that our approximation for the hit ratio derived from block traces is close to reality.

5. RECOMMENDATIONS FOR AN HTTP VIDEO SERVER DESIGN

By studying and analyzing the performance of state-of-the-art multi-tier storage systems for DASH video streaming, we have learned a number of lessons. We summarize these lessons in the form of recommendations for constructing a cost-conscious high-performance HTTP streaming server adhering to the DASH protocol.

Recommendation 1: **No small random writes**: Small random writes are extremely inefficient for MLC flash memory SSDs. There are two possible solutions to this problem. First solution is a logging approach. This approach transforms the random writes to sequential writes that the MLC flash memory SSDs can handle very efficiently. However, logging necessitates frequent invocation of the garbage collection anytime it needs to clean obsolete blocks and make room for new data blocks that need to be written. Clearly, this is detrimental to real-time performance such as timely video delivery, since foreground read operations can be stymied and delayed resulting in missing application deadlines. Therefore, logging is not an appropriate solution for the small random write problem in a real-time system like video streaming. A more preferred solution is to write using a much larger granularity. If write operations are requested in multiples of the flash memory's erase block size, and their offset is aligned with multiples of the erase block size, write amplification will not occur, and MLC flash memory SSDs can handle the writes very efficiently even if the access pattern is completely random.

Recommendation 2: **No flash writes on the critical path**: Writes to the cache while servicing a cache miss should not be in the critical path of serving the requested segment to the application. Hardware caches in a processor are routinely designed in this fashion, wherein the missing data (due to load instruction) is supplied to the processor in parallel with updating the cache. Failing to do this in a video server guarantees that a read request that misses in the cache, will incur the additional penalty of write to the cache when the data is brought from the hard disk. ZFS solves this problem using an evict-ahead policy by which a separate thread copies blocks that are supposed to be evicted soon from RAM to the flash [15, 11].

Recommendation 3: **Higher priority for reads**: Flash reads are more important than flash writes because the former needs to be served before their deadline while the latter is not time critical. Therefore, flash reads should have a higher priority than flash writes when they compete for resources. Both flashcache and ZFS do not consider this point.

Recommendation 4: **Object-level caching**: Cache replacement policies such as LRU or its variants which operate at the block level (e.g., single page) have been successfully used for the OS buffer cache. However, caching at such a fine granularity is not appropriate for flash memory since it would trigger frequent small writes to the flash device that are detrimental to performance. For a given price, flash provides a much larger capacity than RAM; therefore, we can increase the granularity of caching for video objects. For example, with a 60 GB flash, we could cache up to 56 most popular video objects in the the flash memory. Assuming a 0.271 zipf distribution, 55.4% of the video accesses could be served out of the flash memory. This hit ratio is much better than the hit ratios which we observed on flashcache (25.7%) and ZFS (11.1%). Moreover, a conservative cache replacement based on the long term history of video access frequency can reduce the amount of write operations to the flash, and consequently, it can lower the chance of interference with the read operations serving videos from the flash.

6. CONCLUSIONS

Due to the cost and size advantage of flash memory compared to DRAM, a multi-tiered storage hierarchy, wherein a flash-based SSD serves as an intermediate level cache appears to be an attractive strategy for constructing a cost-efficient high performance video streaming server. However, we found through extensive performance studies that two state-of-the-art multi-tiered storage systems exhibited disappointingly poor performance for HTTP video streaming using the DASH protocols. We performed careful analysis to uncover the sources of poor performance in both these systems. Based on our analysis, we have recommendations for constructing an HTTP streaming server that avoids the pitfalls in designing such a server. Our future work includes building such a server embodying these design principles and carrying out experimental studies to validate these design ideas.

7. REFERENCES

[1] Apache. http://httpd.apache.org.
[2] Blktrace. http://linux.die.net/man/8/blktrace.
[3] DASH dataset. http://www-itec.uni-klu.ac.at/dash/?page_id=207.
[4] Ext4 file system. https://ext4.wiki.kernel.org.
[5] Flashcache. http://www.facebook.com/note.php?note_id=388112370932.
[6] Http/1.1. http://www.ietf.org/rfc/rfc2068.txt.
[7] Hulu. http://www.hulu.com.
[8] ISO/IEC DIS 23009-1.2. http://www.iso.org/iso/iso_catalogue/catalogue_tc/catalogue_detail.htm?csnumber=57623.
[9] Netflix. http://www.netflix.com.
[10] Zettabyte file system. http://solaris-training.com/classp/200_HTML/docs/zfs_wp.pdf.
[11] ZFS L2ARC. https://blogs.oracle.com/brendan/entry/test.
[12] N. Agrawal, V. Prabhakaran, T. Wobber, J. D. Davis, M. Manasse, and R. Panigrahy. Design tradeoffs for ssd performance. In *ATC'08: USENIX 2008 Annual Technical Conference on Annual Technical Conference*, pages 57–70, Berkeley, CA, USA, 2008. USENIX Association.
[13] A. Barbir, B. Cain, R. Nair, and O. Spatscheck. Known content network (cn) request-routing mechanisms. RFC 3568, http://tools.ietf.org/html/rfc3568.
[14] Intel Corporation. Understanding the Flash Translation Layer (FTL) Specification. White Paper, http://www.embeddedfreebsd.org/Documents/Intel-FTL.pdf, 1998.
[15] A. Leventhal. Flash storage memory. *Communications of the ACM*, 51(7):47–51, July 2008.
[16] T. R. G. Nair and P. Jayarekha. A rank based replacement policy for multimedia server cache using zipf-like law. *Journal of Computing*, 2(3):14–22, 2010.
[17] C. Park, W. Cheon, J. Kang, K. Roh, W. Cho, and J.-S. Kim. A reconfigurable ftl (flash translation layer) architecture for nand flash-based applications. *Trans. on Embedded Computing Sys.*, 7(4):1–23, 2008.
[18] C. Partridge, T. Mendez, and W. Milliken. Host anycasting services. RFC 1546, http://tools.ietf.org/html/rfc1546.
[19] M. Ryu, H. Kim, and U. Ramachandran. Impact of flash memory on video-on-demand storage: Analysis of tradeoffs. In *Proceedings of the ACM Multimedia Systems*, San Jose, CA, USA, February 2011.

What Happens When HTTP Adaptive Streaming Players Compete for Bandwidth?

Saamer Akhshabi,
Lakshmi Anantakrishnan,
Constantine Dovrolis,
College of Computing
Georgia Institute of Technology
s.akhshabi, lakshmi3, constantine@gatech.edu

Ali C. Begen
Video and Content Platforms Research and
Advanced Development
Cisco Systems
abegen@cisco.com

ABSTRACT

With an increasing demand for high-quality video content over the Internet, it is becoming more likely that two or more adaptive streaming players share the same network bottleneck and compete for available bandwidth. This competition can lead to three performance problems: player instability, unfairness between players, and bandwidth underutilization. However, the dynamics of such competition and the root cause for the previous three problems are not yet well understood. In this paper, we focus on the problem of competing video players and describe how the typical behavior of an adaptive streaming player in its Steady-State, which includes periods of activity followed by periods of inactivity (ON-OFF periods), is the main root cause behind the problems listed above. We use two adaptive players to experimentally showcase these issues. Then, focusing on the issue of player instability, we test how several factors (the ON-OFF durations, the available bandwidth and its relation to available bitrates, and the number of competing players) affect stability.

Categories and Subject Descriptors

C.4 [**Computer Systems Organization**]: Performance of Systems

General Terms

Performance, Measurement, Algorithms

Keywords

Adaptive streaming, video streaming over HTTP, player competition, available bandwidth competition, stability

Permission to make digital or hard copies of all or part of this work for personal or classroom use is granted without fee provided that copies are not made or distributed for profit or commercial advantage and that copies bear this notice and the full citation on the first page. To copy otherwise, to republish, to post on servers or to redistribute to lists, requires prior specific permission and/or a fee.
NOSSDAV'12, June 7–8, 2012, Toronto, Ontario, Canada.
Copyright 2012 ACM 978-1-4503-1430-5/12/06 ...$10.00.

1. INTRODUCTION

Adaptive video streaming over HTTP is quickly getting adopted as the technology of choice for the delivery of video over IP networks. At the same time, the popularity of Internet-based high-quality streaming for various end-user devices such as HDTVs, mobile phones, gaming devices, and computers is on a steady rise as well. The bandwidth requirement for such devices is rapidly increasing as the content quality is improving to meet end-user demands. With abundant video content and increasing bandwidth demands, it is becoming likely that two or more adaptive streaming players have to share a network bottleneck and compete for available bandwidth. Such competition can take place, for example, when several people in the same house watch different movies at the same time. In that case the residential broadband access link is probably going to be a shared bottleneck. Another instance of such competition is when many users watch the same live event (such as Super Bowl) online. An edge network link may constitute the shared bottleneck in that case. It has been previously observed that such competition can lead to performance issues [1, 3, 4]. However, the dynamics of such competition and the root cause for the previous performance problems are not yet well understood.

Our goal in this paper is to identify the underlying root cause of the performance problems that take place when multiple adaptive streaming players compete. We group these problems into three categories: The first relates to the stability of the players in terms of requested bitrates and video quality. The second is the unfairness among competing players. The third is the potential bandwidth underutilization when multiple adaptive players compete.

We first give a short overview of how a typical adaptive streaming algorithm works. Then, we show that this typical behavior can lead to periods during which the player stays idle – downloading nothing from the server. The player cannot estimate the available bandwidth in the bottleneck during these idle times. Depending on when these idle times start and end for each competing player, the previous three issues (instability, unfairness, and underutilization) can arise. In this paper we only focus on the performance of the players in the Steady-State in which the player has already built its playback buffer. We experimentally evaluate two adaptive streaming players, the Smooth Streaming player [7] and a variant of the AdapTech Streaming player introduced in [2], when two or more players compete with each other. Finally, focusing on the instability issue, we examine how 1) the relative duration of the player idle periods, 2) the "fair share" of each player and its relation to the available bitrates, and 3) the number of competing players, affect the stability of the system.

To the best of our knowledge, there have only been two prior studies focusing on the competition between adaptive streaming players. Cloonan and Allen [3] developed a simulator to explore corner-case scenarios that may occur with competing streaming sessions. They reported requested bitrate oscillations and unfairness when multiple adaptive streaming players compete and they observed that the instability tends to increase with the number of competing players (we disagree with this point in Section 5). Houdaille and Gouache [4] observed instability and unfairness with competing adaptive streaming players and they proposed a traffic shaping method at home gateways to reduce the extent of these problems.

The rest of this paper is organized as follows: In Section 2, we describe the root cause of the previous performance problems when multiple players compete. In Section 3, we describe the experimental methodology and metrics that we use. In Section 4, we showcase how competition in real scenarios can lead to performance degradation. Section 5 focuses on the stability of the competing adaptive streaming players and studies the various factors that can affect it. We conclude the paper in Section 6.

2. MULTIPLE COMPETING PLAYERS

In this section we describe qualitatively three performance issues that can take place when two or more adaptive streaming players share a network bottleneck and compete for available bandwidth. An important point is that the issues we focus on in this paper, are *not* due to TCP dynamics, as is often reported, but they mainly arise from the rate adaptation algorithms at the application layer.

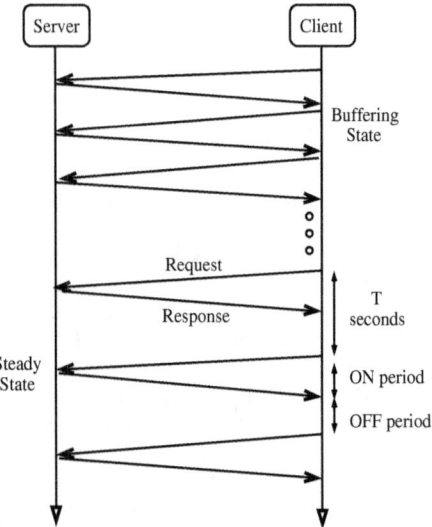

Figure 1: The request-response timing between client and server in the Buffering and Steady states.

An adaptive streaming player typically starts a streaming session in the Buffering-State [1]. At this phase, the goal of the player is to build up its playback buffer as quickly as possible and to reach a maximum buffer size. To do so the

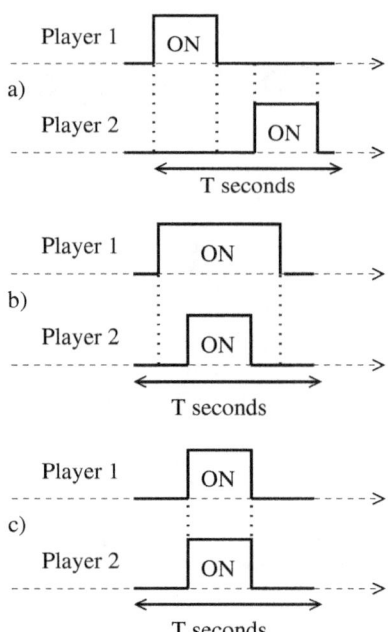

Figure 2: Three instances of the ON-OFF periods of two competing players during one chunk download period.

player requests a new chunk (also known as "fragment" or "segment") as soon as the previous chunk is downloaded.

Once the playback buffer size reaches a certain target (e.g., 30 seconds), the player switches to the Steady-State during which it aims to maintain a constant playback buffer size. Assuming for simplicity that each chunk corresponds to T seconds of content, the player requests one chunk every T seconds (if the download duration is less than T) or as soon as the previous chunk is received (otherwise). This can lead to an activity pattern in which the player is either ON, downloading a chunk, or it is OFF, staying idle. This pattern is illustrated in Figure 1.

In parallel, the player estimates its fair share in the underlying network path by measuring the per-chunk TCP throughput, and computing a running average of those measurements over time [1]. The player then uses that running average to select the bitrate for the next requested chunk.

Depending on the temporal overlap of the ON-OFF periods among competing players, they may not estimate their fair share correctly. This can cause the following three performance problems: instability, unfairness, and underutilization. Specifically, consider a simple model with two adaptive players sharing a bottleneck of capacity C. Suppose that both players have already reached the Steady-State requesting a new chunk every T seconds. Also, let us ignore for now the well-known TCP shortcomings, and assume that a single active connection gets the whole capacity C, while two active connections share the capacity fairly, receiving $\frac{C}{2}$ each. The fair share for each player, denoted by f, in this model is $\frac{C}{2}$. We denote by f_1 and f_2 the throughput received by player-1 and player-2, respectively, during a chunk download period. Ideally, it should be that $f_1 = f_2 = f$.

Figure 2-a shows the case where the ON periods of the two players do not overlap during a chunk download period. Both players measure a per-chunk throughput of C, and so they estimate that $f_1 = f_2 > f$. In other words, both players overestimate their fair share by a factor of two. When both players overestimate their fair share, and depending on the video bitrates, they may request a profile with higher bitrate than f, causing congestion. When that happens, the players will measure that their TCP throughput is less than their previous fair share estimate, and so they will switch back to a lower video bitrate. This oscillatory scenario can repeat, causing instability.

Figure 2-b shows the situation where the ON period of one player falls within the ON period of the other player. This can happen if one player is requesting a chunk with lower bitrate than the other player. In this case, the former observes a throughput of $\frac{C}{2}$ and the latter observes a throughput that is more than $\frac{C}{2}$. So the two players estimate that $f_1 > f_2 = f$, which means that one player overestimates its fair share. When only one player overestimates its fair share, it can be that the two players converge to a stable but unfair equilibrium in which the player with the larger fair share estimate requests a higher bitrate video.

Figure 2-c shows the situation where the ON period of the two players are perfectly aligned. Both players observe a throughput of $\frac{C}{2}$ and so $f_1 = f_2 = f$. In this case the two players estimate their fair share correctly. Note however that even in this case we can have bandwidth underutilization. To illustrate, suppose that the video has two available profiles with bitrates b_1 and b_2, respectively. Then, both examples in Figure 2-b and 2-c can be stable if $b_1 < \frac{C}{2}$, $b_1 + b_2 < C$, and $b_2 > \frac{C}{2}$. However, the case shown in Figure 2-c, where both players request the b_1 profile, causes underutilization, even though it is stable and fair.

Instability can also cause underutilization. Suppose that $b_1 \ll b_2$ and $b_1 + b_2 \approx C$. Consider the case that one player requests b_1 and the other requests b_2, which is stable and the capacity of the bottleneck is completely utilized. On the other hand, consider the case that the players oscillate between b_1 and b_2, given that it is not possible that they both receive the b_2 profile. This oscillatory scenario will lead to significant underutilization, when both players request b_1.

The previous examples illustrate some competition scenarios for two adaptive streaming players. In reality, several other factors can play an important role in the appearance and extent of instability, unfairness and underutilization, such as the exact player adaptation algorithm, TCP dynamics, bandwidth fluctuations, and the variability of the video encoding rate. In the rest of this paper, we use actual adaptive streaming players to demonstrate that the previous issues can still arise in reality.

3. METHODOLOGY AND METRICS

In this section, we give an overview of the experimental methodology and define the metrics we focus on. The experimental set up is similar to that in [1]. The host that runs the video players also runs a packet sniffer (Wireshark [5]) and a network emulator (DummyNet [8]). Wireshark allows us to capture and analyze offline the traffic from and to the HTTP server. DummyNet allows us to control the *downstream available bandwidth* (also referred to as *avail-bw*) that the players can receive. That host is connected to the Georgia Tech campus network through a Fast Ethernet interface. The TCP connections that transfer video and audio streams cannot exceed (collectively) the avail-bw at any time.

We use two different players in the following experiments. The first is a variant of the AdapTech-Streaming player introduced in [2], which is based on the Adobe OSMF player [6]. We have instrumented the player to log its internal parameters such as playback buffer size, requested bitrate, chunk download time, and chunk throughput over time. The second is the commercial Smooth Streaming player [7]. We infer the previous parameters for that player by using packet captures, as described in [1]. Due to space constraints, we do not repeat the details in this paper.

We represent by P_r an encoding bitrate of r Mbps that is available for a given video stream at the server (e.g., $P_{2.75}$). We test competing players under constant avail-bw. We do not, however, control the servers and the content ourselves and so we select the avail-bw according to the bitrates available at the servers. An experiment ends when at least one of the players finishes receiving the whole video.

We define the following three performance metrics:
1. The *instability* metric, denoted by θ, is the fraction of successive chunk requests by a player in which the requested bitrate does not remain constant.
2. The *unfairness* metric (for two players) is the average of the absolute bitrate differences between the corresponding chunks requested by each player.
3. The *utilization* metric is defined as the aggregate throughput during an experiment (measured from the Wireshark captures) divided by the avail-bw in that experiment.

We first test the Smooth Streaming player when two players compete under constant avail-bw. We also use this player to study the effect of two factors: the duration of the ON-OFF periods, and the fair share of each player relative to the available bitrates. Due to resource constraints, for example CPU and GPU power, on the machine hosting the players, we cannot run multiple instances of the Smooth Streaming player to investigate the effect of the number of competing players. Therefore, we have developed a *simpler player* that mimics the behavior of Smooth Streaming at a qualitative level, without actually decoding and displaying the video streams, to study the effect of the number of players (see Section 4.2).

All experiments are performed on a Windows 7 Professional host with an Intel(R) Core(TM)i5 CPU M480 2.67GHz processor, 4.00 GB physical memory, and an Intel(R) HD Graphics processor with 1307 MB total memory.

4. BASIC EXPERIMENTS

We performed many experiments with the Smooth Streaming player and observed that the performance issues described in Section 2 also take place in practice. Due to space constraints, we show results here for only one of those experiments. We also show results from a single experiment with a simpler player, which is based on the AdapTech Streaming player introduced in [2].

4.1 Smooth Streaming Player

We use Microsoft Silverlight Version 5.0.61118.0 provided by Microsoft at the IIS Web site.[1] The manifest file for the video that is provided there declares eight video encoding bitrates ranging from 350Kbps to 2.75 Mbps. Figure 3 shows

---
[1]http://www.iis.net/media/experiencesmoothstreaming

the requested bitrates, the chunk throughputs as well as the number of active (i.e., ON) players for an experiment with two Smooth Streaming players sharing a bottleneck with 1.6 Mbps avail-bw. Note that we only focus on the time interval between $t = 80$ s and $t = 280$ s, when both players are in Steady-State. When the ON periods of the two players do not overlap (i.e., the number of active players is less than two, e.g., between $t = 140$ s and $t = 160$ s), the chunk throughputs are much larger than the fair share (0.8 Mbps). This happens when the players are requesting lower bitrates ($P_{0.47}$ and $P_{0.63}$). We do not know exactly how the Smooth Streaming player uses the chunk throughput measurements to estimate the avail-bw but we can observe that the players decide then to switch to a higher bitrate (e.g., at $t = 157$ s to $P_{0.845}$) that is larger than the fair share, which is unsustainable. The durations of the ON periods increase then, the number of active players becomes two, and the measured throughput by each player decreases. Consequently, the players switch back to the lower bitrates at around $t = 182$ s. This oscillatory pattern continues throughout the streaming session. Overall, this experiment's instability is 12%, the unfairness is 0.085 Mbps, and the utilization is 94%.

follows. Assume that the bitrate of the ith profile is b_i and the rank of the current profile is ϕ_{cur}. Then the index of the next candidate profile ϕ is given by

$$\phi = \max\{i : b_i < c \times \hat{A}\}$$

where c is a slack parameter ($0 < c < 1$) that is necessary due to the variability of the video encoding rate and the temporal bandwidth fluctuations – we use $c=0.8$. The requested profile for the next chunk is determined as follows

---

if $\phi > \phi_{cur}$ **then**
 Increase the requested bitrate by one profile.
else if $\phi < \phi_{cur}$ **then**
 Decrease the requested bitrate by one profile.
else
 Stay with the current requested bitrate
end if

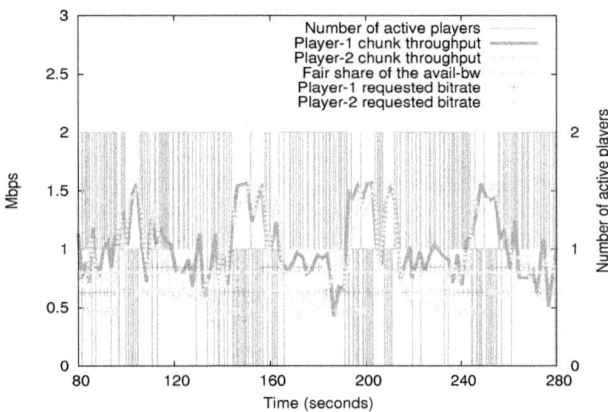

Figure 3: Requested bitrates and chunk throughputs for two competing Smooth Streaming players.

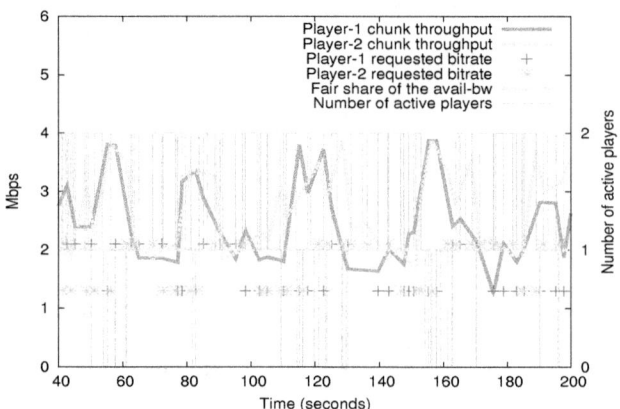

Figure 4: Requested bitrates and chunk throughputs for two competing "simpler" players.

4.2 Simpler Player

Our goal here is to design a simpler player that behaves similar to Smooth Streaming, at least qualitatively, while allowing us to run a large number of players at the same host. To do so, we use a variant of the AdapTech Streaming player introduced in [2]. We simplify the player and choose the parameters of the adaptation algorithm based on our experiments in [2] to match the Smooth Streaming player. This player also has two states: Buffering and Steady-State. The maximum buffer size is set to 30 seconds. The player maintains two throughput-related metrics, the throughput of the latest downloaded chunk, denoted by A, and a running average of A, denoted by $\hat{A}$. If $A(i)$ is the throughput of the i'th chunk, the running average $\hat{A}$ is:

$$\hat{A} = \begin{cases} \delta \hat{A}(i-1) + (1-\delta)A(i) & i > 0 \\ 0 & i = 0 \end{cases}$$

with $\delta = 0.8$.

The player starts a streaming session requesting the lowest available profile. It selects the next profile based on $\hat{A}$, as

In the following experiment, we use a movie trailer ("Freeway") provided by Akamai's HD-video Web site for Adobe HTTP Dynamic Streaming.[2] We use four different encoding bitrates between 0.9 Mbps and 2.5 Mbps. Figure 4 shows the requested bitrates, the chunk throughputs, and the number of active players from $t = 40$ s to $t = 200$ s for two competing players sharing a bottleneck with 4 Mbps avail-bw. The players show an instability pattern similar to that with the Smooth Streaming players. The instability metric for this experiment is around 16%, the unfairness metric is 0.27 Mbps, while the utilization is 92%.

The experiments with Smooth Streaming as well as with our simpler player show that these clients do a reasonable job regarding fairness and utilization. However, the players fail to address the root cause of the instability problem described in Section 2. In the next section, we focus on the instability issue and show how certain key factors affect the stability of the adaptive streaming players.

---

[2]http://zeridemo-f.akamaihd.net/content/inoutedit-mbr/inoutedit_h264_3000.f4m

5. STABILITY

In this section we focus on three factors that affect the instability of competing adaptive players. The first factor is the relative duration of the OFF periods in the activity pattern of each player. The second factor is the fair share of each player relative to the bitrates of the available video profiles. The third factor is the number of competing players. For the first two factors we use the Smooth Streaming player, while for the third factor we use our simpler player. We summarize the metrics and parameters used in this section in Table 1.

Metric	Summary
f	Bandwidth fair share for each player
θ	Instability metric
γ	Fraction of time: exactly one player is idle
μ	Fraction of time: both players overestimate f
λ	Overlap factor
N	Number of competing players

Table 1: List of metrics and parameters in Section 5

5.1 Duration of ON-OFF Periods

How does the duration of the competing players' ON-OFF periods affect their stability? We denote the fair share of each player, i.e., the total avail-bw divided by the number of competing players, by f. We use two competing Smooth Streaming players, starting with $f = 400$Kbps and increasing the fair-share in steps of 100Kbps until $f=3$ Mbps. We repeat each experiment four times for each value of f.

We measure the instability metric θ for each streaming experiment. Additionally, we denote by γ the fraction of the streaming session's duration in which exactly one player is idle, i.e., in the OFF state. $\gamma = 1$ if at any point in time exactly one player is in the OFF state while the other player in the ON state. $\gamma = 0$ when the players' ON-OFF periods are perfectly aligned in time (as in Figure 2-c). We then match each player-1 request to the player-2 request that is closest in time. We denote by μ the fraction of time where both players estimate a throughput that is larger than f, based on these time-matched requests.

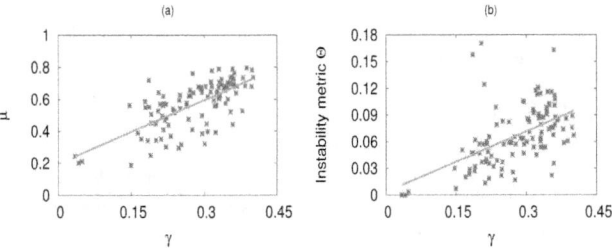

Figure 5: a) μ, the fraction of time where both players estimate a throughput that is larger than their fair share f, and b) the instability metric (θ) as a function of the fraction of time in which exactly one player is idle (γ).

Figure 5-a shows a scatter plot of μ and γ for all experiments. The correlation between the two metrics is 0.70.

When only one player is OFF, the ON player observes the entire capacity and so it overestimates the fair-share f. Recall that the overestimation of f, as described in Section 2 and showcased in Section 4, can trick the player to switch to a bitrate that is higher than f, which is unsustainable. This in turn leads to unnecessary bitrate changes and instability. Figure 5-b shows a scatter plot of the instability metric θ and the fraction γ. Again, we see a clear positive correlation between the fraction of time in which one player is idle (γ) and the instability of the requested bitrates. The correlation coefficient is 0.52.

5.2 Fair Share and Available Profiles

Does the fair share of each player (f) affect the stability of the system? Suppose that there are only two available profiles at the video server. We perform the following set of experiments: start with a fair share that is equal to the lower profile bitrate, and increase f in steps of 50Kbps until it exceeds the higher profile bitrate. For each value of f, two Smooth Streaming players compete for bandwidth. We repeat the experiment eight times for each value of f.

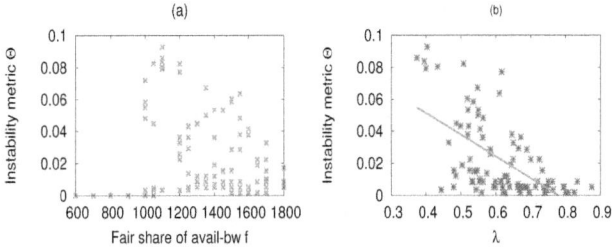

Figure 6: a) The instability metric θ as a function of the fair share f, and b) θ as a function of the player overlap factor λ.

Figure 6-a is a scatter plot showing the instability metric θ as function of the fair-share f. The two profile bitrates are 470Kbps and 1.52 Mbps. Note that instability is always 0 when $f < 1$ Mbps. This is because the avail-bw in that range is not sufficient for even one player to switch to the higher profile (that would require at least 2.1 Mbps of avail-bw, including audio). At the other extreme, if $f \geq 1.8$ Mbps the avail-bw is sufficient for both players to switch to the higher profile and so the instability is again close to 0.

The more interesting case is the range $1 < f < 1.8$ Mbps, in which there is high variability in the stability of the players across different experiments. In this range of f at least one of the players can switch to the higher profile, triggering instability.

However, there are also several experiments in that range of f in which the instability is close to 0. Further analysis of those experiments revealed that they correspond to the case of Figure 2-b, where the ON period of one player almost falls within the ON period of the other. The former is requesting the lower profile, while the latter is requesting the higher profile. To demonstrate this point, we calculate the fraction of the ON duration of one player in which the other player is also ON. We then take the maximum of that value among the two players. We denote this maximum by λ. $\lambda = 1$ if the ON period of one player always falls within the ON period of the other.

Figure 6-b shows a scatter plot with the instability metric θ and the "overlap" factor λ. There is a clear negative correlation between the two metrics (correlation coefficient -0.61). The more *overlapping* the ON periods of the two competing players are, the more stable they become, as expected based on Figure 2-b.

5.3 Number of Competing Players

Assuming that the capacity of the bottleneck link is fixed, is there a relation between the stability of the system and the number of competing players? We examine this question with the following experiments using our simpler player.

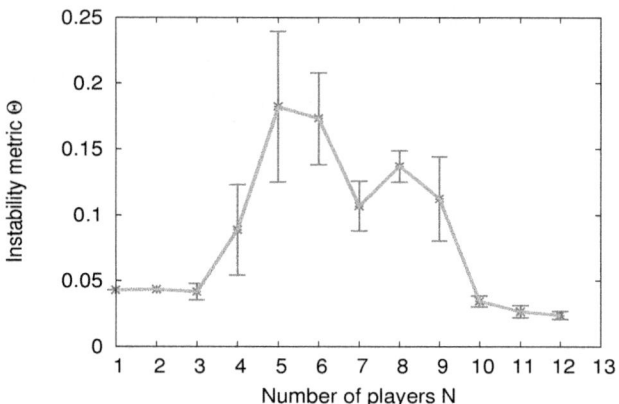

Figure 7: The instability metric θ as a function of the number of competing players N.

Figure 7 shows the instability metric θ as a function of the number of competing players, denoted by N. The players share an 11 Mbps bottleneck. Note that the lowest and highest available profiles are $P_{0.9}$ and $P_{2.5}$ with two other profiles in between. Each point is obtained by repeating the experiment four times and averaging the instability values across all experiments. The corresponding 95% confidence intervals are also shown.

The players start streaming about five seconds apart. When $N < 4$, the fair share of each player f is sufficient for all players to switch to the highest profile $P_{2.5}$. So, the instability factor is then small (only a few initial rate changes before stabilizing). On the other extreme, when $N > 10$, the fair share f is less than 1.1 Mbps and so it is barely sufficient for the players to receive the lowest profile (including the audio stream, which requires 64 Kbps). The players would then stay in the Buffering-State and rarely switch to a higher profile, meaning that the instability is close to 0.

As N increases from 4 to 10, however, f falls within the lowest and the highest available bitrates. Then, the players are mostly in the Steady-State, and they go through the previously discussed ON-OFF activity pattern. The instability increases until it peaks at $N = 5$ or 6. This corresponds to approximately a fair share value that is half way between the lowest and highest profiles. As we increase N further, f decreases, all players are forced to request lower bitrates, and instability decreases.

6. CONCLUSIONS

We described how the competition for available bandwidth between multiple adaptive streaming players can lead to instability, unfairness, and bandwidth underutilization. We identified the root cause of the problem as the behavior of adaptive players in the Steady-State phase; that phase includes periods of activity (ON periods) followed by periods of inactivity (OFF periods). A player cannot estimate the available bandwidth during OFF periods because it does not transfer any data then. We conducted experiments with real adaptive streaming players and showed that the previous issues can arise in practice. Finally, we showed how certain factors, namely the duration of ON-OFF periods, the fair share relative to the available profile bitrates, and the number of competing players, can affect the stability of the system.

In future work, we plan to expand the previous study with analytical and computational models for adaptive streaming systems. Another goal is to propose a solution that takes into account the several dimensions of this problem including the complexity of the player's adaptation logic and its interaction with the underlying transport protocol and congestion control mechanism.

7. REFERENCES

[1] S. Akhshabi, A. C. Begen, and C. Dovrolis. An experimental evaluation of rate-adaptation algorithms in adaptive streaming over http. *ACM MMSys*, 2011.

[2] S. Akhshabi, S. Narayanaswamy, A.C. Begen, and C. Dovrolis. An experimental evaluation of rate-adaptive video players over http. *Signal Processing: Image Communication*, 27:271–287, 2012.

[3] T. Cloonan and J. Allen. Competitive analysis of adaptive video streaming implementations. *SCTE Cable-Tec Expo Technical Workshop*, 2011.

[4] R. Houdaille and S. Gouache. Shaping http adaptive streams for a better user experience. *ACM MMSys*, 2012.

[5] A. Orebaugh, G. Ramirez, J. Burke, and J. Beale. *Wireshark and Ethereal network protocol analyzer toolkit*. Syngress Media Inc, 2007.

[6] OSMF Player. http://www.osmf.org.

[7] Smooth Streaming Player. http://www.iis.net/download/SmoothClient.

[8] L. Rizzo. Dummynet: a simple approach to the evaluation of network protocols. *SIGCOMM CCR*, 27(1):31–41, 1997.

To Chunk or Not to Chunk: Implications for HTTP Streaming Video Server Performance

Jim Summers, Tim Brecht
University of Waterloo
jasummer,
brecht@cs.uwaterloo.ca

Derek Eager
University of Saskatchewan
eager@cs.usask.ca

Bernard Wong
University of Waterloo
bernard@cs.uwaterloo.ca

ABSTRACT

Large amounts of Internet streaming video traffic are being delivered using HTTP to leverage the existing web infrastructure. A fundamental issue in HTTP streaming concerns the granularity of video objects used throughout the HTTP ecosystem (including clients, proxy caches, CDN nodes, and servers). A video may be divided into many files (called chunks), each containing only a few seconds of video at one extreme, or stored in a single unchunked file at the other.

In this paper, we describe the pros and cons of using chunked and unchunked videos. We then describe a methodology for fairly comparing the performance implications of video object granularity at web servers. We find that with conventional servers (`userver`, `nginx` and `Apache`) there is little performance difference between these two approaches. However, by aggressively prefetching and sequentializing disk accesses in the `userver`, we are able to obtain up to double the throughput when serving requests for unchunked videos when compared with chunked videos (even while performing the same aggressive prefetching with chunked videos). These results indicate that more research is required to ensure that the HTTP ecosystem can handle this important and rapidly growing workload.

Categories and Subject Descriptors

H.5.1 [**Multimedia Information Systems**]: Video; D.4.3 [**File Systems Management**]: File organization

General Terms

Performance, Experimentation, Measurement, Design

Keywords

HTTP video, HTTP adaptive streaming, web servers, performance, video segmentation, video chunking, file placement, prefetching

1. INTRODUCTION

Internet video streaming, and in particular video streaming over HTTP, is growing rapidly. For example, one recent measurement study found that 98% of the video traffic on a large cellular network was delivered over HTTP [4]. Advantages of delivery over HTTP include the ability to use conventional web servers, easily exploit CDN services and web caches, and seamlessly traverse firewalls.

Several different approaches are used for video delivery with HTTP. A basic distinction among these approaches concerns the granularity of client requests. Clients may use a single HTTP request to retrieve the entire video, may use multiple HTTP range requests, or may request individual video "chunks" each consisting of a few seconds of video and with its own URL. A recent measurement study of YouTube traffic, for example, found that "PC-players" used the first approach for YouTube video access while "mobile-players" used the second approach [5]. The third approach is used by some systems supporting HTTP adaptive streaming, a technology in which the client is able to adaptively switch among video versions of differing qualities [2].

The granularity of client requests may have important performance implications. For example, the third of the above approaches may more readily accommodate caching of frequently accessed portions of videos at conventional web caches and CDN nodes, since each video chunk can be independently cached as a separate object. Also, it is natural, although not necessary, to match the storage approach used at the server with the approach used for client requests, and to store each video as a single file when clients use single HTTP requests to retrieve videos, or use HTTP range requests, and as multiple files when requests are for video chunks with their own URLs.

In this paper, we consider the question of what impact the granularity of files used to store videos has on the server's throughput. In particular, can similar server performance be achieved when videos are stored with each chunk in a separate file, when compared with storing videos in single files? Our contributions are as follows:

- We describe substantive methodological challenges when attempting to compare different video storage approaches, as arising from the impact of disk layout on throughput, as well as our solutions to these challenges.

- We show that the throughput differences between the two storage approaches are modest for three conventional web servers: `Apache`, `nginx`, and `userver`.

- We show that when videos as stored as single files, a particular prefetching technique, based on asynchronous prefetching through sequentialized disk access, can yield substantial improvements in peak throughput (double in some of our experiments). Only modest improvements from prefetching are found when videos are chunked and stored with each chunk in a separate file.

- We find that even when the `userver` is provided with a list of chunks that comprise the video and it uses that list to aggressively prefetch files from that video, throughput is significantly lower than when using unchunked videos.

2. BACKGROUND AND RELATED WORK

HTTP is rapidly becoming the most widely used method for serving video over the Internet. Companies like Apple, Adobe, Akamai, Netflix, Microsoft, and many others [2] are leveraging the existing HTTP ecosystem to support video streaming using a number of different approaches.

Servers will often support multiple encodings of the same video in order to provide videos of different quality and to permit streaming at different bandwidths over networks of different speeds to devices with a variety of capabilities. The encoding can be selected or changed manually by the user or dynamically by the video player software in order to adapt to changing network conditions (e.g., reductions in available bandwidth). However, clients cannot switch encodings at any arbitrary point in time; videos are encoded in interrelated groups of pictures (GoP), so videos can only be decoded starting from the boundaries between the groups. These boundaries provide natural opportunities for creating video chunks.

With conventional progressive download, clients request the entire video file and begin playback once a sufficient number of bytes have been buffered. With HTTP adaptive streaming (HAS), in contrast, the server provides a manifest to the client that specifies the URLs to request in order to play back the video. Each manifest item identifies a video *segment*. Segments start on GoP boundaries, allowing independent decoding. With knowledge of the time offset associated with each segment, clients are able to easily and seamlessly switch between different encodings.

There are two common approaches to storing the segments on the server. One approach, used by Microsoft's Smooth Streaming for example [14], is to store the entire video in a single file. Each segment is given a distinct URL, and a server-side API is used to map segment URLs into file ranges. Alternatively, segments can be specified using byte ranges enabling clients to use standard HTTP range requests.

A second approach, used by Apple's HTTP Live Streaming for example [14], is to store the video in multiple files (called chunks), with each chunk corresponding to a single segment. In this case the manifest contains the URLs of the different files that comprise the video. We also observe that there is sufficient flexibility to support a third approach; chunks could contain multiple segments, and the manifest file could specify a segment in terms of both a URL and a byte range within the chunk.

One of the clear advantages of dividing videos into chunks, with each chunk corresponding to a single segment, is that because the client player issues normal HTTP requests for entire files, this type of streaming and rate adaptation is well supported by the existing HTTP ecosystem. While we expect that the caching of HTTP range requests may be supported by some clients, proxy caches and CDN nodes, it is unclear how widespread or how well existing implementations have been optimized to support video workloads. Segment durations are chosen based on the desired granularity of adapting to changing conditions, and on characteristics of the encoding. These considerations are largely independent of how videos are stored.

In previous work [15], we developed methodologies for generating HTTP streaming video workloads, benchmarks, and for testing web server performance. Preliminary performance results in that paper suggest that prefetching within a chunk can be beneficial for large chunk sizes. However, those methodologies do not permit a rigorous investigation of the impact of chunk size on server performance. Furthermore, prefetching across multiple chunks of the same video was not considered. In this paper, we extend our methodologies and carry out a fair comparison of different video storage alternatives, in particular chunked (with varying chunk sizes) versus not chunked. This task is complicated by the fact that to enable fair comparisons, we must take care to ensure that when videos are stored using different chunk sizes (or as single files), they are located at equivalent physical locations on disk [1]. If not, differences in performance could be due to the location on disk rather than differences in chunk sizes (e.g., because disk throughput is higher on outer tracks than on inner tracks).

There are many papers that study the effect of file systems and disk storage on the efficiency of servers. One example, [13] investigates the effect of 4 different file systems and numerous tuning options on server performance for 4 representative workloads. However, none of their workloads model HTTP streaming video workloads, so their conclusions may not be applicable to our specific workloads and must be validated experimentally.

A more theoretical discussion of the difficulties of servicing concurrent sequential streams [9] investigates the effect of request size on disk throughput and finds that disk throughput is improved with larger request sizes. These results are not directly applicable to our workload because their server simply reads the data from disk and does not send it to any clients. In previous work [15], we have found that real-world network bandwidth constraints can render techniques that work well without such constraints ineffective.

Recent work by Lederer *et al.* examines the effect of different segment sizes on a dynamic adaptive HTTP streaming workload [7]. Using a single client, while varying network conditions during the experiment, they find that shorter segment sizes (2 or 6 seconds) enable higher average bit rates. Their single client is insufficient to generate high enough demand to test the limits of disk performance. Additionally, their work does not directly address disk storage issues like chunk size being examined in our paper.

3. EXPERIMENTAL ENVIRONMENT

The equipment we use to conduct our experiments was selected to ensure that network and processor resources are not limiting factors in the experiments. We use 12 client machines and one server. All client machines run Ubuntu 10.04.2 LTS with a Linux 2.6.32-30 kernel. Eight clients have dual 2.4 GHz Xeon processors and the other four have dual 2.8 GHz Xeon processors. All clients have 1 GB of memory and four Intel 1 Gbps NICs. The clients are connected to the server with multiple 1 Gbps switches each containing 24 ports. On the clients we use `dummynet` [11] to emulate different types of client networks and a modified version of `httperf` [8] to issue requests.

The server machine is an HP DL380 G5 with two Intel E5400 2.8 GHz processors that each include 4 cores. The system contains 8 GB of RAM, three 146 GB 10,000 RPM 2.5 inch SAS disks and three Intel Pro/1000 network cards with four 1 Gbps ports each. The server runs FreeBSD 8.0-RELEASE. The data files used in all experiments are on a separate disk from the operating system. We intentionally avoid using Linux on the server because of serious performance bugs involving the cache algorithm, previously discovered when using `sendfile` [6].

We use a number of different web servers. Most experiments use version 0.8.0 of `userver`, which has been previously shown to perform well [3, 10] and is easy for us to modify. We also use `Apache` version 2.2.21 and version 1.0.9 of `nginx`. Each server was tuned for performance before executing these experiments.

4. WORKLOAD GENERATION

The workloads and benchmarks used in this paper are based on methodologies developed previously [15] to represent YouTube video and client characteristics that were measured in 2011 [5]. Videos have a Zipf popularity distribution, and we target a disk cache hit rate of about 35% in order to exercise the disk.

Client sessions consist of a series of requests for consecutive 10 second segments of a video. The initial three requests are issued in succession, with each request issued immediately after the previous reply has been completely received (to simulate a play out buffer), while subsequent requests are issued at 10 second intervals. If a segment is not received before a 10 second timeout expires, the client terminates the session and we do not include the final partial transfer in our throughput figures. We chose a 10 second segment duration because it is the value used by Apple's HTTP Live Streaming implementation, and it is longer than the 2 second segments used by Microsoft's Smooth Streaming implementation [2]. We assume a fixed encoding bit rate of 419 Kbps (a common bit rate observed for YouTube), so 10 seconds of video is equal to 0.5 MB of data. Video data is stored in chunks that contain one or more video segments and when chunks contain multiple segments, clients issue HTTP range requests.

To generate the graphs in this paper, we repeat an experiment using a number of different target segment request rates and measure the average aggregate throughput of the server. Our test environment uses multiple clients, so the request rate is an aggregate value over all clients. To calculate the rate at which new client sessions are initiated, the target request rate can be divided by the average number of segments per session: 15.445 for 0.5 MB segments.

For this paper, we extend our previous methodology by introducing a new procedure for creating file sets. Care is taken to ensure that the same number of bytes of data are being requested whether the video is stored in chunks or not. Additionally, all of the data associated with each video is as close to the same location as possible on disk irrespective of the size and number of chunks used to store the video. This is required because the throughput of disk reads can be significantly impacted by the location of the files being read. In the following sections, we describe the procedure for creating different file sets and for confirming that videos are stored at comparable disk locations.

4.1 Determining File Placement

File system details are hidden behind a layer of abstraction. Applications are able to create directories and files within a hierarchy of directories, but cannot control where files are physically placed on disk. The kernel is responsible for placing files, and it is difficult for applications to even determine where the files are placed.

We determine the physical location of each file on disk using `dtrace` and the Unix `wc` utility. `dtrace` is a framework that allows us to insert probes into the kernel to monitor when specific kernel functions are called, and to record the arguments to those functions. While `dtrace` is monitoring the kernel, we run a script that uses `wc` to read every byte in every file in the file set. We use `dtrace` to collect information about all calls to the internal kernel functions `open`, `close`, and `bufstrategy`. We capture the names of files from the `open` call, and track the `close` calls to determine which files are associated with `bufstrategy` calls. The arguments to `bufstrategy` provide the logical block addresses (LBA) where the files are stored on disk.

After collecting the LBAs accessed for each file, we post-process the `dtrace` logs to compute the average LBA for each chunk. Similarly, when a video is stored in multiple chunks, we compute the average LBA for the video. The computed average LBAs can be used to compare the disk locations of videos that are stored using different chunk sizes (and to produce the graphs shown in Section 4.3).

4.2 File Set Generation

Our goal is to be able to directly and fairly compare the performance of videos stored with different granularities and to examine the impact that decision has on web server performance. As a result, we develop a methodology to control where files are placed on disk so that we can use the same locations on the same disk to store different file sets (i.e., chunked and unchunked).

We use three different file sets: one using a 0.5 MB chunk size, one using a 2.0 MB chunk size, and one that stores videos unchunked. Because video durations may not be exact multiples of each of the chunk sizes, we pad the file sizes (with data that is never requested) to ensure that a video occupies the same amount of space on disk, regardless of the chunk size. This helps to ensure that for each chunk size examined, the same video data can be placed in approximately the same location on disk.

We create a file set by starting with a freshly created file system, then writing all file chunks in a single directory. When a video consists of multiple chunks, we create the chunks consecutively on disk, but we create videos in a randomized order so there is no particular relationship between the location of a video and the number of times it is viewed. Using the same creation order for the different file sets, all chunks for the same video will be stored contiguously on disk, and at very close to the same physical locations for each of the different file sets. Unfortunately, this procedure does not produce repeatable results because the FreeBSD file system does not place directories in the same location each time the file system is recreated. Figure 1 and Figure 2 show examples of the potential variation in file placement that can occur, depending on the unpredictable choice of the kernel.

We work around this problem by creating a large number of directories (in this case 500), while using `dtrace` to determine the location of each directory. We then create the file set in the directory with the lowest LBA.

This procedure for creating file sets is expected to place files at the fastest locations on disk, with the chunks that comprise a video placed consecutively and with minimal file fragmentation. This layout permits significant performance optimizations that might not be possible with file sets that are heavily fragmented. We expect this layout could be achieved in most commercial video environments where video deletions are relatively uncommon, so it is a reasonable and consistent basis for comparing file sets.

4.3 File Set Locations

Figure 1 shows the average locations of each video when the file sets are created using our procedure. This figure shows that the files are placed in sequential order, with some small deviations, and videos created earlier have lower average locations. The results show that the videos for different workloads are generally created at the same locations across all three file sets.

Figure 2 shows the result when we alter our file set creation procedure to use a directory that is placed at a high LBA. The files are placed consecutively and at comparable positions for the different file sets; but files placed at these higher LBAs will be slower to access than the files in Figure 1, even though there is no apparent difference between the file sets at the application level.

4.4 Potential File System Performance

Using the file sets shown in Figures 1 and 2 we conducted experiments to determine the potential throughput that can be obtained

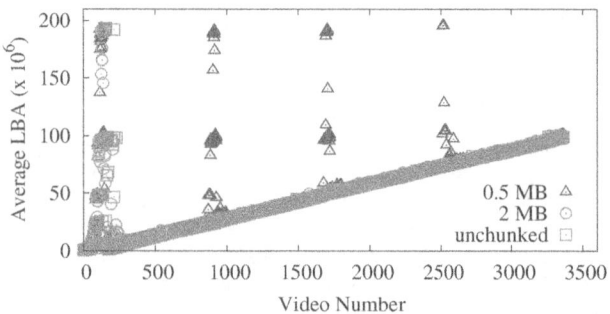

Figure 1: Video locations at low block numbers

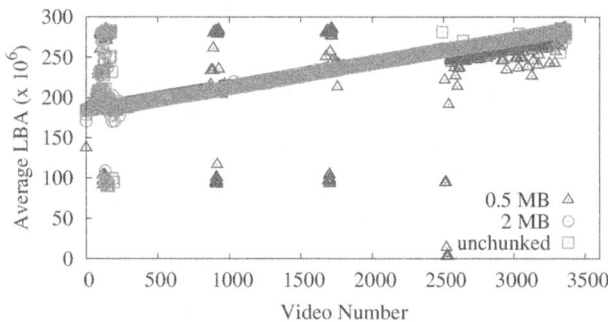

Figure 2: Video locations at high block numbers

while reading those videos files. We used `wc` to read all the chunks used for all videos in the file set. The chunks making up a particular video are read in sequential order, but the videos are chosen in a random order. We repeated the experiments 15 times for each file set while using `iostat` to measure average disk throughput. We calculated 95% confidence intervals using a t-distribution for the results for each file set, which are shown in Table 1.

file set	mean (MB/s)	95% c.i.
low unchunked	94.90	0.062
low 2 MB chunks	57.33	0.023
low 0.5 MB chunks	34.84	0.118
high unchunked	77.66	0.057
high 2 MB chunks	50.02	0.016
high 0.5 MB chunks	31.91	0.085

Table 1: Average Throughput using `wc`

Throughput is 10 to 25% higher when the file sets are placed at low positions on disk compared to high positions. These results demonstrate that placement has a significant effect on access speed and further illustrate the importance of placement when conducting a fair comparison between file chunk sizes. For consistency, we use the low file sets for all other experiments in this paper.

The results also show there is a significant difference caused by the choice of chunk size; the larger the chunk size, the higher the throughput. The following sections explore whether the throughput differences that occur when using `wc` also occur when a web server accesses the file set.

5. EXPERIMENTS

We use our HTTP streaming video workload generator [15] to evaluate the performance of three different web servers: `nginx`, `Apache` and `userver`. Specifically, we evaluated workloads where clients request 0.5 MB segments at a time, for 3 different chunk sizes (0.5 MB, 2 MB, and unchunked). We first look at the throughput of these web servers at different target request rates. Figure 3 shows the results for `userver` and Figure 4 shows the results for `nginx` and `Apache`. From these results, we see that `userver` and `nginx` perform similarly, with `Apache` generally trailing in performance. The relative performance of the web servers is consistent with previous measurements [15]. More importantly, the file chunk size has only a modest impact on throughput for all three web servers, with the largest performance increase occurring when changing from 0.5 MB to 2 MB chunks.

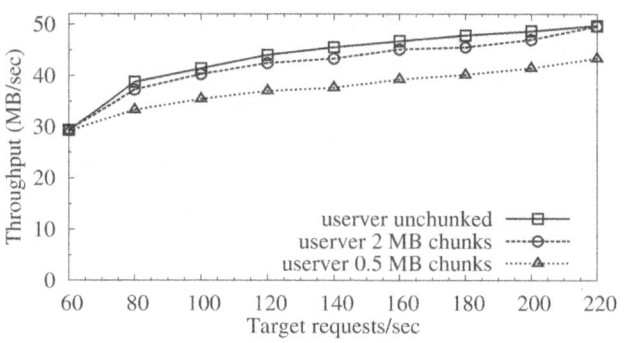

Figure 3: `userver` Throughput

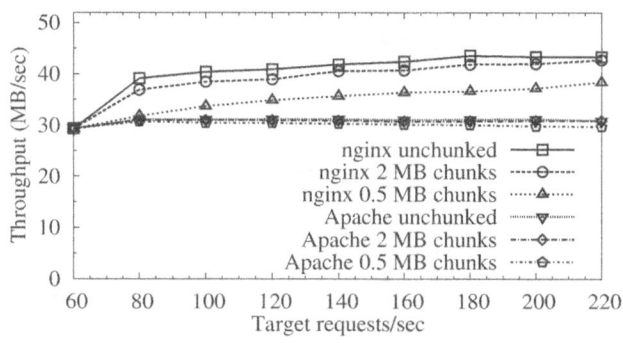

Figure 4: `Apache` and `nginx` Throughput

Given the results using `wc` in Table 1, we were surprised by the small difference in performance from increasing the chunk size for the web servers. These performance results led us to examine the contributions of the disk in isolation, as the throughput results in Figures 3 and 4 combine the throughput of both the cache and disk. We used `iostat` to measure the disk throughput using a workload with a target request rate of 80 requests/sec. The results were similar for both `nginx` and `userver`: 26.5 MB/s, 25.7 MB/s and 22.6 MB/s for unchunked, 2 MB, and 0.5 MB file sets, respectively. These throughput values are far below the peak disk throughput in the top half of Table 1, which were generated using the same file sets. These results suggest that neither `userver` nor `nginx` are efficiently reading from disk, and that the chunk size has a small impact on disk read performance for these servers.

5.1 Aggressive Prefetching

We had originally expected that the operating system could, without additional hints or modifications, significantly leverage the larger chunks to improve disk performance. However, the low disk throughput suggests that a workload specific, application-level disk scheduler and prefetcher may help the web servers take advantage of larger chunk sizes and achieve higher throughput.

Therefore, we utilize modifications previously made to userver to perform sequentialized reads and aggressive prefetching [15]. These modifications use an option in the FreeBSD implementation of sendfile that causes the system call to return an error code rather than blocking to read from disk [12]. When this occurs, we send a message to a helper thread which reads a portion of the file and signals the main userver thread after the data is read. The helper thread uses a FIFO queue and services requests sequentially. It prefetches a configurable amount of data prior to servicing each request. For this paper, we made additional modifications to userver that allow us to specify all of the files that comprise each video. This information is used to prefetch multiple consecutive chunks of the same video when the desired prefetch amount is larger than a single chunk. This is done for comparison purposes rather than as something we would expect a server to implement. It permits us to study the throughput of the server when files are stored in different sized chunks, while prefetching the same amount of data.

Figure 5 shows the throughput of the prefetch userver when using the different file sets. For each of these experiments, userver was configured with a prefetch size of 2 MB. We chose 2 MB because, in experiments not included here, it performed well compared with other prefetch sizes and it is a multiple of the chunk sizes, 0.5 MB and 2 MB. As expected, we also found that if the prefetch size was too large, throughput actually degraded. This is a result of prefetching data that is evicted from the cache before it can be transmitted to clients.

In the case of the 0.5 MB chunk size experiment, userver was configured to prefetch four consecutive chunks, to total 2 MB. The results show that throughput increases when the chunk size is increased.

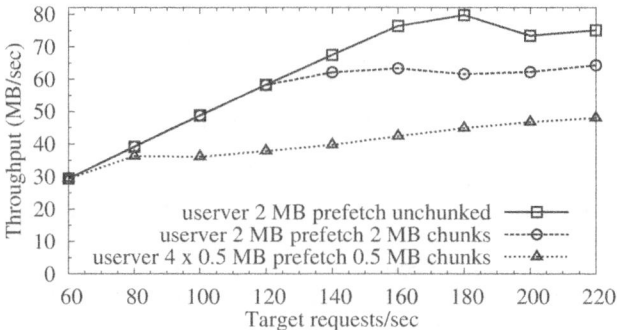

Figure 5: Throughput using a 2 MB prefetch size

These results show that, using sequentialized reads and aggressive prefetching, the size of chunks used to store videos has a large effect on server throughput. Server throughput is lowest with 0.5 MB chunks, it is improved by approximately 20 MB/s with 2 MB chunks, and is improved by an additional 20 MB/s with unchunked files. It also shows that prefetching the same amount of data from multiple chunks performs significantly worse than prefetching from an unchunked video.

Figure 6 compares the throughput of four web servers when using the unchunked video file set. Up to double the throughput is achieved when userver is configured to prefetch 2 MB at a time from an unchunked file set, showing the clear benefit of using unchunked files when the server also uses aggressive prefetching.

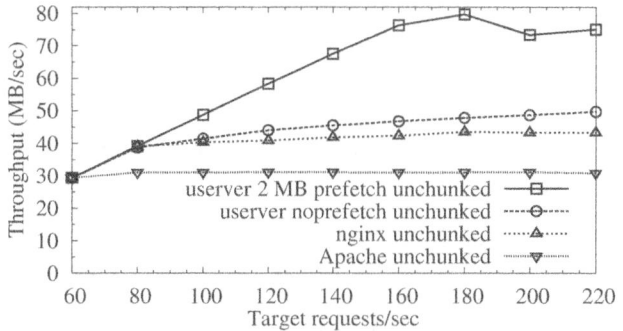

Figure 6: Throughput using an unchunked file set

5.2 Effect of Segment Size

From our experiments, we have found that most web servers use suboptimal methods to read from disk. Furthermore, web servers, when servicing client requests, do not generate an efficient disk workload. We found that we could use prefetching to change the disk access pattern, and improve throughput by reading large amounts sequentially from disk.

Another method that changes the client request pattern, and therefore potentially affects disk access patterns, is to change the size of segments that the clients request. This can be accomplished without modifying the web server implementations by simply generating a new workload with a different segment size. Figure 7 shows the results of experiments using a workload with 2 MB segments, which represent 40 seconds of video. We chose a size of 2 MB to equal the prefetch size we have been using, not because we know of any HTTP streaming video implementation that uses this segment length; most implementations use shorter segment sizes that optimize network performance [7]. We cannot compare the results of these experiments directly to the results in Figure 6 because the different segment size changes the workload. For example, there is an average of 15.445 segments per session using the 0.5 MB segment size compared to an average of 4.263 segments per session with 2 MB segments, so the target requests per second are significantly different for the two workloads. Comparing only the experiments in Figure 7 that use a 2 MB segment size, it is clear that increasing the segment size does not have the same effect as prefetching. It appears that segment size has little effect on throughput, and we intend to develop a methodology that allows us to compare workloads with different segment sizes so we can investigate the precise effect of changing the segment size.

6. DISCUSSION

In our experiments with three conventional web servers, using HTTP streaming video workloads, we found that the video storage granularity had only a small impact on performance. The impact

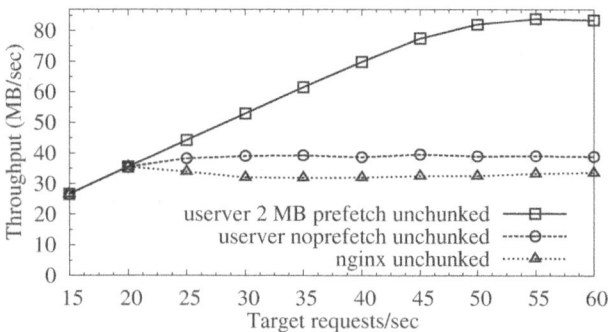

Figure 7: Throughput servicing 2 MB segments

was small since the efficiency of disk access with these servers did not substantially improve when storage granularity increased. Even in experiments where each video was stored in a single file, these conventional servers were only able to read from disk at a fraction of the disk's peak throughput rate. We also found, however, that with modifications to one of the servers, so as to aggressively prefetch and sequentialize disk accesses, the throughput could be doubled when videos were stored in single files rather than in small chunks. These results clearly suggest that for optimized servers, storing videos in single files rather than chunks may offer substantial performance benefits, at least on the server side.

What is less clear is the performance impact of video chunking on the rest of the HTTP ecosystem. Some web caches are currently unable to cache range requests on a large file, or fall back to full file caching. The latter may be less than ideal for video streaming workloads, as video files are generally large and most sessions only require portions of their requested videos. In contrast, frequently accessed video chunks can be cached in the same manner as other popular web objects. On the other hand, note that the same disk access efficiency issues that we observed for web servers, may arise at web caches and CDN nodes, and there may be a substantial impact on the potentially achievable performance if cached videos are stored in many small chunks rather than in single files. Examining the performance implications of video chunking on the rest of the HTTP ecosystem is a topic for future work.

7. CONCLUSIONS

The shift towards using HTTP for serving streaming video is largely the result of pragmatic decisions made by content providers to take advantage of the existing HTTP ecosystem. However, as most studies of web server performance are focused on serving small static files from cache that do not reflect streaming video workloads, this shift raises a number of performance issues.

In this paper, we developed a methodology to fairly compare the performance of server storage alternatives, specifically storing each video in a single file versus in many small files, and applied this methodology to investigate the performance implications of the two approaches. Our findings suggest that there is little difference in performance with these approaches when using conventional web servers. However, by introducing aggressive prefetching and sequentialized disk access to one of the web servers, we obtain as much as a two-fold improvement in throughput when storing each video as a single large file.

8. AVAILABILITY

The source code for our modified version of `httperf` and the log files we used to run the benchmarks in this paper are available at http://cs.uwaterloo.ca/~brecht/papers/nossdav-2012.

9. ACKNOWLEDGMENTS

Funding for this project was provided by the Natural Sciences and Engineering Research Council of Canada. The authors also thank Tyler Szepesi and Adam Gruttner for their help with modifications to `httperf`.

10. REFERENCES

[1] N. Agrawal, A. C. Arpaci-Dusseau, and R. H. Arpaci-Dusseau. Generating realistic impressions for file-system benchmarking. In *Proc. FAST*, 2009.

[2] A. C. Begen, T. Akgul, and M. Baugher. Watching video over the web: Part 1: Streaming protocols. *IEEE Internet Computing*, 15(2):54–63, 2011.

[3] T. Brecht, D. Pariag, and L. Gammo. accept()able strategies for improving web server performance. In *Proc. USENIX Annual Technical Conference*, 2004.

[4] J. Erman, A. Gerber, K. Ramakrishnan, S. Sen, and O. Spatscheck. Over the top video: the gorilla in cellular networks. In *Proc. IMC*, 2011.

[5] A. Finamore, M. Mellia, M. Munafo, R. Torres, and S. Rao. YouTube everywhere: Impact of device and infrastructure synergies on user experience. In *Proc. IMC*, 2011.

[6] A. Harji, P. Buhr, and T. Brecht. Our troubles with Linux and why you should care. In *Prof. 2nd ACM SIGOPS Asia-Pacific Workshop on Systems*, 2011.

[7] S. Lederer, C. Müller, and C. Timmerer. Dynamic adaptive streaming over HTTP dataset. In *Proc. MMSys*, 2012.

[8] D. Mosberger and T. Jin. httperf: A tool for measuring web server performance. In *Proc. 1st Workshop on Internet Server Performance*, 1988.

[9] G. Panagiotakis, M. Flouris, and A. Bilas. Reducing disk I/O performance sensitivity for large numbers of sequential streams. In *ICDCS*, 2009.

[10] D. Pariag, T. Brecht, A. Harji, P. Buhr, and A. Shukla. Comparing the performance of web server architectures. In *Proc. ACM EuroSys*, 2007.

[11] L. Rizzo. Dummynet: a simple approach to the evaluation of network protocols. *SIGCOMM Comput. Commun. Rev.*, 27(1):31–41, 1997.

[12] Y. Ruan and V. S. Pai. Understanding and addressing blocking-induced network server latency. In *Proc. USENIX Annual Technical Conference*, 2006.

[13] P. Sehgal, V. Tarasov, and E. Zadok. Optimizing energy and performance for server-class file system workloads. *ACM Transactions on Storage*, 6(3), 2010.

[14] T. Stockhammer. Dynamic adaptive streaming over HTTP: standards and design principles. In *Proc. MMSys*, 2011.

[15] J. Summers, T. Brecht, D. Eager, and B. Wong. Methodologies for generating HTTP streaming video workloads to evaluate web server performance. In *5th Annual International Systems and Storage Conference (SYSTOR)*, 2012.

Interactions Between HTTP Adaptive Streaming and TCP

Jairo Esteban* Steven Benno* Andre Beck*

Yang Guo* Volker Hilt† Ivica Rimac†

<firstname>.<lastname>@alcatel-lucent.com *Bell Labs Research, USA †Bell Labs Research, Stuttgart, Germany

ABSTRACT

HTTP adaptive streaming (HAS) is quickly becoming a popular mechanism for delivering on-demand video content over the Internet. The chunked transmission and application-layer adaptation create a very different traffic pattern than traditional progressive video downloads where the entire video is downloaded with a single request.

In this paper, we investigate experimentally the interplay between HAS and the network transport control protocol (TCP). We investigate the impact of network delay on achievable throughput and discover that HAS streams cannot fully utilize the available bandwidth due to the start and stop nature of HAS traffic patterns and its interaction with TCP. We investigate TCP pacing as a potential solution to this issue, particularly for packet losses that occur as a result of bursting packets into the network at the start of a transmission. We find that pacing can significantly increase a TCP flow's congestion window but it does not necessarily translate into higher throughput. Instead, we find that packet losses at the end of chunk transmission have a greater impact on throughput.

Categories and Subject Descriptors

C.2.2 [**Computer-Communication Networks**]: Network Protocols—*Applications*

General Terms

Algorithms, Measurement, Performance, Design

Keywords

Adaptive Streaming, Video Streaming, TCP, HTTP

1. INTRODUCTION

Over the past few years HTTP Adaptive Streaming (HAS) has become a popular method for streaming video over the Internet. As such, understanding HAS and its impact on Internet infrastructure warrant thorough analysis.

Each HAS video is encoded at several different quality levels. Each encoding is divided into small 'chunks'-video segments typically no more than a few seconds in length. A HAS client requests one video chunk at a time via HTTP. With each download, it measures the received bandwidth then runs a rate determination algorithm (RDA) to determine the quality of the next chunk to request based on factors such as available bandwidth and buffer fullness.

The bursty nature of chunked transmissions creates a specific traffic pattern. This pattern is very different from progressive video downloads where the entire video is downloaded with a single request without adaptation.

In this paper, we analyze TCP behavior in the context of this start-and-stop traffic pattern. We look at the inability of HAS to fully utilize the available bandwidth and look at pacing as a solution to the problem of bursts of TCP packets entering the network and overflowing bottlenecks, such as DSLAM buffers, which are small in comparison to those found in network service routers.

As part of our analysis, we break down a data transfer into three phases, the initial burst, ACK clocking phase, and trailing ACK phase. We analyze the impact of packet losses in each of these phases and use this understanding to conclude that pacing/shaping may improve throughput in some cases but not all, and, in fact, may even reduce performance.

The paper is structured as follows: in Section 2 we briefly describe relevant work related to TCP and describe our lab environment in Section 3. We discuss the impact of network delay on HAS throughput in Section 4 and analyze the interactions between HAS and TCP in Section 5. Section 6 investigates the use of pacing for HAS streams which is followed by our conclusions in Section 7.

2. RELATED WORK

The study presented in this paper focuses on the interplay between HAS and the underlying network transport control protocol (TCP), and explores TCP pacing as a means for HAS players to fully utilize the available bandwidth. Pacing has been studied extensively to reduce the burstiness of TCP traffic at the slow start phase and at the restart phase of idle TCP connections [3, 4, 11, 12]. The benefits of TCP pacing depend on the TCP variants, application requirements, and the configuration of underlying network routers/switches.

While pacing is beneficial to many applications in providing fairness and lower packet drop rates, it occasionally suffers from lower throughput due to delayed congestion signals and is at a disadvantage when competing for bandwidth against nonpaced flows [3]. In [12], pacing was found to increase synchronization among flows and reduce the effectiveness of selective acknowledgements (SACK) because SACK blocks tend to be more fragmented.

Permission to make digital or hard copies of all or part of this work for personal or classroom use is granted without fee provided that copies are not made or distributed for profit or commercial advantage and that copies bear this notice and the full citation on the first page. To copy otherwise, to republish, to post on servers or to redistribute to lists, requires prior specific permission and/or a fee.
NOSSDAV'12, June 7–8, 2012, Toronto, Ontario, Canada.
Copyright 2012 ACM 978-1-4503-1430-5/12/06 ...$10.00.

3. HAS TESTBED

We conducted a number of experiments in an emulated network consisting of one or more instrumented Microsoft Smooth Streaming clients [10] and an Apache server with the Smooth Streaming module [1] running on a Linux server. Additionally, the testbed includes a Linux server that runs an instance of the caching proxy Squid [2] and a FreeBSD server running Dummynet [7] to shape the download bandwidth and delay between the HAS client, cache, and server. Unless otherwise noted we configured Dummynet to use a 'tail drop' packet drop policy and a buffer size equal to two times the bandwidth delay product (BDP). Setting the buffer size to 2xBDP ensures that the network throughput is not limited by the size of the buffer. All servers used TCP CUBIC [8].

All experiments used the same 10-minute video clip which was encoded into 7 quality levels and divided into 300 two-second chunks. The seven quality levels are 300, 427, 608, 866, 1233, 1636, and 2436 Kbps.

4. THROUGHPUT VS. DELAY

In order to understand the impact of round trip time (RTT) on HAS throughput, we conducted a series of experiments in our emulated network with a single client requesting content directly from the video server for both HAS and FTP streams. We varied the available bandwidth and round trip delay (RTD) between the client and server for each run.

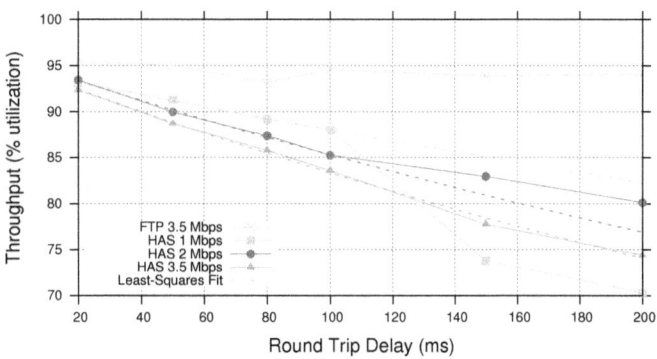

Figure 1: Average HAS Throughput - 3.5 Mbps Connection

We ran experiments with the bandwidth set to 1, 2 and 3.5 Mbps, and the RTD set to 20, 50, 80, 100, 150, and 200 ms. Figure 1 shows that the 1 Mbps HAS connection experienced a sudden drop in throughput for delays greater than 100 ms. This is related to the fact that Silverlight has separate chunks for audio and video streams and both media may be requested over the same TCP connection. Smaller audio chunks tend to reduce the TCP congestion window (cwnd). Conversely, the 2 Mbps connection performed better than projected due to fewer audio chunks sharing the same TCP connection. Since our router's buffer is sized to 2xBDP, this phenomenon does not occur for shorter delays because the size of the small audio chunks are closer to the router's limit. Other HAS schemes, such as Apple's HTTP Live Streaming (HLS), combine audio and video into one chunk, avoiding this problem altogether.

Anomalies aside, the results in Figure 1 show that HAS throughput drops off at a rate roughly inversely proportional to 2xRTD, i.e., each chunk download incurs a 2xRTD penalty on average. The FTP stream, in comparison, is robust to delay, using 93% of the available bandwidth even with 200 ms RTD. Because the FTP download is so large, it is able to sustain a continual stream of bytes in-flight and returning ACKs necessary for a quick recover from congestion

events. As a result of its longer download times, the initial burst, timeouts, and retransmissions that occur during the trailing ACK phase become negligible border effects. The difference between FTP and HAS throughput represents the performance penalty for dividing a video into chunks and requesting them separately.

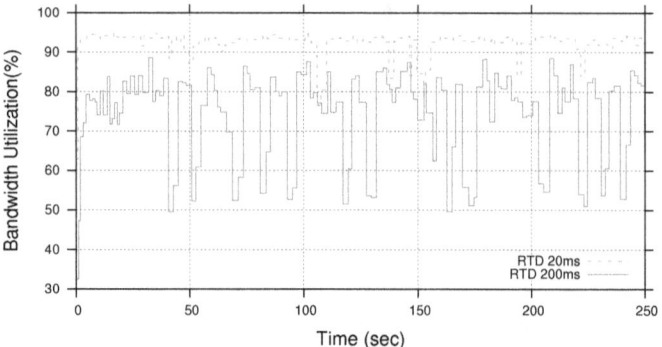

Figure 2: Chunk Download Rates - 3.5 Mbps Connection

In order to understand the performance degradation for HAS streams, we look first at individual chunk download rates. Figure 2 plots the bandwidth utilization for each chunk download for the cases where RTD equals 20 ms and 200 ms. For the 200 ms RTD case, many chunks are downloaded with over 80% efficiency while the worst case download used only 50% of the available bandwidth. This variation in efficiency was unexpected, especially given that the experiments were conducted in a controlled environment under static conditions. In comparison, the 20 ms case performs well, with most downloads utilizing 90% or more of the available bandwidth. To analyze the cause of these fluctuations, we examined network traces to understand how TCP dynamics affect bandwidth utilization for HAS streams.

5. TCP ANALYSIS

HAS streams generate sequential HTTP requests every few seconds. The on-off traffic pattern it creates is a challenge for TCP, which performs best when there is a steady stream of data packets and returning ACKs to keep the network pipeline full.

In order to understand the consequence of this traffic pattern, we divide TCP transmissions into 3 phases 1) Initial Burst, 2) ACK Clocking, and 3) Trailing ACKs, which are illustrated in a time-sequence graph in Figure 3.

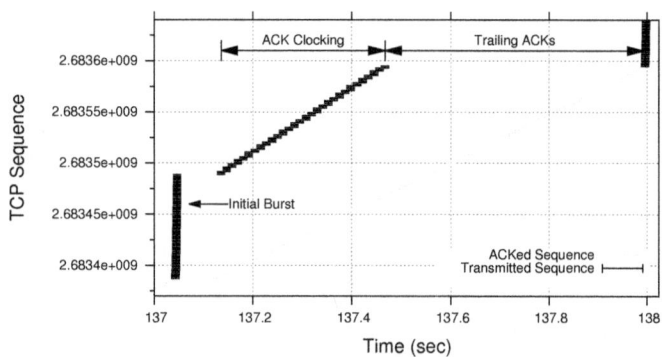

Figure 3: Three phases of TCP data transfer

For large transfers, most data is transferred during the ACK clocking phase where data and ACKs fill the network pipeline in both directions. The initial burst and trailing ACK phases are merely edge effects, explaining why the FTP transfer in Figure 1 is able to utilize 95% of the available bandwidth even as the round trip time increases.

HAS requests, on the other hand, are relatively small and a significant portion of the transmission duration is spent in the initial burst and trailing ACK phases, especially for large-delay networks. Indeed, if the congestion window is large enough and the data is small enough, the entire transmission could occur during the initial burst, eliminating the ACK clocking phase. The start-and-stop traffic pattern is similar to that of small web objects.

Next, we look at each phase in more detail and the impact of a packet loss during each of these phases.

5.1 Initial burst

The initial burst occurs when the sender fills its congestion window quickly at the start of each response, which has grown over time from previous transmissions. Once the window is full, the sender waits for returning ACKs before sending more packets and growing the congestion window further.

When the congestion window gets too large, the burst causes multiple packet loss at the bottleneck in the network, triggering congestion avoidance or even slow start. The start and stop nature of HAS requests encourages this inefficient sequence of events.

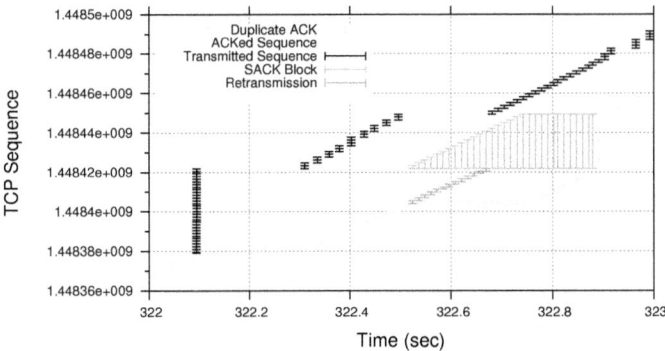

Figure 4: Packet loss from initial burst

Figure 4 shows a time-sequence graph of lost packets from the initial burst and their retransmission. The burst of packets overflowed the router's buffer, but left the reverse direction essentially empty. The losses sent the server into congestion avoidance even though the network's full duplex pipeline is half empty. As a result, the sender's congestion window does not reach the network limit. This is discussed more in Section 6.

As a side note, the benefit of the selective ACK (SACK) option is evident in Figure 4 as SACK blocks prevent unnecessary retransmissions of packets that were successfully received.

5.2 ACK clocking

The ACK clocking phase occurs when the sender receives ACKs from the receiver and has more data to send. In this phase, the network pipeline is full in both directions because the sender has filled the congestion window. Additional packets are clocked into the network by returning ACKs and the TCP stack's *cwnd* growth curve.

Figure 5 illustrates a packet loss during the ACK clocking phase. This phase is the most desirable phase to suffer a packet loss because TCP packets are in the network pipeline in both directions, allowing the mechanics of TCP, such as fast retransmit/fast recovery, to quickly detect and retransmit lost packets.

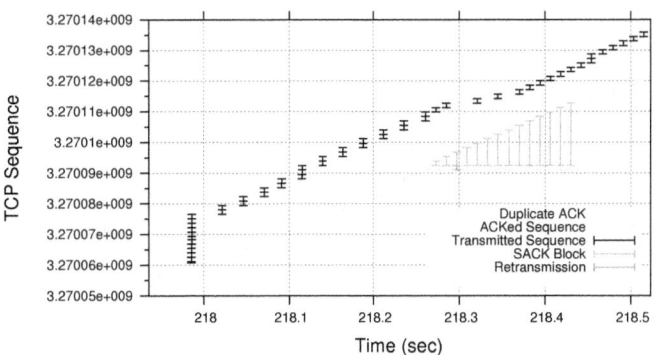

Figure 5: Packet loss during ACK clocking phase

5.3 Trailing ACKs

The trailing ACK phase is when the sender has sent all packets belonging to a chunk at least once and is waiting for outstanding ACKs to return. During this phase, the bytes-in-flight decreases with each returning ACK as there are no new packets to transmit.

We label a retransmission as one occurring during the trailing ACK phase if the sender runs out of new data to transmit before the end of the recovery phase. During the trailing ACK phase, fast retransmission is still possible as long as the packet loss occurs before the last three ACKs are sent. Fast recovery, however, is not possible since the sender has no new data for all or part of the recovery phase. If one of the last three data packets is dropped, the loss may require a retransmission timeout (RTO) to trigger a retransmission, increasing the download time by the RTO timer plus a full RTT.

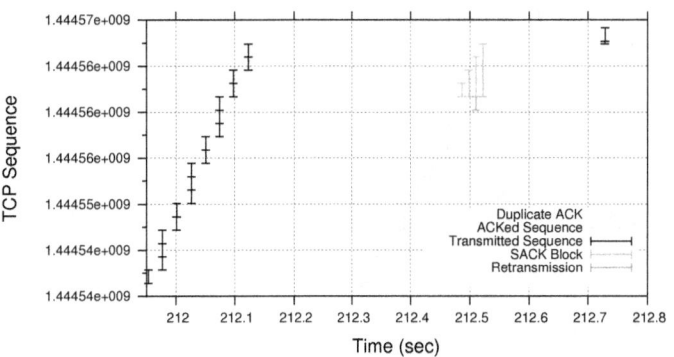

Figure 6: Packet loss during trailing ACK phase

This is the least desirable phase for packet losses to occur for two reasons. First, download times may be significantly increased due to idle time waiting for ACKs of retransmissions sent at the end of the transfer. Figure 6 shows a retransmission occurring at the end of a chunk transfer. The connection is idle for more than 100 ms while waiting for the packet to be ACKed.

Trailing packet losses reduce the throughput of the next chunk to be sent as well because the congestion window is reduced in response to the shrinking number of bytes-in-flight as trailing ACKs are received by the sender. RTO is a worst-case scenario because not only is the connection idle waiting for RTO timer to expire and the retransmitted data to be sent and ACKed, but the sender also goes into slow start to recover from RTO, incurring multiple round trip delays for the next chunk.

Even when RTO is avoided, the congestion window is reduced as a result of the shrinking number of bytes-in-flight with each returning ACK, as illustrated by the bytes-in-flight graph in Figure 8. When there are no packet losses, the initial burst quickly fills the congestion window to its last value at the end of the previous chunk. When packets are lost, the number of bytes-in-flight at the time of the retransmission becomes the new target window size which is significantly smaller than the window size prior to the packet loss. In this sense, flows that incur packet losses during the trailing ACK phase are penalized because they do not have new data to send for fast recovery, and, as a result, their congestion window shrinks well below where it would have had it not run out of data. This problem is not unique to HAS. Small web objects also create similar traffic patterns but the problem is more critical for HAS because chunks have a real-time constraint.

5.4 Slow-start

Slow-start causes large changes in throughput that can cause the client's RDA to become unstable. This reduction in throughput due to slow start is well understood [3] and HAS video is particularly vulnerable to it. When a HAS client needs to fill up its buffer, it will request chunks back-to-back. When the buffer is full, it will request the next chunk only after memory is freed when a chunk is consumed to be rendered by the player. During this waiting period, the retransmission timer could expire, sending the connection into slow start. Videos with longer chunk durations are more vulnerable because of their extended wait times. Furthermore, the start-and-stop nature of HAS flows creates more opportunities for a packet loss in the trailing ACK stage, which could trigger slow-start too.

Several solutions have been proposed [5, 9, 11]. According to our experiments, this area of research is central to performance improvements for HAS, especially for long-delay networks.

6. TCP PACING

Originally introduced for geostationary satellite links in heterogeneous networks with small buffers [6], TCP pacing is an attractive solution to address the bursty traffic created by HAS. It is a technique for spreading the transmission of TCP packets across the entire duration of the estimated RTT instead of sending bursts. By spacing the sent packets, router queues are less likely to overflow, reducing lost packets and increasing bytes-in-flight.

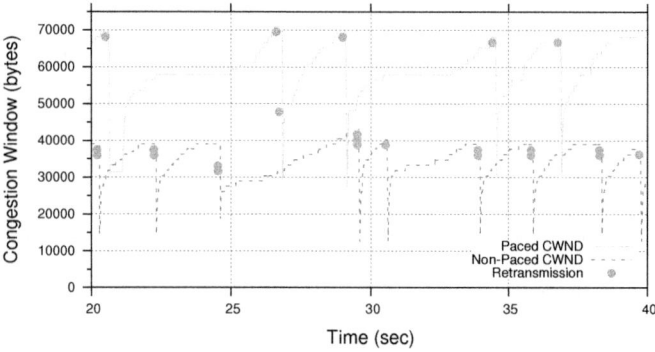

Figure 7: Comparison of estimated CWND for paced and unpaced flows in network with a 70 KB buffer limit

In order to investigate the effects of pacing for HAS streams, we prototyped a light-weight algorithm for pacing at the application level. We modified Squid source code so that the size of the first TCP send operation is always smaller than the size of the network buffer in our testbed (2xBDP). Our modified Squid cache also adds a delay equal to half the RTD between the client and the cache

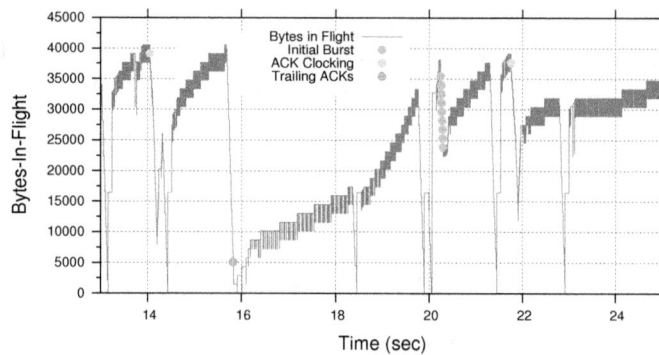

Figure 8: Packet losses in all three phases

before sending the remainder of the chunk data which should then be governed by the ACK clocking regime.

Using bytes-in-flight to estimate the congestion window, Figure 7 shows that the paced flow achieves the network limit of 70 KB whereas the non-paced flow achieves roughly half that amount. This indicates that unpaced flows saturate the network in one direction, leaving the reverse direction under-utilized. In addition, the paced flow reduced retransmissions by 62.2%. Despite these promising metrics, the paced flow realized only a 4.8% improvement in throughput because the connection reached its saturation point. This raises questions as to the conditions when pacing is and is not effective.

Although pacing can be effective at avoiding packet losses caused by the initial burst, it does not guarantee increased throughput. We know from Section 5.3 that packet losses in the trailing ACK phase can be even worse. Pacing can reduce throughput if it shifts losses from the beginning of the transmission to the end. This point is illusted by examining the bytes-in-flight in Figure 8 from a paced, 2 Mbps connection. In the 10 second window shown, the connection still suffers packet losses in all 3 phases despite pacing. Even though there are multiple packets lost during the initial burst, the connection is able to grow cwnd quickly after the retransmissions. For the trailing ACK loss that occurs at 16 sec., on the other hand, cwnd is sharply reduced after the recovery stage because of a lack of new data, impacting the throughput for the next 2 chunks.

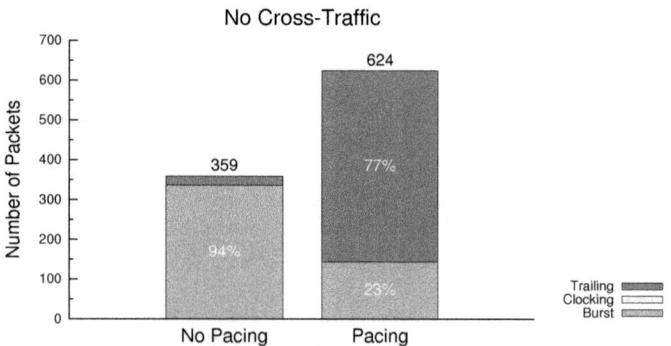

Figure 9: Distribution of packet losses/retransmissions for paced and unpaced flows without cross-traffic

Figure 9 shows the down-side of pacing. In this experiment we configured the network emulator for a 15 Mbps pipe with 80 ms RTD. In order to reduce the number of variables, we forced the requested video bitrate to 1.6 Mbps to eliminate artifacts from the client's rate determination algorithm (RDA) and controlled the idle time between requests to prevent the TCP idle timer from expiring. Since nearly all of the packet losses for the unpaced flow were caused by the initial burst, we expected that pacing would improve throughput. However, not only did the number of packet losses increase, but most of the packet losses migrated to the trailing ACK phase, the least desirable phase for losses. Consequently, the throughput was 14% lower for the paced flows.

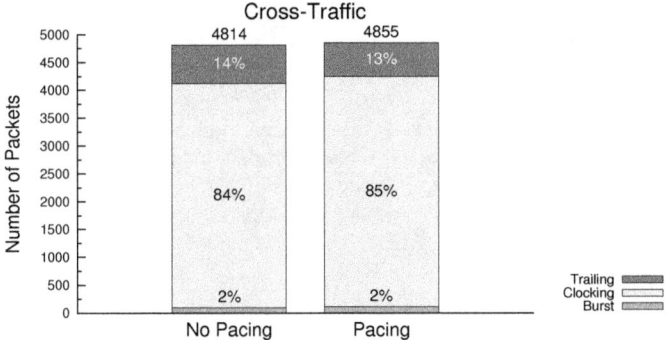

Figure 10: Distribution of packet losses/retransmissions for paced and unpaced flows over 15 Mbps pipe with cross-traffic

The above experiment is unrealistic in that it was conducted with a single HAS client without cross-traffic. We repeated the same experiment with the addition of 5 greedy TCP flows competing for bandwidth in the 15 Mbps pipe to simulate the multiplexing of flows that occurs over the public Internet. Figure 10 shows that after running the experiment 5 times, there are a very small number of initial burst packet losses, rendering pacing an ineffective tool for improving performance.

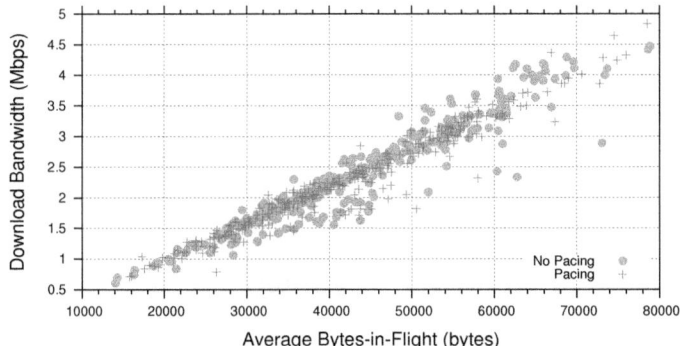

Figure 11: Throughput vs. bytes-in-flight for paced and unpaced flows over 15 Mbps pipe

Figure 11 shows the strong linear relationship between bytes-in-flight and throughput and that pacing was ineffective at increasing the bytes-in-flight. These results are representative of similar experiments we conducted where we varied the idle time, network buffer size, and where the client's RDA was allowed to determine which chunks to request and when to request them. In each case, throughput for the paced experiments was either comparable to or less than the throughput for the unpaced scenarios, as illustrated in Figure 12.

To corroborate our testbed results, we used the same client to request the same video over the public Internet via DSL. Ping times indicated that the RTT between client and server was 60 ms and the pacing algorithm was adjusted accordingly. Comparing the DSL

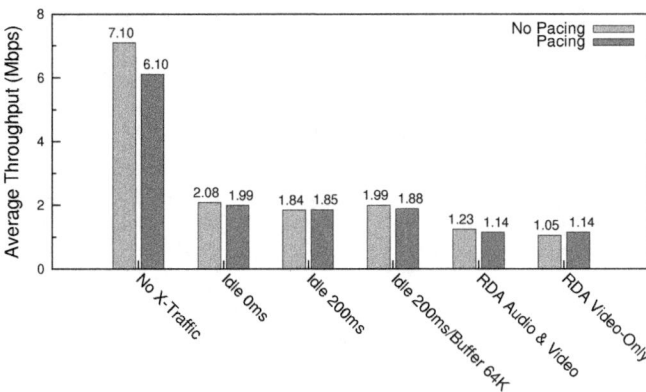

Figure 12: Throughput for various testbed experiments over a 15 Mbps connection with 80 ms RTD

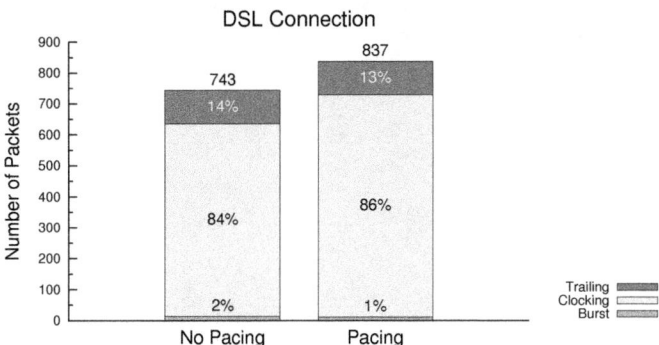

Figure 13: Packet loss statistics on the public Internet via DSL

pattern of packet losses to the testbed experiments, the proportion of packet losses in Figure 13 is nearly identical to those in Figure 10 where the HAS client was competing against the greedy TCP cross-traffic for bandwidth, with the majority of losses occuring during the ACK clocking phase. The lack of initial burst packet losses in the DSL experiment indicates that there is sufficient multiplexing of packets from other flows in the core network to shape the burst of packets before it reaches the bottleneck in the DSLAM, making pacing ineffective. Indeed, repeated DSL tests showed no significant difference in throughput for paced vs. non-paced flows.

7. CONCLUSIONS

In this paper we examined the TCP traffic patterns created by HAS video and divided the transmission into 3 phases, the initial burst, ACK clocking, and trailing ACK phases. We examined the impact of packet losses in each phase, determining that packet losses are most damaging during the trailing ACK phase and are least disruptive during the ACK clocking phase.

Intuitively, we expected that packet bursts should be a problem for HAS flows because of the start-and-stop nature of its traffic pattern, and that TCP pacing should improve throughput performance. Although TCP pacing is reported to improve performance in some scenarios, we found that burst losses do not occur as often as anticipated and that pacing was ineffective at improving throughput for HAS streams.

In future work, we intend to explore new TCP pacing strategies that aim to prevent packet losses due to the initial burst and in the trailing ACK phase by monitoring the location patterns of packet losses.

8. REFERENCES

[1] Smooth Streaming Module for Apache. http://smoothstreaming.code-shop.com/trac/wiki/Mod-Smooth-Streaming-Apache.

[2] Squid. http://www.squid-cache.org.

[3] A. Aggarwal, S. Savage, and T. Anderson. Understanding the performance of TCP pacing. In *INFOCOM 2000. Nineteenth Annual Joint Conference of the IEEE Computer and Communications Societies. Proceedings. IEEE*, volume 3, pages 1157–1165. IEEE, 2000.

[4] M. Allman and E. Blanton. Notes on burst mitigation for transport protocols. *ACM SIGCOMM Computer Communication Review*, 35(2):53–60, 2005.

[5] M. Allman, S. Floyd, and C. Partridge. Increasing TCP's initial window. RFC 2861, October 2002.

[6] C. Barakat, N. Chaher, W. Dabbous, and E. Altman. Improving TCP/IP over geostationary satellite links. In *Global Telecommunications Conference, 1999. GLOBECOM'99*, volume 1, pages 781–785. IEEE, 1999.

[7] M. Carbone and L. Rizzo. Dummynet revisited. *ACM SIGCOMM Computer Communication Review*, 40(2):12–20, 2010.

[8] S. Ha, I. Rhee, and L. Xu. CUBIC: A new TCP-friendly high-speed TCP variant. *ACM SIGOPS Operating Systems Review*, 42(5):64–74, 2008.

[9] M. Handley, J. Padhye, and S. Floyd. TCP congestion window validation. RFC 2861, June 2000.

[10] Microsoft. Microsoft Expression Encoder 2 SDK. http://www.microsoft.com/downloads/en/details.aspx?FamilyID=9a077a3d-58ce-454c-b486-153f0578be4a.

[11] V. Visweswaraiah and J. Heidemann. Improving restart of idle TCP connections. Technical report, Technical Report 97-661, University of Southern California, 1997.

[12] D. Wei, P. Cao, S. Low, and C. EAS. TCP pacing revisited. In *Proceedings of IEEE INFOCOM*, 2006.

Quiver: a Middleware for Distributed Gaming

Giuseppe Reina
Technicolor - Eurecom
France
giuseppe.reina@technicolor.com

Ernst Biersack
Eurecom
Sophia Antipolis, France
ernst.biersack@eurecom.fr

Christophe Diot
Technicolor
Paris, France
christophe.diot@technicolor.com

ABSTRACT

Massively multiplayer online games have become popular in the recent years. Scaling with the number of users is challenging due to the low latency requirements of these games. Peer-to-peer techniques naturally address the scalability issues at the expense of additional complexity to maintain consistency among players.

We design and implement Quiver, a middleware that allows an existing game to be played in peer-to-peer mode with minimal changes to the engine. Quiver focuses on achieving scalability by distributing the game state. It achieves consistency by keeping the state synchronized among all the players. We have built a working prototype of Quake II using Quiver. We analyze the changes necessary to Quake II and discuss how generic a software like Quiver can be.

Categories and Subject Descriptors

H.3.4 [**Information Storage and Retrieval**]: Systems and Software; C.2.4 [**Computer-Communication Networks**]: Distributed Systems

Keywords

Distributed Gaming, Peer-to-peer Systems, First-Person Shooter Games, Middleware Design, Distributed Gaming Challenges

1. INTRODUCTION

Over the last decade, the industry of multiplayer online games has seen a rapid growth in popularity and revenue. With the rise of Massively Multiplayer Online Games (MMOGs) large scale gaming infrastructures allow thousands of players to share a consistent experience over the Internet.

Most networked games rely on centralized architectures. The virtual world is managed by a game server that stores the game state and performs the game simulation, while coordinating remote players. The game server can be either located on dedicated hardware (*i.e.* a single dedicated machine or a cluster of servers) or on a player machine. The players remotely interact with the game using a client component that provides a graphical front-end to the remote simulation. The success of the centralized architecture comes from many advantages, namely ease of implementation, manageable game consistency (all players have the same view), cheating prevention, access control and billing.

Centralized architectures have drawbacks: (i) the cost of hardware is high, as game servers must be deployed on high-end servers that have to be operated and maintained; (ii) scalability is limited to the number of players that a server can support; (iii) finally, the presence of single points of failure makes the architecture not robust. Fast paced games such as First Person Shooter (FPS) games are more affected by the previous limitations. In FPS, the player controls the movements and actions of its avatar by looking at the world in a first-person perspective. The goal of such games is to compete in gun-based combats (*e.g.* kill the opposite team, steal the flag, etc.) as effectively as possible. The strict real time constraints limit the scale and the size of a FPS game session; only few players with limited network delays can interact.

Peer-to-peer (p2p) mechanisms naturally address these drawbacks by using players resources and offloading the servers from performing game management tasks. However, the absence of a central coordination entity leads to a number of new design challenges, including an efficient coordination of the distributed simulation, data storage and discovery, handling player churn, load balancing, consistency and latency related issues. These problems are extremely difficult to address, typically require low-level programming skills and a deep knowledge of the game architecture.

Our objective is to study the feasibility of a software that allows any existing single player game or centralized multiplayer game to be played in p2p mode (*i.e.* to be distributed among the players) with minimal changes to the game engine.

In this paper, we first study the basic *modus operandi* of a generic game engine (Section 2), we isolate the main functional components and we analyze how to distribute the game on multiple machines while maintaining an unaltered game experience (Section 3). We realize that design such a software to be as generic as possible is a challenge and we focus our analysis on understanding to which extent it is possible, and what the limitations are with current game engines.

We introduce Quiver (Section 4), a middleware for distributed multiplayer online games that can be applied to both, existing games and newly developed games. Our middleware implements p2p techniques to achieve system scalability and game state consistency. Quiver is designed to be "plugged" to any commercial game with minimal changes. It acts as a distributed entity storage that allows the game programmer to develop a p2p multiplayer game without the need to comprehend the low-level message exchange.

We show the feasibility of our approach by integrating Quiver with Quake II (Section 5). We show that the integration of Quiver in the Quake II game engine requires minimal code modifications and we discuss about the the limit of this approach.

2. BACKGROUND
2.1 Game features

Games have specific requirements that depend on the gameplay. We identify some fundamental properties that are common to most networked games, namely consistency, responsiveness, data persistency, scalability, and security.

The first and most important requirement of networked games is *consistency*, it is achieved when the following two properties are satisfied (i) the virtual world state is equally perceived by all the players at any time and (ii) the outcome of a user action to the virtual world reflects the intentions of the user (*e.g.* the action of shooting a player should damage the targeted avatar). Due to a number of issues, such as delayed traffic on the Internet and unpredictability of the user demand, this task is considered to be one of the most challenging in networked games.

Reactiveness is a strict requirement for fast-paced games. In such games, the user must perceive quickly enough the changes in the virtual world state, *e.g.* neighbor avatar movements or missile explosions. This requires the game architecture to communicate the result of a user action, as well as it's consequences within a time period that preserve natural interaction (*i.e.* $\leq 100ms$ for FPS games [4]).

Scalability indicates the ability of the game to handle high number of participants without sacrificing the user-experience. Precisely, a networked game architecture is required to sustain a theoretically unbounded growth in the user demand with a sub-linear impact on the user experience. In FPS games, the real-time gameplay imposes strict reactiveness requirements that affect both consistency, due to increased latency, and scalability, due to the high workload of the simulation. In most centralized games, only few players can interact in order to preserve consistency and reactiveness.

Persistency is the capability of the networked game architecture to guarantee that information, *e.g.* objects or scores, are not lost during the evolution of the virtual world.

Finally, *security* is one of the most sensitive requirement of multiplayer games. MMOGs have created complex virtual economies as well as fierce competitions among users. Therefore, a networked game architecture needs to guarantee security in order to ensure fairness among its users (*i.e.* cheating prevention) as well as privacy of user information.

2.2 Game architecture

The software component behind a game is called the **game engine**. It is responsible of capturing and processing player intentions coming from input devices (*i.e.* mouse, keyboard, controller, etc.). It stores and simulates the virtual world and finally renders the most updated state to the output devices (*i.e.* screen, speakers, etc.). A game engine includes several subsystems such as a physics engine, graphics and audio rendering, artificial intelligence, networking, and others depending on the genre and complexity of the game.

Regardless of whether the game is played locally or over the Internet, few recurring abstractions are required to describe it, namely the *entity*, the *command* and the *game loop*.

The dynamic part of the game state, can be described as a collection of virtual objects that make up the virtual world. Each virtual object is stored in a data-structure called **entity**. Every part of the

---

Algorithm 1 Game loop
function tick():
cmds ← fetchCommands(inputs_state)
gameState$_i$ ← executeCommands(cmds, gameState$_{i-1}$)
foreach *entity* in gameState$_i$
    gameState$_i$ ← simulatePhysics(*entity*)
    gameState$_i$ ← checkCollision(*entity*, gameState$_i$)
    gameState$_i$ ← *entity*.think(gameState$_i$)
end
graphicRendering(gameState$_i$)

---

game that can change its state is described by an entity, this includes avatars, monster, bullets, explosions, moving doors etc.

The **command** is a representation of the player intentions obtained by processing the user inputs. The command encapsulates an action that can be performed by the player on the subset of entities that he can control. The execution of a command by the game engine causes a change on the entities state.

Finally, at the very heart of the game engine there is the **game loop**, a single threaded execution process that periodically fetches and executes user commands, invokes all the subsystems to perform the simulation, and finally gives back the feedback to the player by rendering the player view (see *alg.* 1 above). At each step of the loop (often called *tick*), the simulation is performed by iteratively simulating each entity of the game state in terms of physics, collisions, and some internal behavior, often named *think function* that usually wraps time-triggered behaviors or calls to the artificial intelligence subsystem.

2.3 Multiplayer gaming

Multiplayer games give a single machine the authority to modify the game state. This architecture is called *client/server* or *centralized*.

The authoritative machine (*i.e.* the server) has the duty to communicate with the remote players (*i.e.* the game clients), to execute the player commands and to run the simulation that alters the virtual world. The client "packs" user inputs into commands to marshal to the game server and receives the view to render to the player. The game state can only be altered by the server, whereas the clients provide the players with the game interface to remotely interact with the state. The client also includes techniques to predict the future state of the game in order to compensate for the latency in the communication with the remote server [7, 11, 2].

While clients are deployed on player machines, the server component can be either deployed on a dedicated machine or hosted by one of the player machines. Scalability is often affected by the reactiveness requirement of the game. In FPS, for example, due to the high pace of simulation (20-60 ticks per seconds) and the high amount of commands sent by the users, a single server can often support as little as 20 players in a match.

3. PEER-TO-PEER GAMING
3.1 Requirements

The implementation of a scalable p2p game is still a research topic, whose challenges have been identified by the community [6, 10]. While the scalability issue can be intuitively solved by a p2p approach, it is challenging to perform the game simulation (see 2.2) in a distributed way while preserving the main features of the game consistency, reactiveness, scalability, persistency and security.

In addition, we identify churn and load balancing as two important features for a distributed gaming architecture.

Churn is a major problem in p2p games. The dynamics of player participation can change during the game: a player can join the ongoing game or can leave it with or without notifying the network, e.g. for a connection drop or a general failure. In a P2P game scenario, churn affects data availability, communication paths, and game state consistency, as the amount of available resources for computing and distributing the game state changes. *Load balancing* can be described as a set of methodologies for the distribution of computational, storage and bandwidth workload among the actual available resources, with the aim of maximizing the overall quality of experience. Thus, load balancing can be exploited for both handling churn and maximizing resource consumption.

In this work, our objective is to provide a system that scales with the number of users, while providing a level of consistency that ensures a satisfactory game experience.

Game distribution.

In a p2p environment, the tasks of game simulation and state storage, which for centralized architectures are performed by a single machine, need to be performed in a distributed manner. The distribution of a game can be divided in three subproblems: (i) state partitioning, (ii) state discovery, and (iii) distributed simulation.

State partitioning.

The state of the world, represented as a set of entities, must be stored and managed by multiple nodes, making sure that each node maintains in its local store only the relevant fraction of the virtual world. Scalability is affected by how the virtual world is distributed as smaller fractions of the virtual world require less resources in the player machines.

State discovery.

State discovery is a direct consequence of the state partitioning algorithm. It takes care to dynamically fetch the part of the game state that becomes relevant to the player. When new parts of the map are explored, the peer node must locate the remote peers responsible for the missing portions of the newly discovered state and fetch it from them.

Distributed simulation.

In the centralized architecture, the presence of a single authority (the server) guarantees to all the players a consistent view of the game. The p2p architecture inherently introduces a distributed parallel execution of the simulation that should allow the players to concurrently modify the game state. State replication and synchronization is needed to achieve consistency in the distributed environment.

A modification of one of the replicas should be propagated in a consistent manner to all the other instances in the remote nodes. The system should also provide collaborative algorithms for conflict resolution to address the problem of concurrent modifications of the same object.

4. QUIVER

4.1 Design

We present Quiver, a middleware for distributed multiplayer online games. We design and implement Quiver to be portable across different games (*i.e.* not based on any specific game engine[1]) and to

[1]Although FPS are the focus of this study we try to keep a broad

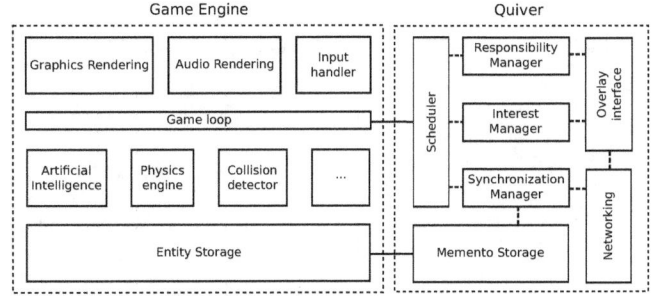

Figure 1: Quiver architecture and its interaction with the game engine

be as little intrusive as possible for the game engine (*i.e.* few modifications are required to integrate Quiver into an existing game). Quiver can be applied to both existing games and newly developed games by working with the abstractions of commands, entity and game loop discussed in section 2.2.

Quiver provides the game engine with object replication through a distributed storage facility that enforces game synchronization. Two high level predicates, the *responsibility* and the *interest*, are used as a means to respectively store and discover the game state. The distributed storage allows the game programmer to manipulate entities without the need to comprehend the low-level message exchange of the underlying distributed algorithms.

Quiver extends the basic functionalities of the game engine by scheduling its internal modules at each tick of the game loop and providing them with high level networking channels and an overlay network. We defined three abstract modules to address the challenges described in the previous section, namely the *Synchronization Manager* for distributed simulation, the *Responsibility Manager* for state partitioning, and the *Interest Manager* for state discovery (*fig.* 1). Each of these modules, together with the overlay network, can have multiple implementations depending on the requirements of the gameplay.

Object replication for distributed simulation.

We choose to implement the distributed simulation at entity level by providing a shared data-storage to the game engine. This way, the game state is distributed among the peers by replicating single entities ensuring that any entity can be instantiated in at least one peer. Quiver enforces consistency by handling the communication between the different replicas over the network.

Quiver treats the simulation phase at each tick of the game loop as a *black box*. Upon its invocation, Quiver enables the synchronization module to detect modifications applied to the game entity during the simulation phase by monitoring the evolution of the fields that describe the game entity.

The game synchronization module, defines the mechanisms that propagate and remotely apply local modifications to the game entity. Moreover, it specifies the conflict resolution policy upon concurrent write access to the same entity by two different peers in the network.

We believe that the shared data-storage approach best satisfies the *portability* and *non intrusiveness* requirements of Quiver. Precisely, as opposed to methodologies based on user commands or events exchange, such as the *Lockstep algorithm* [7], *Trailing State Synchronization* [5] and others [11, 12, 13, 8], the shared data-

view on other game genres, spanning from role-playing games to real-time strategy games

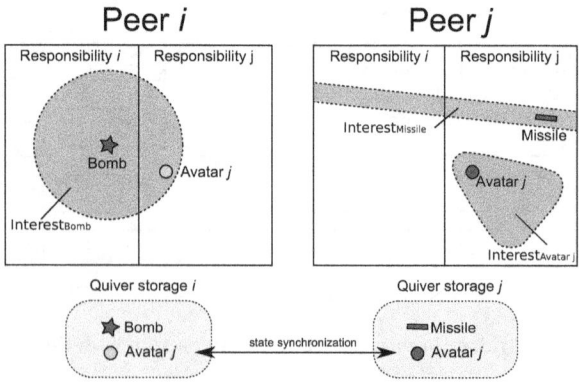

Figure 2: The three main modules in action: object replication and synchronization using spatial interest and spatial responsibility.

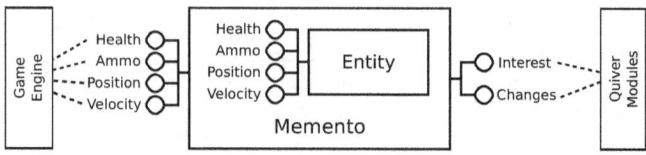

Figure 3: Entity/Memento wrapping and its interaction with the two layers

storage enforces a better decoupling from the logic of the game engine components that perform the game simulation. Moreover, the event-based approach would require the simulation to be performed only once all the events from the other peers have been received [9], thus violating the reactiveness requirement.

Responsibility Management and state partitioning.

We define the notion of **responsibility** to partition the game state and to assign replicas every peer.

A responsibility is a *predicate* assigned to each peer in the network, that applied to an entity returns true, if the object should be replicated on the peer, false, otherwise. The responsibility of a peer defines a subset of the game state that should be locally replicated. We use the responsibility as a means to cluster entities onto peers and ensure that for each entity there exists at least one peer responsible for storing the entity. Peers trade and negotiate responsibilities in the overlay network to achieve state persistency in an application specific manner.

State partitioning can be performed spatially by clustering entities according to their location inside the virtual world. This specific case of spatial responsibility, called *area of responsibility*, makes sure that the entities located inside the region are locally replicated (*fig. 2*).

Interest Management and state discovery.

While *Responsibility Management* defines how entities are disseminated among the peers, the state discovery defines how the peers communicate in order to fetch replicas of an entity located outside their responsibility. There are two main cases in which a peer should store a replica of an entity for which it is not responsible:

- The entity is "physiologically sensed" by the avatar of the player (*i.e.* eyesight, hearing, etc.)

- The entity is accessed by the simulation of a local replica during the execution of the local game loop.

We define the **interest** as a predicate of an entity that applied to another entity returns true if the latter should be locally available in the data-store, false otherwise. There are two kinds of interests, the *interest of an entity* and the *interest of the player*.

The *interest of an entity* is used to fetch all the the entities that can be modified during the future simulation of the local replica. Every moving entity has a default spatial interest of a sphere centered around the object so that all the other objects close to it can be processed by the physics and collision engine. In addition, when a moving entity implements a think function, the interest is used to pre-fetch all the other entities that the think function can modify.

The *interest of the player* is a special kind of interest, and recalls the *area of interest* used in centralized games [11]. Every player perceives the virtual world by looking at the view rendered by its client. Such a view depends on the specific game genre, FPS, for example, renders the view as the player is seeing the world through the eyes of his avatar, while real-time strategy games renders a bird-eye view that can be controlled by the player. The peer, therefore, must specify an interest in order to fetch all the objects that are required to render to the view of the player, regardless of the local responsibility.

Figure 2 summarizes the described modules through a simple scenario.

4.2 Implementation

Quiver has been implemented in Java and it has been designed to be modular and extensible. The main scheduler (*fig.* 1) manages the execution of three main modules that perform *Synchronization Management* to achieve per-entity eventual consistency, *Interest Management* for state discovery and *Responsibility Management* for state partitioning. Quiver provides the developer with a library of different implementations of such modules that can be used by the game engine or extended to meet specific game requirements. The low-level description and the implementation details of these modules is out of the scope of this paper.

Quiver defines its own data-structure for the entity, called *Memento*. The Memento exposes functionalities to both the game engine and the middleware providing a shared data-structure for the two communicating layers (*fig.* 3). The Memento keeps track of the modifications applied to the entity from the game engine allowing the underlying layer to detect when the entity state must be negotiated with the remote peers. In addition, the memento exposes the *Interest* of the entity at each step of the game simulation. Finally, the memento data-structure supports a transparent per-field serialization used by the Synchronization module to marshal entity updates across the network.

The *Networking* module provides the other Quiver modules with high-level networked channels to communicate using message exchanges that can be either reliable or best effort.

Game Integration.

Integration of Quiver with a game engine is straightforward and consists of three steps.

- Invoke the Quiver scheduler at the end of each tick of the game loop

- Adopt the Quiver storage to store the game objects (*i.e.* insertion, deletion and simulation must be notified to the middleware).

- Link or wrap each entity using a Memento.

In order to provide a single data-structure shared by the game engine and middleware, some functionalities must be defined in the Memento data-structure. In particular, a Memento must specify, at each tick of the simulation, the Interest of the game entity used for state discovery by the Interest Management module. The Interest is used in the overlay network to *subscribe* for the portion of the virtual world that is relevant to the entity associated. For example, an avatar Memento is "interested" in the portion of the world it can perceive, while a bomb is "interested" in the portion of the world that can damage upon its explosion.

Quiver requires the entity to expose a bitmask that indicates which fields or parts of the entity have been changed during the last tick. The bitmask is used to reduce conflicts caused by simultaneous modification of the game entity by acting at field-level rather than object-level. Moreover, the bitmask is used to produce delta-encoded updates to reduce load of the synchronization messages on the network.

5. ANALYSIS

5.1 Quake case study

We evaluated Quiver with Quake II, the popular FPS developed by idSoft (*fig.* 4). Quake II is the first FPS game that offered excellent game-play in online matches. Moreover, Quake II has been the object of several mods by the open source community that spawned some of the most played free FPS such as WarSow and CodeRED: Alien Arena.

We chose a Java version of Quake II called Jake2[2] created by faithfully translating the original C code of Quake II into Java code[3]. We chose the Java implementation since we need a rich environment of tools for testing and debugging, moreover Java makes the game easily portable to different hardware architectures and operating systems. Versions of Jake 2 have been ported to multiple architectures spanning from embedded systems such as Android to browser integrated HTML5 WebGL

We integrate Quiver with the server component of Jake2 maintaining the decoupling with the client component. This integration can be used for both, a pure p2p mode by simultaneously activating both the client, the server and the middleware component in each player machine, and multiple server architecture, by activating only the server and the middleware on dedicated machines, while players connect to them by using ordinary clients.

We use Aspect Oriented Programming (AOP) and AspectJ [1], to integrate the middleware into Jake2. AOP enabled us to inject calls of the middleware without modifying the original game code. Using AOP, we were able to decorate the entity state into a Quiver's Memento intercepting single reads and writes to the fields of the entity and injecting control code used to monitor the evolution of the entity state.

The resulting number of lines of code of the bridge between Quiver and Quake is 8k, versus the 150k for Quiver. Due to the verbosity of the Quake entity and the triviality of the wrapping operations, the code related to the entity-Memento integration has been automatically generated using a compiler to Java code.

Game distribution modules.

In order to evaluate the middleware we implement some strategies for the game distribution modules.

We adopt the replication strategy described by Bharambe *et al.*

Figure 4: Screenshot of Quake II in p2p using Quiver

[3] for game synchronization. Entities are replicated among the peers either as primary copy or as a secondary copy. For each entity in the virtual world, there exists a unique primary copy and the peer that owns the primary copy is the authoritative peer for the entity. The peers that can interact with the entity locally replicate the remote entity by holding a secondary copy. The primary copy owner acts as a central coordinator for all the secondary copies and taking care of forwarding entity updates and managing conflicts upon simultaneous modification of the same entity.

The game state is partitioned into *disjoint* spatial responsibilities, or area of responsibility (AoR), such that each primary copy is assigned to one and one peer only. We use the BSP tree nodes of the Quake II map both to partition the game map into AoR's and to define Interests of the avatars and monsters. Negotiation of responsibilities and interests are done over an DHT network based on Kademlia that has been adapted to better work with the BSP tree nodes of Quake.

We establish that in order to reduce message exchanges between the peers, and reduce conflicts caused by simultaneous modifications, the primary copy is the only copy that can be simulated[4].

We handle parallel write attempts of an entity at the peer who owns the primary copy. The primary copy decides which of the concurrent modifications should win the race condition. The decision on how to resolve the conflict comes from the entity itself and its properties. By default, changes are applied in a first-come, first-served basis in order to boost reactivity. Therefore, conflicts between a primary and a secondary are always won by the owner of the primary copy due to the direct modification by the game engine.

There are, however, entities that need a different resolution mechanism. For example, the effect of rollback on an avatar position negatively affects the game experience of the player controlling it. Rollback of an avatar to an old position causes a change of the whole view of the player and this operation must be avoided as much as possible. In this context, we prefer to give priority to the update coming from the machine that handles the player, regardless of whether it stores a primary or a secondary copy.

Play experience.

The resulting prototype provides a good play experience. Operation of handing-over of an entity due to its migration from a responsibility to an other is lightweight enough to not be noticed by the players. The effects of rollback due to modification conflicts of an

---

[2]Jake2. http://www.bytonic.de/html/jake2.html
[3]Unofficial Jake2 Resource.
https://wiki.in-chemnitz.de/bin/view/RST/Jake2

[4]In FPS games, the high pace of simulation causes frequent changes in the state of an entity.

entity are significantly reduced by the adoption of the Memento bit-mask that allows multiple peers to simultaneously modify different disjoint subsets of the entity fields. However, due to its early state of development the prototype suffers from the classic inconsistencies introduced by latency (jerky movements of the other players outside the local responsibility).

5.2 Limits and future development

During our study we found two main limitations with our approach. First, the animations of entities that are synchronized by remote peers appear jerky. This is a common problem in networked games and is caused by the latency in the p2p communication. Our choice of decoupling the game engine from the middleware, makes the adoption of well known centralized techniques for latency compensation [2] challenging. We are currently working on a new prediction system able to work on our distributed environment without sacrificing the modularity of our current design.

The second limitation regards inconsistencies inherently caused by the object replication methodology. In particular, when executing the game loop it may happen that a think function (*e.g.* a bomb exploding near a group of avatars) or a player command (*e.g.* a spell is casted upon a team), can modify multiple entities at the same time. Since each entity follows an isolated process of update propagation, it may happen that the changes made locally on a subset of objects are reverted back to an old state due to a remote conflict. The result is that entities are not modified by the command or simulation (*i.e.* an avatars survives the bomb explosion, or a player is not affected by the spell) thus violating the consistency requirement.

Finally, we plan to support *churn* in the next version of Quiver to allow each player in the game to freely join and leave the game at any moment. The resources allocated by the leaving peer will be redistributed to the remaining peers in a timely manner without affecting the gameplay of other players.

6. CONCLUSIONS AND OUTLOOK

A scalable solution for p2p gaming requires to properly address the following questions: (i) How to distribute the game state (ii) How to discover the game state and (iii) How to perform the game simulation on the game state in a distributed way.

We designed a middleware, called Quiver, that addresses the three previous questions. Quiver encapsulates each aspect in one of its modules. Precisely, the game state is distributed by defining a *Responsibility* for each peer. The game state is discovered by subscribing to the *Interest* exposed by each entity. Finally, entities are replicated on the machines according to their Responsibility and the Interest. We proved the feasibility of our approach by creating a working prototype with a popular FPS game (*i.e.* Quake II).

We showed that our approach allowed us to abstract from the internal design of the game and can be adopted with minor modification to an existing engine: few entry points are required to Quiver to interact with Quake II. Using Aspect Oriented Programming as a methodology, we were able to integrate Quiver with Quake II by simply injecting code into the game engine.

As future work, we plan to evaluate the performance of Quake II comparing the centralized version against the Quiver-integrated version. The results obtained will allow us to define the architectural direction for the next generation of Quiver. Finally, we will integrate Quiver in more recent and diverse games in order to conduct performance comparisons between different game genres.

7. REFERENCES

[1] Aspectj framework, cross-cutting objects for better modularity. *http://eclipse.org/aspectj/*.

[2] Y. Bernier. Latency compensating methods in client/server in-game protocol design and optimization. *http://bit.ly/wGNhMO*, 2001.

[3] A. Bharambe, J. Pang, and S. Seshan. Colyseus: a distributed architecture for online multiplayer games. In *Proceedings of the 3rd conference on Networked Systems Design & Implementation*, NSDI'06, Berkeley, CA, USA, May 2006.

[4] M. Claypool and K. Claypool. Latency and player actions in online games. *Commun. ACM*, 49(11), November 2006.

[5] E. Cronin, A. Kurc, B. Filstrup, and S. Jamin. An efficient synchronization mechanism for mirrored game architectures. pages 7–30, Hingham, MA, USA, May 2004. Kluwer Academic Publishers.

[6] L. Fan, P. Trinder, and H. Taylor. Design issues for peer-to-peer massively multiplayer online games. *Int. J. Adv. Media Commun.*, pages 108–125, March 2010.

[7] G. Fiedler. What every programmer needs to know about game networking. *http://bit.ly/7jSZ15*, January 2011.

[8] L. Gautier and C. Diot. Design and evaluation of mimaze, a multi-player game on the internet. In *Proceedings of the IEEE International Conference on Multimedia Computing and Systems*, ICMCS '98, pages 233–, Washington, DC, USA, 1998. IEEE Computer Society.

[9] S. Hu, S. Chang, and J. Jiang. Voronoi State Management for Peer-to-Peer Massively Multiplayer Online Games. In *Consumer Communications and Networking Conference*, CCNC '08, pages 1134–1138, 2008.

[10] C. Neumann, N. Prigent, M. Varvello, and K. Suh. Challenges in peer-to-peer gaming. *SIGCOMM Comput. Commun. Rev.*, 37(1):79–82, October 2007.

[11] A. Steed and M. Oliveira. *Networked Graphics: Building Networked Games and Virtual Environments*. Morgan Kaufmann publishers, 2009.

[12] J. Steinman. Breathing time warp. In *Proceedings of the seventh workshop on Parallel and distributed simulation*, PADS '93, pages 109–118, New York, NY, USA, 1993. ACM.

[13] J. Steinman and J. Wong. The speedes persistence framework and the standard simulation architecture. In *Proceedings of the seventeenth workshop on Parallel and distributed simulation*, PADS '03, pages 11–, Washington, DC, USA, 2003. IEEE Computer Society.

Cloud Transcoder: Bridging the Format and Resolution Gap between Internet Videos and Mobile Devices

Zhenhua Li
EECS, Peking University
Beijing, China
lzh@net.pku.edu.cn

Yan Huang
Tencent Research
Shanghai, China
galehuang@tencent.com

Gang Liu
Tencent Research
Shanghai, China
sinbadliu@tencent.com

Fuchen Wang
Tencent Research
Shanghai, China
futurewang@tencent.com

Zhi-Li Zhang
EECS, University of Minnesota
Minneapolis, MN, US
zhzhang@cs.umn.edu

Yafei Dai
EECS, Peking University
Beijing, China
dyf@pku.edu.cn

ABSTRACT

Despite the increasing popularity, Internet video streaming to mobile devices is still challenging. In particular, there has been a format and resolution "gap" between Internet videos and mobile devices, so mobile users have high demand on video transcoding to facilitate their specific devices. However, as a computation-intensive work, video transcoding is greatly challenged by the limited battery capacity of mobile devices. In this paper we propose and implement "Cloud Transcoder", which utilizes an intermediate cloud platform to bridge the "gap" via its special and practical designs. Specifically, Cloud Transcoder *only requires* the user to upload a *video request* rather than the video content. After getting the video request, Cloud Transcoder downloads the original video from the Internet, transcodes it on the user's demand, and transfers the transcoded video back to the user *with a high data rate* via the intra-cloud data transfer acceleration. Therefore, the mobile device only consumes energy in the last step – fast retrieving the transcoded video from the cloud. Running logs of our real-deployed system confirm the efficacy of Cloud Transcoder.

Categories and Subject Descriptors

C.2.4 [**Distributed Systems**]: Distributed Applications

Keywords

Cloud computing, video transcoding, mobile devices

1. INTRODUCTION

In recent years, mobile devices, such as smartphones and tablets, have become more and more popular. Gartner reports [1] that worldwide sales of mobile devices have far exceeded the PC shipments. Besides the conventional web surfing, nowadays more and more accesses from mobile devices are headed for Internet video streaming and the mobile video traffic tends to dominate the total Internet mobile traffic in the near future [2]. Despite the increasing popularity, Internet video streaming to mobile devices is still challenging for a number of reasons. In particular, there has been a format and resolution "gap" between Internet videos and mobile devices.

Due to relatively small but highly diverse screen resolutions, embedded processors and low battery capacities, mobile devices usually support limited video formats and resolutions [3]. For example, iPhone4S, one of the most popular and powerful smartphones at present, typically supports MP4 videos up to 640*480 pixels and does not support Adobe Flash videos (FLV). However, today's Internet videos, either uploaded by common users or supplied by large video content providers, are still PC oriented – most videos possess a single format and very limited resolutions. For instance, Youtube usually transcodes its own videos into three resolutions (240p, 360p and 480p) in FLV format in advance to *approximate* its users' devices and bandwidths. As to a mobile device, it often still has to transcode the downloaded video to *match* its specific playback capability, i.e., to *fill the "gap"* between Internet videos and mobile devices.

By reason of the abovementioned "gap", mobile users have high demand on *video transcoding* to facilitate their specific devices. However, as a computation-intensive work, video transcoding is greatly challenged by the limited battery capacity of mobile devices. The computation complexity of video transcoding is equal to that of simultaneously viewing (decoding) multiple videos [4, 5], so locally performing video transcoding in mobile devices (e.g., by using the mobile applications like [6, 7]) can easily consume up their battery capacity. Consequently, today's mobile users often have to utilize their PCs with auxiliary software (like iTunes or AirVideo [8]) to transcode the original videos and then transfer the transcoded videos back to mobile devices, which is very inconvenient especially when they are out of office/home.

Recent years have seen a worldwide upsurge of cloud service deployments [9] that gradually move computation intensive works from light-weight end users onto heavy-weight data centers. This upsurge provides us with a novel perspective to consider the "gap" problem. It is natural to imagine

---

Permission to make digital or hard copies of all or part of this work for personal or classroom use is granted without fee provided that copies are not made or distributed for profit or commercial advantage and that copies bear this notice and the full citation on the first page. To copy otherwise, to republish, to post on servers or to redistribute to lists, requires prior specific permission and/or a fee.
NOSSDAV'12, June 7–8, 2012, Toronto, Canada.
Copyright 2012 ACM 978-1-4503-0752-9/12/06 ...$10.00.

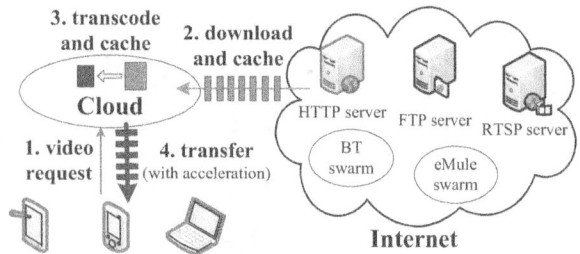

Figure 1: Working principle of Cloud Transcoder.

using cloud utilities to perform video transcoding for mobile users on their specific demands. To provide such *on-demand* video transcoding service, the existing cloud-based transcoding solution (e.g., [10, 11, 12]) typically lets the user upload her/his original video ($\leq$ 100 MB) to the cloud which subsequently transcodes the original video and transfers the transcoded video back to the user. This solution may work well for transcoding audios and short videos, but is not fit for transcoding *long videos* like movies – the difficulty lies in that it would be time-consuming (and thus energy-consuming) for the user to upload his (long) original video to the cloud, because most users access the Internet in an asymmetric manner (i.e., their upload bandwidth is lower than their download bandwidth) and the size of the original movie is usually larger than that of the transcoded movie.

Taking all above into consideration, in this paper we propose and implement "Cloud Transcoder", which utilizes an intermediate cloud platform to bridge the format and resolution gap between Internet videos and mobile devices. As depicted in Figure 1, Cloud Transcoder *only requires* the user to upload a *video request* rather than the video content. The *video request* contains a *video link* and the *user-customized transcoding parameters* including the format, resolution, etc., so it looks like:

<*video link*; *format, resolution, · · ·* >, [1]

where the *video link* can be an HTTP/FTP/RTSP link or a BitTorrent/eMule/Magnet[13] link. After getting the video request, Cloud Transcoder downloads the original video (says v) using the video link (from the Internet, e.g., a HTTP/FTP/RTSP server or a P2P swarm where the original video is stored) and stores v in the cloud cache, then transcodes v on the user's demand and caches the transcoded video (says v'), and finally transfers v' back to the user *with a high data rate* via the intra-cloud data transfer acceleration. Nowadays, web/P2P download has become the major way in which people obtain video content, so it is reasonable for Cloud Transcoder to require its users to upload their video requests rather than the video content. Therefore, the mobile user only consumes energy in the last step – fast retrieving the transcoded video from the cloud. In a nutshell, Cloud Transcoder provides energy-efficient on-demand video transcoding service to mobile users via its special and practical designs trying to minimize the user-side energy consumption.

---

[1]For a "naive" user who cannot decide what format and resolution he should specify, he can leave the transcoding parameters empty and then Cloud Transcoder will recommend some possible choices to him.

Since Cloud Transcoder moves all the video download and transcoding works from its users to the cloud, a critical problem is how to handle the resulting heavy *download bandwidth pressure* and *transcoding computation pressure* on the cloud. To solve this problem, we utilize the *implicit data reuse* among the users and the *explicit transcoding recommendation and prediction techniques*. First of all, for each video v, Cloud Transcoder only downloads it from the Internet when it is requested for the first time, and the subsequent download requests for v are directly satisfied by using its copy in the cloud cache. Such implicit data reuse is completely handled by the cloud and is thus oblivious to users. Meanwhile, the transcoded videos of v (note that v may correspond to multiple transcoded videos in different formats and resolutions which are collectively denoted as $T(v)$) are also stored in the cloud cache to avoid repeated transcoding operations.

Moreover, when a user uploads a video request referring to a video v and the cloud cache has stored several transcoded videos of v (i.e., $T(v)$) that do not match the user-customized parameters, Cloud Transcoder will *recommend* $T(v)$ to the user for a possible choice, so as to further reduce the transcoding computation pressure. Finally, when the transcoding computation pressure falls down at night, we also utilize the video popularity based *prediction* to transcode some videos into specific formats and resolutions in advance, so as to satisfy future potential user requests in daytime for load balancing. According to the real-world performance of Cloud Transcoder, the cache hit rate of download tasks reaches 87% while the cache hit rate of transcoding tasks reaches 66%.

Since May 2011, we have implemented Cloud Transcoder as a novel production system [2] that employs 244 commodity servers deployed across multiple ISPs. It supports popular mobile devices, popular video formats and user-customized video resolutions. Still at its startup stage, Cloud Transcoder receives nearly 8,600 video requests sent from around 4,000 users per day, and 96% of the original videos are long videos ($\geq$ 100 MB). But its system architecture (in particular the cloud cache) is generally designed to serve 100,000 daily requests. Real-system running logs of Cloud Transcoder confirm its efficacy. As an average case, a mobile user needs around 33 minutes to retrieve a transcoded video of 466 MB. The above process typically consumes around 9%/5% of the battery capacity of an iPhone4S/iPad2 ($\approx$ 0.47 WH/1.25 WH, 1 WH = 1 Watt Hour = 3600 J). And the average data transfer rate of transcoded videos reaches 1.9 Mbps, thus enabling the users' view-as-download function. In conclusion, the system architecture, design techniques and real-world performance of Cloud Transcoder provides practical experiences and valuable heuristics to other cloud system designers planning to offer video transcoding service to its users.

The remainder of this paper is organized as follows. Section 2 describes the system design of Cloud Transcoder, including its system architecture and critical design techniques: transcoding prediction, cloud cache organization and data transfer acceleration of transcoded videos. Section 3 evaluates the performance of Cloud Transcoder via its real-system running logs. Finally, we discuss about the possible future work in Section 4.

---

[2]The implementation of Cloud Transcoder is based on a former production system [14] which only downloads videos on behalf of users.

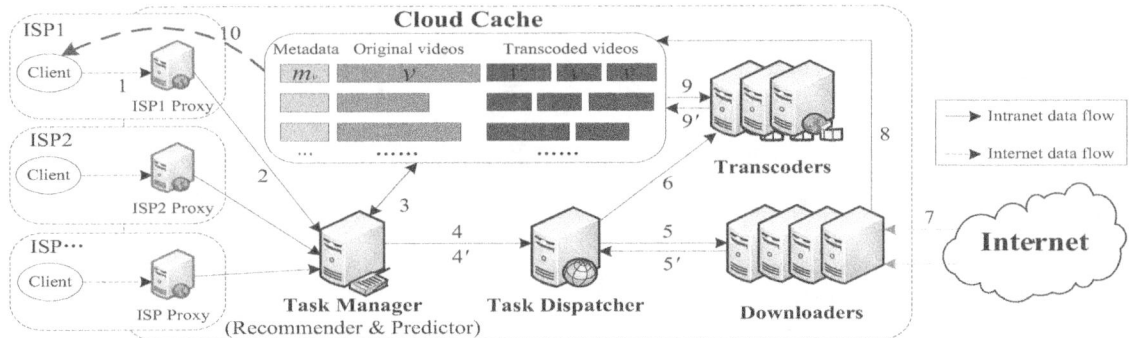

Figure 2: System architecture of Cloud Transcoder.

2. SYSTEM DESIGN

2.1 System Overview

The system architecture of Cloud Transcoder is composed of six building blocks: 1) *ISP Proxies*, 2) *Task Manager*, 3) *Task Dispatcher*, 4) *Downloaders*, 5) *Transcoders* and 6) *Cloud Cache*, as plotted in Figure 2. The system utilizes 244 commodity servers, including 170 chunk servers making up a 340-TB cloud cache, 20 download servers with 6.5 Gbps of Internet bandwidth, 15 transcoding servers with 60 processing cores @2.4 GHz, 23 upload servers with 6.9 Gbps of Internet bandwidth, and so forth. Such hardware composition (in particular the cloud cache) is generally designed to serve 100K (K=1000) daily requests, though the current number of daily requests is usually below 10K. Below we describe the organization and working process of Cloud Transcoder by following the message and data flows of a typical video request.

Firstly, the user uploads his video request to the corresponding ISP Proxy (see Arrow 1 in Figure 2). Each ISP Proxy maintains a *task queue* to control the number of tasks (video requests) sent to the Task Manager (see Arrow 2), so that the Task Manager is resilient to task upsurge in any ISP. Presently, Cloud Transcoder maintains ten ISP Proxies in the ten biggest ISPs in China: Telecom [15], Unicom [16], Mobile [17] and so on. If a user (occasionally) does not locate at any of the ten ISPs, his video request is sent to a random ISP Proxy. On receiving a video request, the Task Manager checks whether the requested video has a copy in the Cloud Cache in two steps (see Arrow 3):

- *Step 1. Checking the video link.* Inside the Cloud Cache, each original video v has a unique hash code and a series of video links pointing to v in its corresponding metadata m_v. If the video link contained in the video request is a P2P link, the Task Manager examines whether the Cloud Cache contains a video that has the same hash code with that contained in the P2P link [3]. Otherwise, the Task Manager directly examines whether the video link is repeated in the Cloud Cache. If the video link is not found, the Task Manager initiates a *video download task* and sends it to the Task Dispatcher (see Arrow 4).

- *Step 2. Checking the transcoded video.* If the video link (pointing to the original video v) is found in the Cloud Cache, the Task Manager further checks whether $T(v)$[4] contains an existing transcoded video matching the user-customized transcoding parameters. If the requested video actually has a copy, the user can directly and instantly retrieve the video from the Cloud Cache (see Arrow 10). Otherwise, the Task Manager recommends $T(v)$ to the user for a possible choice so as to reduce the transcoding computation pressure on the cloud; thereby, the Task Manager also acts as the "Task Recommender". If the user does not accept any recommendation but insists on his customized transcoding parameters, the Task Manager initiates a *video transcoding task* and sends it to the Task Dispatcher (see Arrow 4').

On receiving a video download task from the Task Manager, the Task Dispatcher assigns the download task to one server (called a "downloader") in the Downloaders (see Arrow 5). For example, if the video link contained in the download task is a P2P link, the assigned downloader will act as a common peer to join the corresponding peer swarm. On receiving a video transcoding task from the Task Manager, the Task Dispatcher assigns the transcoding task to one server (called a "transcoder") in the Transcoders for video transcoding (see Arrow 6).

The Task Dispatcher is mainly responsible for balancing the download bandwidth pressure of the 20 downloaders and the transcoding computation pressure of the 15 transcoders. Each downloader executes multiple download tasks in parallel (see Arrow 7), and the Task Dispatcher always assigns a newly incoming video download task to the downloader which has the lightest download bandwidth pressure. Likewise, a newly incoming video transcoding task is always assigned to the transcoder which has the lightest computation pressure.

As long as the downloader accomplishes a download task, it computes the hash code of the downloaded video and attempts to store the video into the Cloud Cache (see Arrow 8). The downloader first checks whether the downloaded video has a copy in the Cloud Cache (using the hash code) [5]. If the video is repeated, the downloader simply

---

[3] A P2P (BitTorrent/eMule/Magnet) link contains the hash code of its affiliated file in itself, while an HTTP/FTP/RTSP link does not.

[4] $T(v)$ denotes all the existing transcoded videos of v in different formats and resolutions stored in the Cloud Cache.
[5] It is possible that multiple downloaders are downloading the same video content with different video links

discards it. Otherwise, the downloader checks whether the Cloud Cache has enough spare space to store the new video. If the Cloud Cache does not have enough spare space, it deletes some cached videos to get enough spare space to store the new video. The concrete cache capacity planning and cache replacement strategy will be investigated in Section 2.3. When the abovementioned video store process is finished, the downloader notifies the Task Dispatcher (see Arrow 5') for further processing.

When a transcoder receives a video transcoding task, it first reads the corresponding original video from the Cloud Cache (see Arrow 9) and then transcodes it according to the transcoding parameters contained in the video transcoding task. Specifically, each transcoder employs the classic open-source FFmpeg codec software [18] for video transcoding and it supports most popular video formats like MP4, AVI, FLV, WMV and RMVB, as well as user-customized video resolutions. After finishing the transcoding task, the transcoder also needs to check whether the Cloud Cache has enough spare space to store the new transcoded video (see Arrow 9').

Finally, the requested video is available in the Cloud Cache and the user can usually retrieve it with a high data rate (see Arrow 10). Since the user's ISP information can be acquired from his video retrieve message, the Cloud Cache takes advantage of the intra-cloud ISP-aware data upload technique (elaborated in Section 2.4) to accelerate the data transfer process.

2.2 Transcoding Prediction

When the *computation pressure* of the transcoders stays below a certain threshold during a certain period (currently the threshold is empirically set as 50% and the period is set as one hour), the Task Manager starts to predict which videos are likely to be requested for transcoding into which formats and resolutions, based on the video popularity information. The *transcoding computation pressure* is indicated by the *average CPU utilization of the transcoders*. Such prediction often happens at night, when the Task Manager (now behaving as the "Task Predictor") first updates the video popularity information using the user requests received in the latest 24 hours. The video popularity information is twofold: 1) the number of request times of each video and 2) the most popular transcoding parameters. Currently, the Task Manager picks the top-1000 popular videos and top-3 popular transcoding parameters to initiate transcoding tasks. If a certain popular video has been transcoded into a certain popular format and resolution in the past, the corresponding transcoding task should not be repeated.

Each predicted (non-repeated) transcoding task is sent to the Task Dispatcher to satisfy future potential requests of users, so that part of the transcoding computation pressure in "hot" time has been moved to "cold" time for load balancing (see Figure 3). Besides, we discover the average CPU utilization of the 15 transcoders in the whole day (with prediction) is 34.13%, indicating that 15 transcoders can support at most $\frac{8600}{34.13\%} \approx 25K$ daily requests (8600 is the total number of video requests received in the whole day). Consequently, in order to support 100K daily video requests, we still need to add at least 45 more transcoders in the future (if the cache hit rate of transcoding tasks does not change significantly).

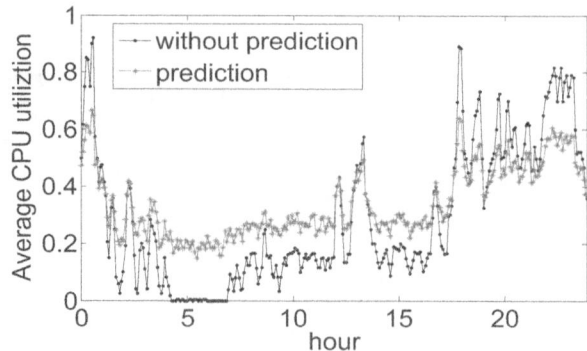

Figure 3: Average CPU utilization of the transcoders in one day (with prediction) and the other day (without prediction), respectively.

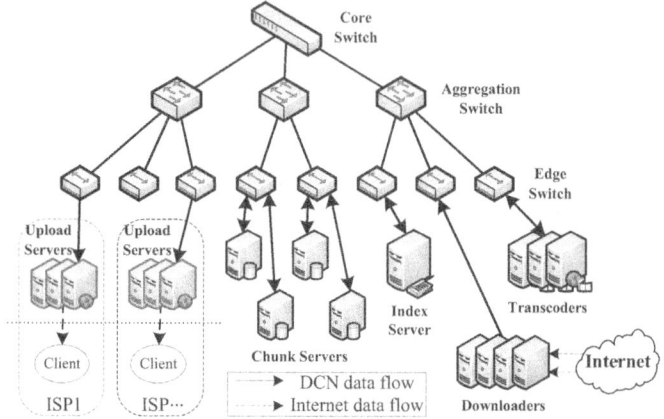

Figure 4: Hardware organization of Cloud Cache.

2.3 Cloud Cache Organization

Cloud Cache plays a kernel role in the system architecture of Cloud Transcoder by storing (caching) all the videos and their metadata and meanwhile transferring the transcoded videos back to users. As depicted in Figure 4, the Cloud Cache consists of 170 chunk servers, 23 upload servers and 3 index servers, connected by a DCN (data center network). The DCN adopts the traditional 3-tier tree structure to organize the switches, comprising a core switch in the root of the tree, an aggregation tier in the middle and an edge tier at the leaves of the tree. All the chunk servers, upload servers, index servers, downloaders and transcoders are connected to edge switches. A specific number of *upload servers* are placed in each ISP, approximately proportional to the data traffic volume in each ISP.

Every video (whether original or transcoded) is segmented into chunks of equal size to be stored in the chunk servers, and every chunk has a duplicate for redundancy, so the 170 chunk servers can accommodate a total of $C = \frac{170 \times 4 \text{ TB}}{2} = 340$ TB unique data. In order to achieve load balance and exploit the chunk-correlation in the same file, all the chunks of a video are stored together into the chunk server with the biggest available storage capacity. The duplicate chunks of a video must be stored in another chunk server. There is an index server (as well as two backup index servers) which maintains the metadata of videos.

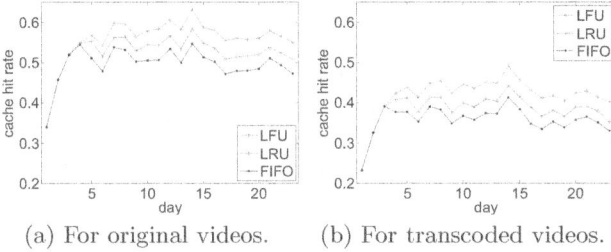

(a) For original videos.   (b) For transcoded videos.

Figure 5: Cache hit rates in simulations.

The 340-TB cloud cache accommodates both original and transcoded videos. Below we first present the cache capacity planning and then discuss the cache replacement strategies. Cloud Transcoder is designed to handle up to 100K daily video requests. Since the average size of original videos is 827 MB (refer to Figure 7) and every video is stored in the cloud cache for at most 12 days (refer to the user service policy [19]), the total storage capacity of the original videos should be: 827 MB × 100K × 12 = 969 TB to well handle 100K daily requests *when there is no data reuse among the users*. According to the running logs of our real-deployed system, the current data reuse rate of original videos is about 87% and thus the storage capacity of the original videos is planned as: $C_1 = 827$ MB$\times 100K \times 12 \times (1-87\%) = 126$ TB. On the other hand, an original video is associated with three transcoded videos in average and the average size of transcoded videos is 466 MB (refer to Figure 8), so the storage capacity of the transcoded videos is planned as: $C_2 = 3 \times 466$ MB $\times 100K \times 12 \times (1-87\%) = 213$ TB. As a result, the total cloud cache capacity should be $C = C_1 + C_2 \approx 340$ TB.

Although the current number of daily video requests is much smaller than 100K, it is possible that this number will exceed 100K some day. If the huge upsurge in request number really happens, some data must be replaced to make efficient utilization of the limited cloud cache capacity, where the cache replacement strategy plays a critical role. Here we investigate the performance of the most commonly used cache replacement strategies for both original and transcoded videos via real-trace driven simulations, i.e., FIFO (first in first out), LRU (least recently used) and LFU (least frequently used). The trace is a 23-day system log (refer to Section 3 for detailed information) of all the video requests and the simulated cloud cache storage is 30 TB ($\approx \frac{8600}{100K} \cdot 340$ TB, where 8600 is the current average number of daily requests). From Figure 5 we discover that for both original and transcoded videos, FIFO performs the worst and LFU performs the best to achieve the highest cache hit rate.

2.4 Accelerating the Data Transfer of Transcoded Videos

A critical problem of Cloud Transcoder is how to accelerate the transfer process of the transcoded videos from the cloud to the user in order to save the users' energy consumption in retrieving their requested videos. Considering that the cross-ISP data transfer performance degrades seriously and the inter-ISP traffic cost is often expensive, we solve this problem via the *intra-cloud ISP-aware data upload technique*. Since the user's real-time ISP information can be acquired from his video retrieve message, the Cloud Cache takes advantage of its ISP-aware upload servers to restrict the data transfer path within the same ISP as the user's, so as to enhance the data transfer rate and avoid inter-ISP traffic cost.

Specifically, suppose a user A locating at ISP1 wants to retrieve a video v' stored in a chunk server S, and the Cloud Cache has placed 3 upload servers (U_1, U_2 and U_3) in ISP1 (see Figure 4). The chunks of v' are first transferred from S to a random upload server (says U_3) in ISP1, and then transferred from U_3 to the user A. The transfer process is not store-and-forward but pass-through: as soon as U_3 gets a complete chunk of v', U_3 transfers the chunk to A. v' would not be cached in U_3 because the intra-cloud end-to-end bandwidth is quite high (1 Gbps) and we do not want to make things unnecessarily complicated.

3. PERFORMANCE EVALUATION

We use the complete running log of Cloud Transcoder in 23 days (Oct. 1–23, 2011) to evaluate its performance. The log includes the performance information of 197,400 video transcoding tasks involving 76,293 unique videos. The daily statistics are plotted in Figure 6. For each task, we record its *user device type*, *video link*, *transcoding parameters*, *original size*, *transcoded size*, *download duration time* (of the cloud downloader), *transcoding time*, *retrieve duration time* (of the user) and so on. 85% of the video links sent from users are P2P links. The most popular transcoding parameters include MP4-1024*768 (10%, mostly coming from iPad users), MP4-640*480 (38%, mostly coming from iPhone and Android smartphone users) and 3GP-352*288 (27%, mostly coming from Android smartphone users). As shown in Figure 7 and Figure 8, the average file size of the original videos is 827 MB, as 1.77 times as that of the transcoded videos (466 MB). 96% of the original videos are long videos ($\geq$ 100 MB).

As an average case, a mobile user needs around 33 minutes to retrieve a transcoded video (see Figure 9) with the help of the intra-cloud data transfer acceleration. The above process may consume 6.1%/5.5% of the battery capacity of an iPhone4S/iPad2 *in theory*, given that the battery of iPhone4S/iPad2 is claimed to support about 9/10 hours' WiFi data transfer. To check the practical energy consumption, we use our own iPhones/iPads to retrieve a long enough transcoded video from Cloud Transcoder (via WiFi) for 33 minutes and then record their battery consumptions. All the other user applications are closed, and the screen brightness is set to 25% with "auto-adjustment" disabled. The results are listed in the following table, indicating that the iPhone battery consumption is typically around 9% ($\approx$ 0.47 WH) while the iPad battery consumption is typically around 5% ($\approx$ 1.25 WH).

Data transfer rate ($\approx$KBps)	50	100	200	300
iPhone battery consumption (%)	8.7	8.9	9.0	9.2
iPad2 battery consumption (%)	4.5	4.8	5.0	5.1

As a contrast, Figure 10 illustrates the average download duration time for a downloader (in Cloud Transcoder) to get an original video is 189 minutes (as 5.72 times as the average retrieve duration time), because each downloader directly gets data from the Internet in the common way (without designated acceleration). Finally, Figure 11 indicates that the average data transfer rate of transcoded videos reaches

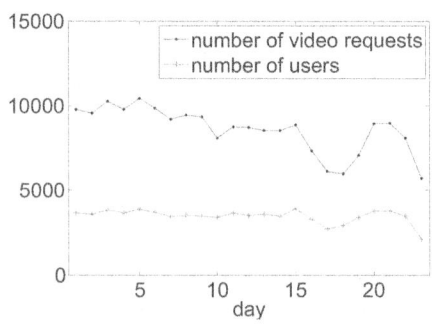
Figure 6: Daily statistics.

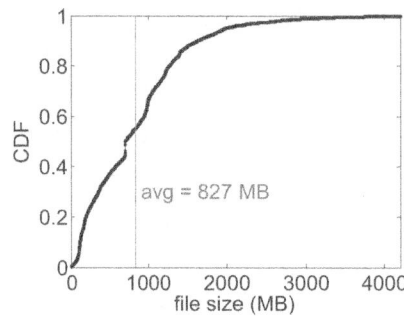
Figure 7: Original file size.

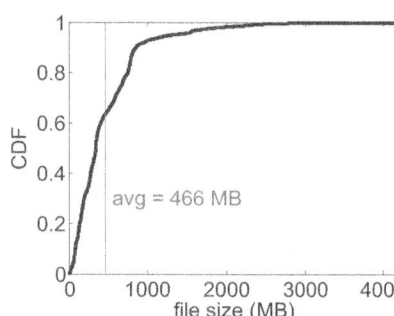
Figure 8: Transcoded file size.

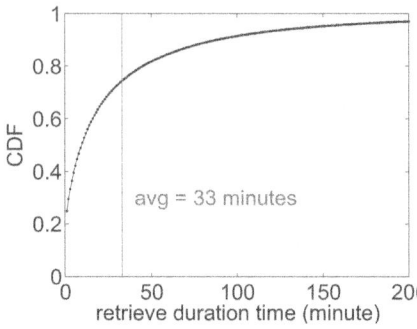
Figure 9: Retrieve duration.

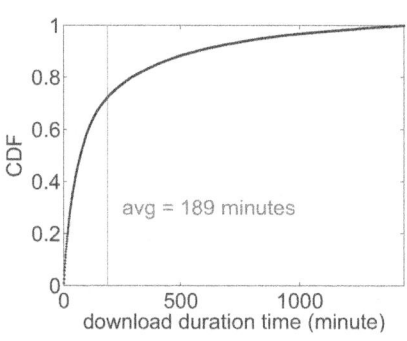
Figure 10: Download duration.

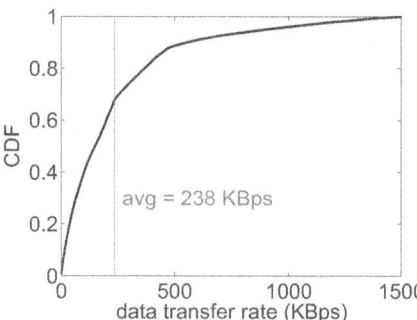
Figure 11: Data transfer rate.

238 KBps (= 1.9 Mbps), thus enabling the users' view-as-download function.

4. FUTURE WORK

Still some future work remains. First, as a novel production system still at its startup stage, Cloud Transcoder tends to adopt "straightforward and solid" designs in constructing each component so that the deployment and debugging works are easy to handle. We realize there is still considerable optimization space for better design to take effect and this paper is the first step of our efforts.

Second, some web browsers also start to provide video transcoding service. For example, UCWeb [20], the most popular mobile web browser in China, has employed cloud utilities to transcode web flash videos into three resolutions: 144*176, 176*208 and 240*320, in order to facilitate its mobile users. Amazon has recently claimed that its novel Silk web browser [21] will transcode Internet videos to certain formats and resolutions (especially fit for its 7-inch Kindle Fire Tablet) by using its EC2 cloud platform. We have begun to explore integrating the service of Cloud Transcoder to the QQ web browser [22].

5. ACKNOWLEDGEMENTS

This work is supported in part by the China "973" Grant. 2011CB302305, China NSF Grant. 61073015, and US NSF Grants CNS-0905037, CNS-1017647 and CNS-1117536.

6. REFERENCES

[1] http://www.gartner.com/it/page.jsp?id=1848514.
[2] Cisco traffic report. http://www.cisco.com/en/US/solutions/collateral/ns341/ns525/ns537/ns705/ns827/white_paper_c11-520862.pdf.
[3] Y. Liu, F. Li, L. Guo, B. Shen, and S. Chen. "A Server's Perspective of Internet Streaming Delivery to Mobile Devices," IEEE INFOCOM, 2012.
[4] J. Ostermann, et al. "Video coding with H.264 /AVC: tools, performance and complexity," IEEE Circuits and Systems magazine, vol. 4, no. 1, 2004.
[5] Z. Huang, C. Mei, L. Li, and T. Woo. "CloudStream: Delivering high-quality streaming videos through a cloud-based SVC proxy," IEEE INFOCOM, 2011.
[6] Android Media Converter. https://market.android.com/details?id=com.ghostmobile.mediaconverter.
[7] Android VLC Pro. https://market.android.com/details?id=com.gmail.traveldevel.android.vlc.license.
[8] http://itunes.apple.com/app/id306550020.
[9] M. Armbrust, et al. "A view of cloud computing," Communications of the ACM, vol. 53, no. 4, 2010.
[10] YouConvertIt. http://www.youconvertit.com.
[11] Online-convert. http://www.online-convert.com.
[12] Mov-avi. http://online.movavi.com.
[13] http://en.wikipedia.org/wiki/Magnet_URI_scheme.
[14] Y. Huang, Z. Li, G. Liu, and Y. Dai. "Cloud Download: Using Cloud Utilities to Achieve High-quality Content Distribution for Unpopular Videos," ACM Multimedia, 2011.
[15] China Telecom. http://www.chinatelecom.com.cn.
[16] China Unicom. http://www.chinaunicom.com.cn.
[17] China Mobile. http://www.10086.cn.
[18] FFmpeg web site. http://ffmpeg.org.
[19] http://xf.qq.com/help_video.html.
[20] UCWeb browser. http://www.ucweb.com.
[21] Amazon Silk. http://amazonsilk.wordpress.com.
[22] QQ web browser. http://browser.qq.com.

A Content Replication Scheme for Wireless Mesh Networks

Zakwan Al-Arnaout, Qiang Fu, Marcus Frean
School of Engineering and Computer Science
Victoria University of Wellington
Wellington, New Zealand
{zakwan.arnaout, qiang.fu, marcus.frean}@@ecs.vuw.ac.nz

ABSTRACT

Wireless Mesh Networks (WMNs) extend Internet access in areas where the wired infrastructure is not available. A problem that arises is the congestion around gateways, delayed access latency and low throughput. Therefore, object replication and placement is essential for multi-hop wireless networks. Many replication schemes are proposed for the Internet, but they are designed for CDNs that have both high bandwidth and high server capacity, which makes them unsuitable for the wireless environment. Object replication has received comparatively less attention from the research community when it comes to WMNs. In this paper, we propose an object replication and placement scheme for WMNs. In our scheme, each mesh router acts as a replica server in a peer-to-peer fashion. Our scheme exploits *graph partitioning* to build a hierarchy from fine-grained to coarse-grained partitions. The challenge is to replicate content as close as possible to the requesting clients and thus reduce the access latency per object, while minimizing the number of replicas. Using simulation tests, we demonstrate that our scheme is scalable, performing well with respect to the number of replica servers and the number of objects. The proposed scheme can give improved performance in terms of convergence time, throughput, hop count and hit ratio.

Categories and Subject Descriptors

C.2.1 [**Network Architecture and Design**]: Wireless communication; G.1.2 [**Approximation**]: Minimax approximation and algorithms

General Terms

Algorithms, Performance, Design

This work is funded in part by InternetNZ (http://internetnz.net.nz).

Permission to make digital or hard copies of all or part of this work for personal or classroom use is granted without fee provided that copies are not made or distributed for profit or commercial advantage and that copies bear this notice and the full citation on the first page. To copy otherwise, to republish, to post on servers or to redistribute to lists, requires prior specific permission and/or a fee.
NOSSDAV'12, June 7–8, 2012, Toronto, Ontario, Canada.
Copyright 2012 ACM 978-1-4503-1430-5/12/06 ...$10.00.

Keywords

Replica Placement, Distributed Algorithm, Wireless Mesh Network, Peer-to-peer Networking

1. INTRODUCTION

Wireless Mesh Networks (WMNs) are a promising solution to extend Internet access to wider areas with high bandwidth [1]. They are generally composed of three types of nodes: Mesh Clients (MCs), Mesh Routers (MRs), and Gateways (GWs). WMNs can be used in community, enterprise, home and Local Area Networks (LANs) for hotels, parks and trains. MRs compose the backbone layer through multi-hop wireless communications. A MC connects to other MCs or the Internet through its access MR. With their extended coverage and low cost, WMNs have attracted a lot of attention for both of research community and industry. However, similar to other wireless networks, WMNs also face challenges arising from resource constraints of wireless communications. One of the key challenges for the development of WMNs is improving the data access efficiency and Quality of Experience (QoE), which determines the satisfaction degree of service users. Furthermore, as the Internet traffic flows through a limited number of GWs, heavy congestion around these GWs presents a serious problem. WMNs have the potential to increase network capacity by adding resource-sharing services such as content caching and replication. It has been observed that, for a given client population, a significant workload *locality* exists in both Internet [2] and WMNs [3] content retrieval. Locality means that multiple users request the same content over time (and possibly at the same time). Web content caching and replication are two techniques that exploit locality to reduce the Internet traffic and access latency.

In this paper, we propose a new object replication scheme and placement heuristic called *SP-DNA* (Single Partition per Delegate Node Assignment). *SP-DNA* is a distributed and scalable scheme that exploits workload locality in WMNs. Our scheme finds the number of replicas needed per object (e.g. video file for a video on demand service) in a time window, and takes into account the variation of content popularity over time. We use *graph-partitioning* techniques to distribute the replica placement problem on *the Delegate Nodes* (DNs). A DN is responsible for replica placement within its partition. The challenge of minimizing object access cost is more serious in WMNs than the Internet. Minimizing the hop count may not be an issue in the wired network, as long as there is sufficient bandwidth between the requesting client and the replica server. In WMNs, the contention between neighboring mesh nodes for the wireless channel, together with the interference from the adjacent wireless links, results in a significant reduction in throughput over a long path. Therefore, MRs that are far from the GWs suffer from long access latency and low throughput. We consider minimizing the demand-weighted distance between the requesting node and the replica server. The simulation results show that *SP-DNA* can give improved performance in terms of convergence time, throughput, hop count and hit ratio.

The rest of the paper is organized as follows. Section 2 reviews the related work. The proposed object replication and placement scheme is described in section 3. Section 4 describes the evaluation methodology and section 5 discusses the results. Section 6 concludes the paper.

2. RELATED WORK

Many caching and replication algorithms have been proposed for the Internet and ad hoc networks, but there has been much less effort devoted to schemes tailored for WMNs. On one hand, many replica placement algorithms designed for the Internet are centralized and incur a high computational cost. On the other hand, caching and replication schemes in ad hoc networks focus on issues such as low bandwidth and energy constraints. In [4], the goal is to find a placement strategy that minimizes the distance that needs to be searched to find an arbitrarily chosen piece of content. However, it does not consider content popularity at different nodes since they formulate the problem as the *k-center* problem. In [5], *P2PMesh* is proposed for P2P file sharing system over WMNs. It aims to reduce both the number of failed lookups and the file lookup latency. However, replica placement was not considered.

[6] proposes a strategy to determine the optimal number of replicas to minimize object access cost (defined as the Euclidean distance from the requester to the nearest replica) in WMNs when the prior knowledge on the global popularity of objects is available. [7] is probably the most relevant work in the sense that it solves the problem of placing replicated objects in a peer-to-peer fashion and formulates the problem as *p-median* problem. The authors have shown the problem to be NP-Complete and proposed four heuristics for object replica placement of different origin servers (*Random, Popularity, Greedy-Single* and *Greedy-Global*). They found using simulations that the global heuristic outperforms the other three heuristics. However, their model assumes equal object size and proportional popularity, while we assume variable object sizes and adjust replication to be fair with unpopular objects. Furthermore, it incurs high convergence time as we show in section 5. In this paper, we compare our proposed scheme with the four heuristics in [7]. From now on, we refer to the four heuristics as *KRR* after the authors' names.

3. THE PROPOSED SCHEME

In this section we describe the proposed scheme. Since WMNs usually have scarce resources and therefore, it is not feasible to put the burden of replica placement on one single entity. To distribute the replica placement problem, we simplify the *p-median* problem by *partitioning* the network graph into p graphs where p represents a potential number of replicas. Then we select for each partition a *Delegate Node* (DN), which will be responsible for placing an object replica within its partition. *Graph partitioning* algorithms

Table 1: Notation used in the proposed scheme.

N	set of demand nodes indexed by i, and potential replica servers indexed by j.
N'	set of demand nodes within a partition indexed by i', and the set of potential replica servers indexed by j'.
M	total number of distinct objects within the WMN indexed by m.
K	total number of the generated graph partitions indexed by k.
DN_k	delegate node of partition k.
Obj_m	Identifier of object m.
$|Obj_m|$	Size of object m in bytes.
τ	time interval window during which object requests are observed.
$Req_{mi}(\tau)$	number of requests for Obj_m from node i during τ.
$Req_m(\tau)$	total number of requests for Obj_m from all nodes during τ.
$Pr_m(\tau)$	global popularity of Obj_m during τ.
$Pr_{mk}(\tau)$	popularity of Obj_m during τ within partition k.
$Pr_{mi}(\tau)$	popularity of Obj_m at node i during τ.
$p_m(\tau+1)$	no. of replicas of Obj_m needed for $\tau+1$.
d_{ij}	distance between demand node i and potential serving node j. It may reflect several metrics such as hop-count, latency, link quality routing metrics (e.g. ETX).
SC	storage capacity of a node.

such as the one proposed in [8] aim to partition a graph into two or more disjoint subsets of equal size, such that it minimizes the edge cuts between the partitions. In our scheme, we recursively bipartite the graph until the partition size ≤ 2. Since the total number of partitions $= N - 1$, each DN will be assigned at most a single partition. Our scheme involves two phases, the *Network Setup Phase* and the *Content Replication and Placement Phase*. We use the notation in Table 1 to describe our scheme.

3.1 Network Setup Phase

In this phase and before the content replication/placement starts, we assume that all nodes (MRs) are enabled with Alg. 1. The goal of this algorithm is to assign a DN to a partition for which the DN will be responsible. To trigger the network phase, an application process called the *Content Manager* (CM) that can be hosted by a centroid node starts this phase. The CM plays a role in collecting statistical information about different objects' requests, computing $p_m(\tau+1)$, and communicating with the DNs. The CM selects randomly one of the nodes to act as a DN for the whole network and then passes the network graph G to the selected DN which on its turn runs Alg. 1 to bipartite the graph (or partition), select a DN for each partition and then forward each partition to its corresponding DN. The process is recursively repeated until the partitions are fine-grained. When the base case is reached (line 6), the node running the algorithm will select itself as the DN (the term *this* refers to the node itself (line 7)). Then, the DNs in the lowest level partitions reply to their callers (parent node) with a list representing the DN and its partition members.

When the caller receives the lists from its child DNs, it appends its node ID and forwards the resulting list to its caller. Eventually, the CM will receive a list of DNs in the form of a balanced binary tree that we call the *Delegates Binary Tree* (DBT). The CM maps the possible numbers of replicas to their DNs in the DBT, creating a Map-List by running Alg. 2. It recursively divides the possible number of replicas (P) by 2 starting from the root node. When the base case is reached (i.e. $P = 1$), it checks whether the node n is a leaf node in the DBT or not. If it is a leaf node, then it means that node n has to *self-host* the object for P replicas and returns the node ID concatenated with a flag (s) to indicate *self-hosting*. Otherwise, it returns the node ID along with a flag (p) to indicate *partition-hosting* (i.e. the DN will need to find the optimal location for the object within its partition). For every possible P, the CM creates an entry in the form of $\langle P,$ set of DNs$\rangle$ and inserts it in the Map-List structure. This will facilitate for the CM to know *a priori* that for a specific P, which DNs the CM shall communicate with to assign the placement job. Upon completion, the CM broadcasts the Map-List to all the nodes.

Algorithm 1 This algorithm builds the DBT during the network setup phase.

1: **function** BTREE(*Graph g, String s*)
2:     *Graph* g_1, g_2
3:     *Node* n_1, n_2
4:     *String* s_1, s_2
5:     $s_1 \leftarrow s_2 \leftarrow s$
6:     **if** $|g| = 2$ **then**
7:         $n_1 \leftarrow this$
8:         **return** $n_1 \parallel \{g\} \setminus n_1$
9:     **else if** $|g| = 3$ **then**
10:        $n_1 \leftarrow rand(g) \notin s$
11:        $g_2 \leftarrow \{g\} \setminus n_1$
12:        $n_2 \leftarrow rand(g_2) \notin s$
13:        $forward(g_2, s) \rightarrow n_2$
14:        $wait(n_2)$
15:        **return** $n_1 \parallel n_2$
16:    **else**
17:        *Bipartite*(g, g_1, g_2)
18:        $n_1 \leftarrow rand(g_1) \notin s_1$
19:        $n_2 \leftarrow rand(g_2) \notin s_2$
20:        $s_1 \leftarrow s_1 \parallel n_1$
21:        $s_2 \leftarrow s_2 \parallel n_2$
22:        $forward(g_1, s_1) \rightarrow n_1$
23:        $forward(g_2, s_2) \rightarrow n_2$
24:        $wait(n_1, n_2)$
25:        **return** $this \parallel n_1 \parallel n_2$
26:    **end if**
27: **end function**

3.2 Content Replication and Placement Phase

This phase consists of three steps to be performed aiming to collect statistical information about the objects, compute the number of replicas for each object and then find the placement for the replicas. These steps are described as follows:

3.2.1 During the τ period:

Every node maintains a list containing an entry in the form $\langle MR_i, Obj_m, Req_{mi}(\tau)\rangle$ that represents the request count

Algorithm 2 Pseudocode to map the possible number of replicas (P) to their DNs.

1: **function** MAP(*Node n, int p*)
2:     **if** $P = 1$ **then**
3:         **if** n *is leaf* **then**
4:             **return** $n \parallel s$
5:         **else**
6:             **return** $n \parallel p$
7:         **end if**
8:     **else**
9:         **return** $map(n.left, P/2) + map(n.right, P - P/2)$
10:    **end if**
11: **end function**

Req_{mi} for every object Obj_m during τ at node i. A request is defined as the request generated by a MC to its access MR. Regardless of being served by the access MR, any other MR or even the origin server.

3.2.2 At the end of the τ period:

In this step, the DNs send the collected statistical information to the CM. The CM computes $pm(\tau + 1)$ as follows:

a) The partition members of the lowest level DNs forward their object frequency list obtained from previous step to their DN. Each DN aggregates the received lists from its children along with its own list, stores the resulting list and then forwards it to its parent node. The process of aggregate, store and forward is repeated until the root node receives the full list for the whole WMN and then forwards it to the CM.

b) For every Obj_m, the CM computes the global popularity according to Eq (1).

$$Pr_m(\tau) = \frac{\sum_{i=1}^{N} Req_{mi(\tau)}}{\sum_{i=1}^{N} \sum_{m=1}^{M} Req_{mi(\tau)}} \quad (1)$$

c) Since it has been proven in [6] that the optimal density $d_m(\tau)$ of replicas for Obj_m during τ satisfies the relation: $d_m(\tau) \propto \sqrt[3]{Pr_m^2(\tau)}$, the CM computes $p_m(\tau + 1)$ for every Obj_m using Eq (2).

$$p_m(\tau + 1) = \frac{SC \times N \times \sqrt[3]{Pr_m^2(\tau)}}{|Obj_m| \times \sum_{m=1}^{M} \sqrt[3]{Pr_m^2(\tau)}} \quad (2)$$

d) The CM creates a *Replica-List* (RL) that contains the entries $\langle p_m(\tau+1), Obj_m, |Obj_m|, Req_m(\tau)\rangle$ grouped by $p_m(\tau+1)$ in a decreasing order and within each group, the objects are sorted by $|Obj_m|$ in an increasing order. The reason behind this way of sorting is that we give priority for the highly popular objects and then the priority is given to the smaller objects to increase the hit ratio since replicating smaller objects usually results in higher hit ratios [9]. We do not assume equal object size. Instead, we consider dividing the popularity of an object by its size yielding fairness for the small objects against the large ones.

3.2.3 Replica placement:

In this step, the *SP-DNA* heuristic (Alg. 3) is executed. The CM sends a multicast message that contains $\langle p_m(\tau+1), Obj_m, |Obj_m|, Req_m(\tau)\rangle$ to the corresponding DNs obtained from the procedure in Alg. 3. When each DN receives the message, it looks up the Map-List for its role. If it has to *self-host* the replica Obj_m, then it only needs to fetch it. Otherwise (i.e. *partition-host*), it computes $Pr_{mk}(\tau)$ using Eq (3), which represents the popularity percentage of Obj_m within partition k with respect to the whole network.

$$Pr_{mk}(\tau) = \frac{\sum_{i'=1}^{N'} Req_{mi'}(\tau)}{Req_m(\tau)} \quad (3)$$

A decision has to be made (line 12) to find out whether it is feasible to place Obj_m in DN_k partition or forward it to the parent of DN_k in the DBT. The corresponding DN_k compares the ϵ_{mk} value from Eq (4) with a threshold value η_m from Eq (5). ϵ_{mk} represents the benefit gained from forwarding Obj_m to a parent DN. η_m is inversely proportional to the number of replicas $p_m(\tau+1)$, serving as an error margin. This means that, for a given network size, a smaller $p_m(\tau+1)$ or in other words larger partitions yields a larger error margin (η_m). A larger η_m means reduced computation cost at the expense of placement accuracy. Note that, for large partitions, the computation cost is high. This is a tradeoff between computation cost and placement accuracy. The threshold η_m can be tuned using the coefficient θ, to trade off between placement accuracy and computation cost for a given partition size. If ϵ_{mk} exceeds η_m, then DN_k will handoff Obj_m to its parent DN which is responsible for a larger partition where a better placement can take place. The parent DN on its turn will take the decision of placement or handoff.

$$\epsilon_{mk} = \frac{1}{p_m(\tau+1) \times Pr_{mk}(\tau)} - 1 \quad (4)$$

$$\eta_m = \frac{1}{p_m(\tau+1) \times \theta} \quad (5)$$

If ϵ_{mk} is not larger than η_m (line 15), DN_k will compute the demand-weighted total cost for every partition member and assigns Obj_m to the node that minimizes the total cost, provided there is enough storage space to accommodate Obj_m. If the space is not enough, it selects the second best node and so forth. Upon successful assignment, the selected node fetches the object. After fetching Obj_m, the node evicts object(s) from previous τ and inserts Obj_m for $(\tau+1)$.

4. EVALUATION METHODOLOGY

GloMoSim simulator [10] is used in the simulation analysis. We simulated a stationary WMN consisting of different number of nodes N for different scenarios in a mesh topology. We used IEEE 802.11g radio interface with a link bandwidth of 18 Mbps, which gives a good balance between throughput and transmission range. Objects are looked-up using Chord structured P2P network directory service. The mean distance between nodes is 100 meters. We used the OLSR [11] routing protocol with the hop-count as the distance $d_{i'j'}$ since the heuristics we are comparing with; use the hop-count in their cost function. Moreover, hop-count is commonly used as a routing metric in multi-hop wireless networks such as in [12]. The number of MCs per node is 8 on average. Requests follow a *Zipf-like* distribution. The threshold coefficient $\theta = 1$ and the object size ranges from 1 to 3 MB following a Gaussian distribution and the application traffic was set to FTP/GENERIC. We note that in reality, the system will use larger SC and $|Obj_m|$. However, due to simulator limitations on the object size, we were

---

Algorithm 3 The Distributed Replica Placement Heuristic *SP-DNA*.

1: **for** *every group in RL* **do**
2:    *multicast a message containing the group of object*
3:    *replicas to the corresponding list of DNs in Map-List*
4:    *the receiving DN_k performs the following:*
5:    *lookup the $Map - List$ for the given $p_m(\tau+1)$*
6:    **if** DN_k *is flagged s* **then**   ▷ self-hosting
7:       **for all** Obj_m *in the received group* **do**
8:          $fetch(obj_m)$
9:       **end for**
10:   **else**   ▷ partition-hosting
11:       **for all** Obj_m *in the received group* **do**
12:          **if** $\epsilon_{mk} > \eta_m$ **then**
13:             $forward \langle p_m(\tau+1), Obj_m, |Obj_m|,$
14:             $Req_m(\tau) \rangle \rightarrow parent(DN_k)$
15:          **else**
16:             *select the node that minimizes the cost:*

$$Min \sum_{i'=1}^{N'} \sum_{j'=1}^{N'} Pr_{mi'}(\tau) d_{i'j'} \; s.t \; \exists \; SC$$

17:             *assign Obj_m to the selected node*
18:             $fetch(obj_m)$ ▷ selected node fetches Obj_m
19:          **end if**
20:       **end for**
21:   **end if**
22: **end for**

---

scaling down both SC and $|Obj_m|$. The relative increase of both will still make our heuristic viable as in [3]. In each simulation test, the baseline *Random* heuristic was run first, followed by another *KRR* heuristic or *SP-DNA*. For all the heuristics, requests are served from the closest replica server. The simulation tests are carried out in online fashion such that object replica placement is performed whilst clients' requests are generated.

5. RESULTS AND DISCUSSIONS

To evaluate the performance of our scheme, we have implemented the four heuristics presented in *KRR* and the *SP-DNA* heuristic. The performance metrics used for comparison are: convergence time, throughput, hop-count and hit ratio. Each of them is defined in an individual subsection.

5.1 Convergence Time

This is the total time taken to identify the number of replicas and the replica servers and allocate all the object replicas to the corresponding replica servers. We compare the heuristics for small ($N = 25$) and medium ($N = 100$) network size and for different numbers of distinct objects (M). The SC is set to 256 MB, M varies from 500 to 3000 and the Zipfian parameter α is set to 0.95. Fig. 1 shows that the basic heuristics (i.e. *Random*, *Popularity* and *G-S*) converge faster than their counterparts because the placement decision is taken locally without any form of cooperation. *G-G* takes the longest time because it recalculates the cost after every replica placement. Since *SP-DNA* is distributed, the placement decision is performed in parallel by the DNs making it converge faster than *G-G*. We can notice that increasing M and/or N, exponentially increases

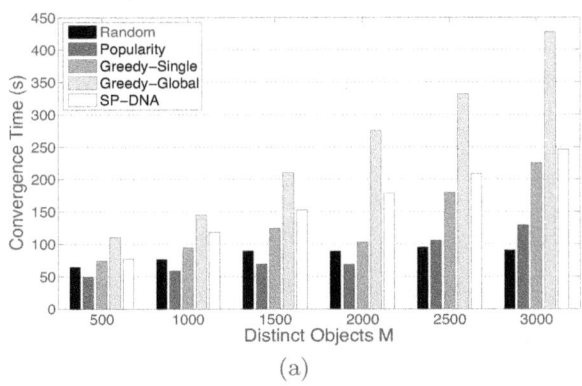
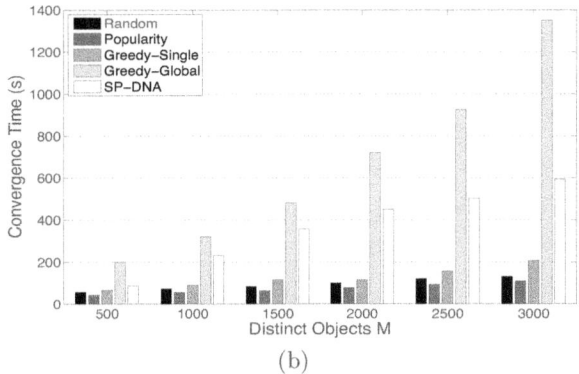

Figure 1: Convergence time comparison between KRR and SP-DNA heuristics. (a) $N = 25$, and (b) $N = 100$.

the convergence time of G-G. Therefore, it does not scale well with respect to M and N. Recall that G-G performs a costly sort operation to find out the *Object-Server* pair that minimizes the access cost. In contrast, SP-DNA runs in a polynomial time as M and/or N increase. A DN locates a replica only within its partition, and as the number of replicas increases the size of the partitions (N') decreases, yielding a shorter convergence time and lower computation cost. Although SP-DNA does not perform better than the basic heuristics, it performs much better than G-G.

5.2 Mean Throughput

This is the summation of all the sizes of served objects divided by the total time taken to complete the transmission of all the packets. In the following experiment, we investigate the throughput performance by varying the Zipfian parameter (α). It has been observed that Web content request follows a Zipf-like distribution [13]. More specifically, the Zipf distribution is defined by a probability p_i of observing the ith ranked element of an infinite sequence of objects in a single random draw from that sequence; where $p_i \propto \frac{1}{i^\alpha}$. The α parameter reflects the tendency of requesting the highly ranked objects. A large α means a small portion of objects are highly popular, while a small α means the distribution of the popularity between the objects is flat. In this experiment, the SC is set to 128 MB, $M = 500$, $N = 25$ and $\tau = 60$ minutes. Fig. 2 shows that both G-G and SP-DNA outperform the basic heuristics with different values of α. However, as α decreases, the performance gain decreases. This is because both G-G and SP-DNA are in favor of popular objects, creating more replicas for the popular objects. However, as α decreases the popularity difference becomes less clear. This results in the convergence of throughput between the schemes. The performance gain of SP-DNA over G-G is due to a few reasons. One reason is low convergence time for SP-DNA. Since G-G requires longer time to converge than SP-DNA and recall that the heuristics are evaluated in online fashion, clients' requests cannot be satisfied from nearby replica servers until the placement heuristic is complete. Another reason is that, given the same popularity, SP-DNA favors small objects over large ones. Moreover, the replication in G-G is proportional to popularity. This is different from the one used by SP-DNA (see Eq (2)). As a result, compared to SP-DNA, G-G is more generous towards popular objects and more frugal towards unpopular objects.

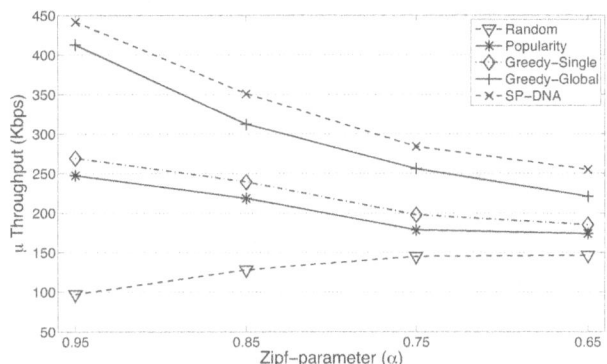

Figure 2: μ Throughput vs. different values of α.

This explains the greater performance gain of SP-DNA over G-G when α is small.

5.3 Mean Hop-Count

This is the total number of hops between the requesting nodes and the serving nodes divided by the total number of served requests. We computed the mean hop-count for all the heuristics. The SC is set to 128 MB, $M = 500$, $N = 25$ and $\tau = 60$ minutes. The results are depicted in Fig. 3. It clearly shows that the cooperative heuristics outperform the basic heuristics. We note that SP-DNA has smaller hop-count than G-G. This means that SP-DNA serves more requests over short paths. In other words, SP-DNA places replicas closer to the requesting nodes. The figure also shows that as α decreases the performance of the heuristics converges. As mentioned earlier, with the decrease of α the popularity difference between the objects becomes less clear. The request behavior tends to be arbitrary instead of favoring popular objects. This results in the convergence between the schemes.

5.4 Hit Ratio

This is the percentage of requests served by local access MRs among all the requests. We set $SC = 128$ MB, $M = 500$, $N = 25$ and $\tau = 60$ minutes. Fig. 4 shows a comparison of the hit ratios between different heuristics. The measured hit ratio includes the local hit observed by the node. In general, the hit ratio increases as the SC increases. It shows that in most cases SP-DNA has the highest hit ratio. This is

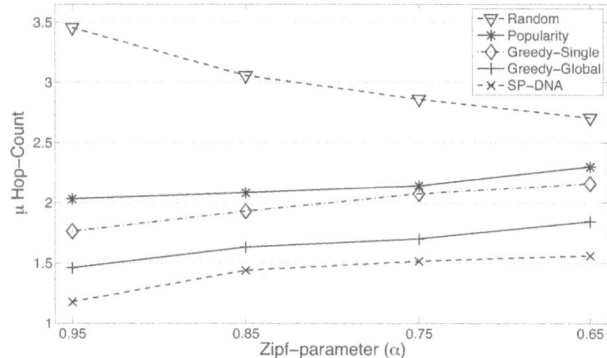

Figure 3: μHop-Count vs. α.

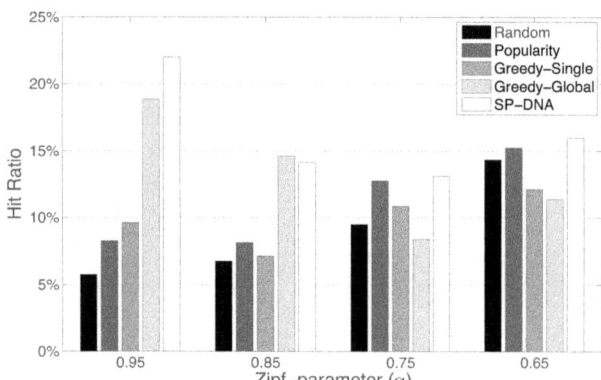

Figure 4: Hit ratio vs α.

because *SP-DNA* favors small objects over large ones given the same popularity. The later factor has not been considered in any of the other heuristics. However, giving priority to small objects can significantly increase the hit ratio leading to improved Quality of Experience.

6. CONCLUSIONS

In this paper, we have designed an object replication and placement scheme for WMNs. To make our scheme distributed and hierarchical, we firstly build a balanced binary tree of multi-level partitions of the network. This is then used to facilitate replica placement and reduce computation cost. The scheme makes the placement decision in a hierarchical way. A delegate node decides to place a replica in its partition when it finds that it is feasible. If not, it forwards the placement job to a larger partition in the hierarchy. As a result, the scheme is capable of making relatively accurate placement without incurring high computation cost. The scheme takes into account the factors of object popularity and size to compute the number of replicas per object. To improve hit ratio, the scheme favors small objects over large ones for the similar popularity. Compared to proportional popularity based replication, which tends to over saturate the network with highly popular objects, the scheme is fair to less popular objects by allocating these objects more space. Moreover, the scheme converges fast due to its distributed nature. To our knowledge this is the first work that exploits graph partitioning to solve the replica placement problem from the perspective of Facility Location Theory. Our simulation results show that the proposed replication scheme can significantly improve network performance in terms of throughput, convergence time (compared to *G-G*), hop count and hit ratio.

7. REFERENCES

[1] I. F. Akyildiz, X. Wang, and W. Wang, "Wireless mesh networks: a survey," *Comput. Netw.*, vol. 47, pp. 445–487, March 2005.

[2] B. Maggs, F. Meyer auf der Heide, B. Vocking, and M. Westermann, "Exploiting locality for data management in systems of limited bandwidth," in *Foundations of Computer Science, 1997. Proceedings., 38th Annual Symposium on*, pp. 284 –293, oct 1997.

[3] S. M. Das, H. Pucha, and Y. C. Hu, "Mitigating the gateway bottleneck via transparent cooperative caching in wireless mesh networks," *Ad Hoc Netw.*, vol. 5, pp. 680–703, August 2007.

[4] B.-J. Ko and D. Rubenstein, "Distributed self-stabilizing placement of replicated resources in emerging networks," *IEEE/ACM Trans. Netw.*, vol. 13, pp. 476–487, June 2005.

[5] A. Al Asaad, S. Gopalakrishnan, and V. Leung, "Peer-to-peer file sharing over wireless mesh networks," in *Communications, Computers and Signal Processing, 2009. PacRim 2009. IEEE Pacific Rim Conference on*, pp. 697 –702, aug. 2009.

[6] S. Jin and L. Wang, "Content and service replication strategies in multi-hop wireless mesh networks," in *Proceedings of the 8th ACM international symposium on Modeling, analysis and simulation of wireless and mobile systems*, MSWiM '05, (New York, NY, USA), pp. 79–86, ACM, 2005.

[7] J. Kangasharju, J. Roberts, and K. W. Ross, "Object replication strategies in content distribution networks," *Computer Communications*, vol. 25, no. 4, pp. 376 – 383, 2002.

[8] B. W. Kernighan and S. Lin, "An efficient heuristic procedure for partitioning graphs," *Bell System Technical Journal*, vol. 49, no. 2, pp. 291–307, 1970.

[9] C. Cunha, A. Bestavros, and M. Crovella, "Characteristics of www client-based traces," tech. rep., Boston, MA, USA, 1995.

[10] X. Zeng, R. Bagrodia, and M. Gerla, "Glomosim: a library for parallel simulation of large-scale wireless networks," in *Proceedings of the twelfth workshop on Parallel and distributed simulation*, PADS '98, (Washington, DC, USA), pp. 154–161, IEEE Computer Society, 1998.

[11] P. Jacquet, P. Mühlethaler, T. Clausen, A. Laouiti, A. Qayyum, and L. Viennot, "Optimized link state routing protocol for ad hoc networks," pp. 62–68, 2001.

[12] P. Nuggehalli, V. Srinivasan, C.-F. Chiasserini, and R. R. Rao, "Efficient cache placement in multi-hop wireless networks," *IEEE/ACM Trans. Netw.*, vol. 14, pp. 1045–1055, October 2006.

[13] L. Breslau, P. Cao, L. Fan, G. Phillips, and S. Shenker, "Web caching and zipf-like distributions: evidence and implications," in *INFOCOM '99. Eighteenth Annual Joint Conference of the IEEE Computer and Communications Societies. Proceedings. IEEE*, vol. 1, pp. 126 –134 vol.1, mar 1999.

Evaluation of Distribution of Panoramic Video Sequences in the eXplorative Television Project

Peter Quax Panagiotis Issaris Wouter Vanmontfort Wim Lamotte

Hasselt University / tUL / IBBT
Expertise Center for Digital Media
Wetenschapspark 2, 3590 Diepenbeek, Belgium
{peter.quax, takis.issaris, wouter.vanmontfort, wim.lamotte}@uhasselt.be

ABSTRACT

In this paper, a scalable solution is presented for distributing panoramic video sequences to multiple viewers at high resolution and quality levels. In contrast to traditional broadcast scenarios, panoramic video enables the content consumer to manipulate the camera view direction and viewport size. By segmenting the panoramic input video into a set of separate sequences, transporting them over standard delivery channels and recombining them at end user side, bandwidth utilization is optimized and the quality of the video that is visualized is increased. The proposed solution, called the segmentation approach, is thoroughly explained and evaluated versus a single-stream solution with regards to several metrics, including bandwidth utilization, encoding speed, objective quality levels and seeking performance.

Categories and Subject Descriptors

H.4 [**Information Systems Applications**]: Miscellaneous

Keywords

Distributed Video Coding, Evaluation

1 Introduction and related work

One of the goals of the eXplorative Television project [4] is to design and evaluate an architecture that is capable of distributing and visualizing panoramic video content on relatively low-end hardware, such as-top boxes and tablet devices. At the same time, the solution should be designed in such a way that the existing distribution infrastructure (consisting mainly of clusters of web servers and a complete end-to-end IP delivery chain) can be utilized and that the load on this back-end (in terms of bandwidth and encoding capabilities) is in line with standard HD transmissions. For capturing panoramic or omni-directional video, either off-the-shelf or custom-built hardware can be used. The output of this stage is a sequence of six or more streams that are to be recorded and (possibly in post-production) stitched together to form a single 360-degree view on the action. Users are able to interact with the video sequences through control over a virtual camera, of which the view direction and zoom

Permission to make digital or hard copies of all or part of this work for personal or classroom use is granted without fee provided that copies are not made or distributed for profit or commercial advantage and that copies bear this notice and the full citation on the first page. To copy otherwise, to republish, to post on servers or to redistribute to lists, requires prior specific permission and/or a fee.
NOSSDAV'12, June 7–8, 2012, Toronto, Ontario, Canada.
Copyright 2012 ACM 978-1-4503-1430-5/12/06 ...$10.00.

Figure 1: **Example of a panoramic frame generated by the capturing process**

factor can be adjusted on the fly. This is fundamentally different from traditional video broadcasts, where a director pre-determines the camera direction and field-of-view. What is specific to the xTV project is that the captured content is to be delivered to the end user in the highest resolution and quality possible, utilizing all camera capabilities available at recording side. To make the solution as generically applicable and future-proof as possible, the architecture was designed to be independent of the codec, container and delivery protocol used.

The European Commission is funding research in its 7th Framework Programme on ICT on panoramic video, e.g. through the FascinatE and FinE projects (no relationship to the results presented here). Traditionally, the technology has been used for the generation of user controllable still image panoramas. Prime examples of this are QuickTime VR [2], MotionVR[6] and Google StreetView. However, the fact that only still images are supported in low resolutions and - for the former two- their non-optimized way of transmitting data (they essentially transport the entire 360 degree panorama to each user, regardless of viewing angle) limits their usage possibilities. Other existing (commercial) solutions utilize a single camera to capture the scene and compress the resulting sequence into a low resolution output stream [5]

The Panocast [9] system and derived PanoMobi solution utilize a spherical video recording as a background to increase the feeling of presence when virtual humans (avatars) are presented to a user. In their solution, the authors capture and process the spherical image to a single image, out of which several viewports are 'cut' at run-time, enhanced with 3D graphics (e.g. the avatar and other objects) and encoded using standard toolchains. As these stages are to be done separately for each user, the system is only capable of handling about 10-15 users on a single server and the output resolution is low. The authors of [3] propose to use an MPEG-7 description to more efficiently compress and distribute panoramic videos. However, the solution proposed does not take into account real-time video streams, but rather image sequences that are updated from time to time. Besides this, the entire panoramic sequence (including all still images) is transmitted as a JPEG(2000) still, making it non-suitable for distribution to large groups of viewers. Automated stitching of images is also included in the solution, but is out of scope for this discussion.

The authors of [1] present pre-processing optimizations to make H.264 codecs better at handling omni-directional video sequences. By performing image warping and resampling, the images are aligned in such a way that intra/inter prediction becomes more viable. There is however no attention paid to the actual transmission of these streams to end users, therefore putting the paper outside of the focus of the discussion. In [8], a system is presented that is able to select viewports from a panoramic video stream, called the Region of Interest (RoI) by the authors. The system focuses on the efficient detection of the whereabouts of the main actors in a video sequence (e.g. a speaker during a lecture) in both the compressed (using P-frame analysis) and uncompressed domain (through feature tracking). However, the tracking is not under direct control of the end user, but is controlled automatically through the system, thereby enabling the transmission of the same video stream to all viewers. This is an essential difference to the system proposed in this paper.

2 Approach
2.1 High level description

In this section, a novel technique is discussed that lowers the requirements for both the back-end and the end user application and is referred to as the 'segmentation approach' in the remainder of this paper. To make the overall architecture as generically applicable as possible, great care was taken to ensure that the solution can make use of existing codecs, containers and delivery mechanisms. This will, for example, enable delivery to devices that have specific requirements in terms of hardware capabilities (e.g. only a specific codec profile that can be decoded using hardware support) or delivery using existing hardware/software in the back-end (e.g. a commodity set of HTTP servers). As an example, the main configuration used for testing the implementation was a Motorola Xoom tablet with a Tegra2 chipset, using full software decoding with FFmpeg (Baseline Profile), a standard Ubuntu installation with Apache2 on a low-end laptop for the back-end and a 802.11G wireless network. The stages of the pipeline are discussed separately for reasons of clarity, in practice most of these are integrated into a single processing flow to optimize the performance.

2.1.1 Stream preparation

First of all, it should be mentioned that the capturing and processing of the frames is out of the scope of this paper. What is to be delivered as input to the processing mechanism is a set of still images, composed of a stitched projection of multiple cameras. In the demonstration case, such images are generated by a Point Grey Ladybug3 camera [7], but can equally be obtained using a custom-developed setup. Typical resolutions for these input images are around 3840 by 2160 pixels (or 4 times Full-HD). An example is shown in figure 1. Higher resolutions are possible using custom camera setups and have also been tested using the described approach but not included in this paper. Once the images are fed into the pipeline, a mosaic is overlaid; segments are cut out from the original sequence based on the boundaries indicated by the mosaic. While the size of these segments can be varied as desired (n.b. the complete frame height/width divided by the segment size needs to be an integer number), experiments have shown that a size of about 250 by 200 pixels provides good results for a normal viewport on a panoramic sequence. The final viewports will, not surprisingly, consist of a number of stitched segments. Available in the back-end is a number of encoder instances that are continuously waiting for input from the segmentation process. It is important to note that these encoders can work in parallel, and that the process can easily be distributed across multiple machines, as each segment is independent of the others.

2.1.2 Stream encoding

Once delivered to the encoders, each segment is encoded using off-the-shelf technology. As in most cases this content will be viewed on mobile devices such as tablets or on low-end hardware such as set-top-boxes, the codec parameters need to be tweaked for optimal decoding afterwards. Therefore, not all advanced (and often bandwidth-saving) techniques may be utilized. In most cases, multiple versions of the same sequence will be generated using varying codec settings. The resulting encoded frames are encapsulated in a container format for storage. The solution is also capable of splitting the video stream into a sequence of fragments of pre-determined duration (more details in the next section), resulting in output that is fully compliant with the HTTP live streaming specification.

2.1.3 Stream delivery

Although the proposed technique can make use of any delivery mechanism currently available, the focus in this paper is on transmission using HTTP. There are several reasons for this choice: first and foremost the ease through which this can be integrated into existing systems in the back-end (using standard web server technology) and the lack of issues with NAT and firewalls. Existing knowledge on web server clustering can be leveraged to ensure the scalability of such a solution. Another clear benefit is that existing CDN technology can be used to deliver content and HTTP proxies can be used to cache contents, speed up delivery and lower the overall requirements on the web server back-end. Two main mechanisms for delivery over HTTP have been integrated and will be discussed further in the evaluation section of this paper: partial downloads of MKV/MP4 container formats (as implemented in the libavformat toolset) and HTTP live streaming (popular on Apple platforms, but also used in the Android OS). Other container formats, such as NUT and MPEG-TS (standard, not HTTP live encapsulated) have also been investigated, but results are not included in the discussion.

2.1.4 Stream decoding and visualization

At client-side, the software determines the size and location of the (virtual) viewport on the entire omni-directional video sequence. These parameters may be based on the processing capabilities of the devices, but also on network parameters

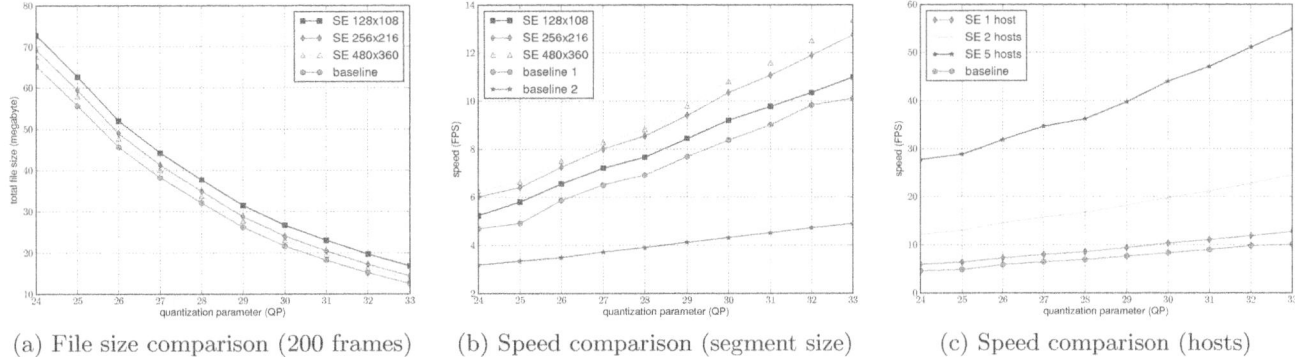

(a) File size comparison (200 frames) (b) Speed comparison (segment size) (c) Speed comparison (hosts)

Figure 2: Quantification of segmentation overhead

or just the available screen space. It is up to the software to instruct the back-end to deliver the right segments, to decode each of them, make sure that they are exactly synchronized and subsequently visualize them in such a way that boundaries between the segments become invisible. To increase the interactivity of the application, segments at the edges of the viewport may be pre-cached, even if not directly needed for visualization.

3 Implementation and test results

3.1 Baseline for comparison

To obtain a baseline against which to compare the proposed solution, the x264 implementation of the ITU-T H.264 / MPEG-4 AVC codec standard was used to generate an encoding of the entire frame in its original resolution (3840 by 2160 pixels). This is similar to the way in which panoramic sequences are delivered to end users in a previously developed solution; however in that case (for practical reasons) the streams needed to be downsized to 1920x1080 resolution before being encoded (resulting in viewports with very low resolution and quality).

For the baseline condition, the H.264 codec parameters were chosen in such a way that they are representative of what the target hardware is typically capable of in terms of decoding (either through hardware assistance or in software). Although under most conditions, a full frame would not be decodable or deliverable in real time due to its size, the frames should intuitively be more easily and efficiently compressed (vs the proposed segmentation approach) and therefore provides a good baseline to compare against. As test sequence for all conditions, a recording was used that was made at the Arras Main Square Festival 2011, with a Ladybug3 camera located on the front stage.

Performance tests on the back-end (encoding and distribution) were run on a cluster of Dell Poweredge 2970 servers that incorporated a Dual 2.3 GHz Quad-core AMD opteron CPU and 8 GB of memory. To avoid any influence of disk I/O delay (which, as a sidenote, is not to be underestimated but not detailed here due to space constraints), the image sequences were copied to a RAM disk before providing them to the encoding software (where relevant).

3.2 Notes on quality and codec settings

To explain the choices made in the comparisons described below, one should understand that it is not possible to target the codec towards a specific bit rate in the segmenta-

Parameter	Value
H.264 Profile	Main
Preset	medium
Tune	fastdecode
GOP size	16
Segment size	256x216
Number of frames	200

Table 1: Test conditions used in section 3.3

tion approach. To do so would result in segments that may vary widely in visual quality. In case they are subsequently stitched back together to form a single high-resolution image, the outcome might look like a patchwork of individual segments rather than a normal composed frame. Therefore, the bitrate is allowed to vary freely, but the quality setting (determined by the Quantification Parameter or QP) is kept at a specific value. As stated in the introduction, one of the main delivery targets are tablet devices, therefore the codec parameters are adjusted to fit those conditions (e.g. not all H.264 features are enabled and a lower profile is chosen, simplifying the decoding process).

3.3 Overhead associated with segmentation

For the results presented in this section, the settings detailed in table 1 were used unless otherwise noted.

When compared to the baseline condition (single encoding of the entire sequence), there will clearly be an overhead factor when cutting the sequence into segments and encoding them individually. Intuitively, this is due to the fact that motion vector ranges are limited to the segment sizes and headers need to be duplicated for each segment. In figure 2(a), the total encoded (stored) file size for 200 frames is shown for various QP settings and for various (representative) segment sizes using the settings as specified in table 1. When calculating the overhead percentage due to segmentation versus the baseline, values of 3 to 8 percent are obtained for large segments and 11 to 28 percent for very small segment sizes. The most realistic conditions are obtained using medium size segments (6 to 14 percent). Unsurprisingly, the overhead is largest when considering very small segments. Note also that for delivery, only a subset of segments is required and not the entire file (as is the case in the baseline condition), so this overhead mainly impacts the storage infrastructure.

An additional overhead might be expected when comparing the speed of the encoding. These results are presented in

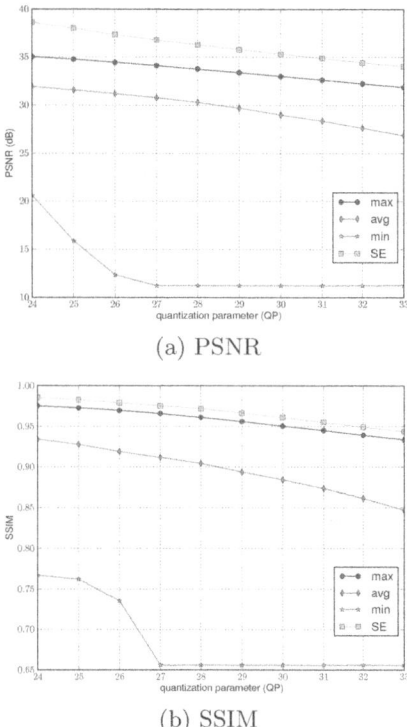

(a) PSNR

(b) SSIM

Figure 3: Quality comparison

Parameter	Value
Segment size	256 x 216
Horizontal segments in viewport	4
Vertical segments in viewport	3
Number of frames	3454
Quantization parameter (QP)	25
Total sequence resolution	3840 x 2160
Total sequence file size HTTP Live	1012 MB
Total sequence file size MKV	759 MB
Total sequence file size MP4	758 MB

Table 2: Test conditions

figure 2(b). In this chart, both baseline data series utilize the same encoder : FFmpeg using libx264. The difference between them is that "baseline 1" represents (full) frames being encoded in parallel using separate threads, while "baseline 2" uses threads to encode slices in parallel (to reduce latency). For both baseline conditions, the FFmpeg codec was allowed to utilize all 8 available cores on the server. It can be seen that even under the simplest condition, the proposed solution provides better results. The segment size (and thus, the total number of segments) is inversely related to the performance. This is mainly due to the fact that the separate codec instances can more easily be distributed over the CPU cores versus the threaded approach in FFmpeg. However, as the number of parallel encodings rises, the overhead due to context switches increases as well. A thread pool as large as the number of available cores is used in the implementation.

As stated before, the segmentation solution also parallelizes easily over multiple hosts, as one can delegate encoding of multiple segments to distinct machines. In case of this test, this was done by subdividing the input sequence into horizontal bands with a height that is a multiple of the individual segment height. As all segments can be independently encoded, these bands are transmitted to other hosts in the cluster in order to be encoded. Results are presented in figure 2(c). Note that a similar approach in case of a single FFmpeg instance would be much harder to achieve, as the encoding depends on information that may or may not be available if the input sequence is split. Using 5 hosts, real-time performance is easily achieved using high quality settings (QP=24) and a segment size of 256 by 216 pixels.

3.4 Quality comparison

As the goal of the proposed solution is to provide the end users with the highest possible quality under specific conditions (bandwidth, CPU resources, screen space), it is vital to compare the quality level that can be obtained with segmentation versus the baseline. For these tests, bandwidth was chosen as the main criterium, as the primary target for deployment of the application is tablet devices. These devices are practically incapable of decoding the sequence generated by the baseline condition (3840 by 2160 pixels) in real-time, thereby nullifying the usefulness of any comparison based on processing power.

To achieve the results in the plot, several conditions were compared. In the charts presented in figure 3, the SE line denotes the PSNR or SSIM value calculated on the segmentation approach. The reader is reminded that for the segmentation approach, the QP is varied instead of using a CBR approach. In practice, this means that the bandwidth will vary over time and will depend on the actual *contents* of the viewport of the user at any given time. An example will be described using frames like figure 1 : under certain conditions (e.g. the user is looking at a piece of the sky), the segments can be compressed to a high degree and the bit rate requirements will be (very) low. In other cases (e.g. looking at the constantly moving crowd of a concert), there is a lot of movement and compression will be relatively poor. As the viewport typically contains multiple segments and the viewport is subject to movement, conditions will average out over time. In table 2, the viewport size is indicated for the test scene in this section.

To compare the quality obtained by the segmentation approach versus the baseline, three bandwidth conditions were chosen: one where compression of segments in the viewport was the highest (cf. the above description, using the least amount of bandwidth, therefore 'min'), one where compression was lowest (highest bandwidth requirements, therefore 'max') and an average condition. The codec used in the baseline condition was instructed to encode the full 3840 by 2160 pixel frames using target bandwidths equal to these values. Note that the x264 codec used in the baseline can do a CBR encoding, as there is no risk of creating patches of different quality levels. It is very important to state again that, when using the segmented approach, only the actual pixels within the viewport need to be transferred (which is just a fraction of the amount of pixels versus the entire frame in the baseline), allowing the codec instances associated with the segments to use more bits per pixel versus the single codec baseline approach. This results in a higher image quality for the segmented approach than can be obtained using the baseline setup under the same bandwidth utilization conditions. The effect is clear both using the PSNR and SSIM metrics (see figures 3(a) and 3(b)).

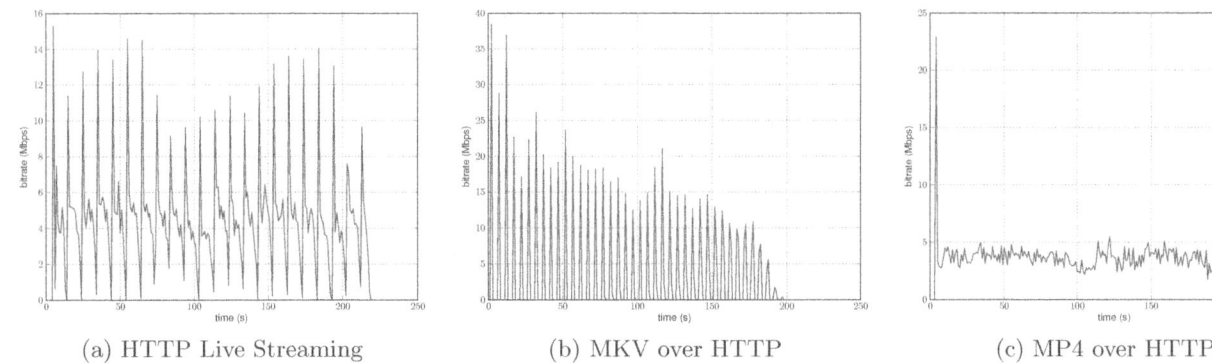

(a) HTTP Live Streaming (b) MKV over HTTP (c) MP4 over HTTP

Figure 4: Bandwidth comparison

3.5 Bandwidth utilization

To clarify some of the results shown below, it is essential to point out that the bandwidth evaluation was performed on a non-restricted local area network. An abstraction from the access network technology is required (wireless/wired networks and WAN technologies), which is accomplished by provisioning a high capacity back-end link for testing. The only practical limitation is the buffer sizes allocated within the software and the TCP/IP stack limitations (sender and/or receiver buffer sizes). This approach will expose the differences in streaming strategies to the maximal extent possible.

Figure 4 shows results from a test run using the parameters detailed in table 2. Mean bandwidth figures are: 4.5 Mbps for HTTP live streaming (HLS), 3.6 Mbps for MP4 over HTTP and 3.5 Mbps for MKV over HTTP. However, the way in which this bandwidth is consumed is fundamentally different. This is due to the internal workings of the different delivery mechanisms and will be explained in the following paragraphs. Note that the results presented here are different from a generic testing scenario of the streaming technologies, as multiple streams are actually requested at the same time (which is not normally the case).

In figure 4(a), the HTTP live delivery mechanism is used (HLS). This technology requires video sequences to be cut into pieces of equal duration. Most often, this duration is kept short, to eliminate the need for long downloads. This also facilitates seeking, as only the file containing the required frame (which can easily be tracked by matching the timestamp vs the duration) needs to be downloaded. In practice, the sequences in this case are 10 seconds long. The list of files needed for a complete sequence is stored in an index file, which is also placed on the HTTP server. The spikes in the bandwidth chart clearly show this behavior, as every 10 seconds a new file has to be downloaded. Note here that the behavior is amplified by the fact that each 10 seconds, an additional file is required for all 12 segments that make up the viewport. Downloading finishes rather quickly, as buffers are read by the program quite soon after the data arrives (making room for more data to be delivered over TCP).

Figure 4(b) shows results from the same test run, using the standard HTTP delivery method and the MKV container. The standard delivery method does not require the sequences to be cut into units of short duration; each segment is contained within a single .mkv file. If needed, the delivery mechanism supports partial HTTP downloads, in order to quickly obtain data e.g. in the middle of the sequence. An example would be if a seek operation to a future time stamp was initiated in the software. For this test case, the content was played back continuously and the feature was therefore not needed. As can be seen, the behavior is quite different from the HLS case. Here, the application requests the entire MKV file for a specific segment and fills its buffer to the maximum. Once enough data is obtained, the buffer is flushed in its entirety to the application, which will start decoding the frames within. Once additional frames are required that are not yet within the buffer, the application performs additional read operations and the buffer will fill up again.

In contrast, the MP4 container, when used with the same delivery mechanism, shows a completely different behavior (see figure 4(c)). After filling the initial buffer, the application will read only as much information as is needed for a single frame to be decoded. The window size is then adjusted accordingly and the TCP throttling mechanism will enable a relatively small amount of data to be delivered. It should come as no surprise that the bandwidth chart here shows a much smoother download characteristic (which may or may not be desired).

3.6 Synchronization and seeking

To ensure perfect synchronization between the segments that make up the final viewport to be rendered on the screen of the end user, exact seeking within each stream is clearly required. FFmpeg, the open source library containing the most extensive set of codec and container format support (used throughout the implementation of the proposed system) provides generic methods for seeking. Unfortunately, some of them are either completely broken, present unexpected or inconsistent results or consistently seek to the wrong moment in time. Additionally, seeking methods are implemented in such a way that they provide a pointer to the closest I-frame - a solution that is fine for general use, but not for frame-precise synchronization as required here.

To cope with these issues, the available seeking methods have been extended to enable single-frame precision. First, a rough seek operation is performed using the standard functionality, after which the exact frame is retrieved by either slowing down (in case a pointer is received to a 'future' I-frame) or speeding up ('past' I-frame) the decoding process. Although it is impossible to directly show the exact frame, at least visualizing something in the same GOP will ensure that the user is not presented with missing picture elements in the

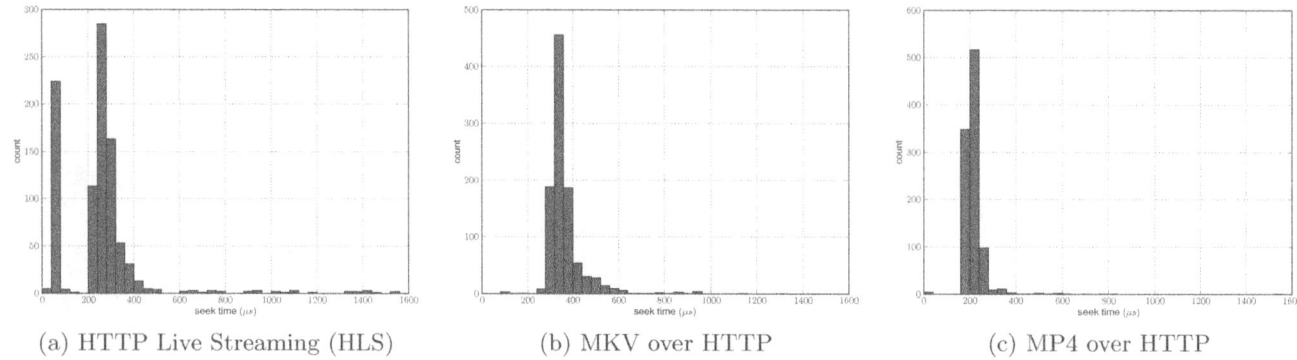

(a) HTTP Live Streaming (HLS)   (b) MKV over HTTP   (c) MP4 over HTTP

Figure 5: Seeking speed comparison

visualization. By using the described technique, the exact frame can be found and decoded quickly (typically within a few milliseconds after discovery of the reference I-frame). The work presented here also includes an implementation of a seeking method to be used in HLS, something that was not previously possible using standard FFmpeg functionality. This functionality is now part of the official distribution.

Seeking is further sped up by indices in the container formats, facilitating tracking the whereabouts of a specific I-frame within the sequence (vs a complete binary search).

Figure 5 presents histograms showing the seeking speed comparison between the various container formats. A set of 1000 randomly selected time stamps was used within a panoramic video sequence of 3.5 minutes, uniformly distributed over the duration of the file. The application was instructed to do a seek operation to the nearest I-frame. Included in the duration was the time to retrieve the data from the server and demultiplex the video frame where required; decoding of the exact frame is left out of the equation.

Note that for HLS, the separate index file is used that details the different files that make up the entire sequence for a segment (split into 10 second durations). Once the correct fragment is found and downloaded, the generic seeking method is used within the 10 second fragment (direct seeking cannot be performed due to the unavailability of an index in the MPEG-TS container in FFmpeg). For the MKV and MP4 containers, the integrated index is utilized.

The difference in seek times between the various methods may be explained by the internal buffer sizes used by the libavformat library. As figure 4 illustrates, FFmpeg's behavior varies greatly when utilizing different demultiplexers over HTTP. For HLS, if the frame requested is within the current fragment, seeking is near instantaneous. In the other methods, buffer sizes are markedly smaller and a partial HTTP download is needed to first retrieve the requested data.

4 Conclusion and future work

In this paper, the segmentation approach was proposed as a means to deliver panoramic video sequences to end users at a resolution and quality level that is as close to the recorded video material as possible. At the same time, attention was paid to the integration of existing technologies, bandwidth utilization, the performance in the back-end infrastructure (encoding and serving of the sequences) and interactivity levels (i.e. seeking speed). A thorough evaluation has shown that the encoding performance is better than the baseline approach, especially as the process can be easily parallelized. The quality level that can be obtained under a fixed bandwidth condition is increased markedly. Three different delivery mechanisms have been compared in terms of their bandwidth utilization characteristics and seeking performance. While MP4 over HTTP delivers the overall 'best' results, the availability of software in the back-end also has to be taken into account (e.g. re-use of an HLS delivery infrastructure for on-demand video).

Future work consists of a formal subjective quality comparison of various codec settings, as PSNR/SSIM metrics may not yield realistic results for the specific type of video sequences in the panoramic use case. Also, the implementation is to be tested on a larger scale in a living labs testbed.

5 Acknowledgments

Part of this work is funded by the IBBT ICON xTV Project. The authors would like to thank Telenet and Androme NV for creating the end user application.

6 References

[1] I. Bauermann, M. Mielke, and E. Steinbach. H.264 based coding of omni-directional video. In *Computer Vision and Graphics*, volume 32, pages 209–215. Springer, 2006.

[2] S. E. Chen. Quicktime vr: an image-based approach to virtual environment navigation. In *Proceedings of SIGGRAPH'95*, pages 29–38.

[3] A. Glowacz, M. Grega, P. Romaniak, M. Leszczuk, Z. Papir, and I. Pardyka. Compression and distribution of panoramic videos utilising mpeg-7-based image registration. *Springer MTAP*, 40:321–339, 2008.

[4] IBBT xTV Project. http://www.ibbt.be/en/projects/overview-projects/p/detail/xtv-2.

[5] Kogeto Dot. http://kogeto.com/dot.php.

[6] MotionVR Technology Corporation. http://www.motionvrworldwide.com/.

[7] PointGrey Ladybug 3. http://www.ptgrey.com.

[8] X. Sun, J. Foote, D. Kimber, and B. S. Manjunath. Panoramic video capturing and compressed domain virtual camera control. In *Proceedings of ACM Multimedia 2001*, pages 329–347. ACM.

[9] B. Takacs, A. Beregszaszi, and G. Komaromi-Meszaros. Panocast: A panoramic multicasting system for mobile entertainment. *Information Visualisation, International Conference on*, 0:883–887, 2007.

Collaborative View Synthesis for Interactive Multi-view Video Streaming

Fei Chen, Jiangchuan Liu, Yuan Zhao
School of Computing Science
Simon Fraser University
Burnaby, British Columbia
Email: {feic, jcliu, yza173}@sfu.ca

Edith Cheuk-Han Ngai
Department of Information Technology
Uppsala University
Uppsala, Sweden
Email: edith.ngai@it.uu.se

ABSTRACT

Interactive multi-view video enables users to enjoy the video from different viewpoints. Yet multi-view dramatically increases the video data volume and their computation, making realtime transmission and interactions a challenging task. It therefore calls for efficient view synthesis strategies that flexibly generate visual views. In this paper, we present a collaborative view synthesis strategy for online interactive multi-view video streaming based on Depth-Image Based Rendering (DIBR) view synthesis technology, which generates a visual view with the texture and depth information on both sides. Different from the traditional DIBR algorithm for single view synthesis, we explore the collaboration relationship between different viewpoints synthesis for a range of visual views generation, and propose Shift DIBR (S-DIBR). In S-DIBR, only the projected pixels, rather than all the pixels of the reference view, are utilized for next visual view generation. Therefore, the computation complexity of projection transform, which is the most computation intensive process in the traditional DIBR algorithm, is reduced to fulfill the requirement of online interactive streaming. Experiment results validate the efficiency of our collaborative view synthesis strategy, as well as the bandwidth scalability of the streaming system.

Categories and Subject Descriptors

H.5.1 [**Multimedia Information Systems**]: Video; C.2.1 [**Network Architecture and Design**]: Networking Communication

General Terms

Design, Performance, Experimentation

Keywords

multi-view streaming, depth-image based rendering, collaborative view synthesis

1. INTRODUCTION

With the rapid development of electronic and computing technology, multi-view video has recently attracted extensive interest due to greatly enhanced viewing experience. A variety of applications have emerged, such as, immersive teleconference, 3DTV and free viewpoint video. In those applications, the users can choose an arbitrary viewpoint to visualize sports or dynamic art actions. Furthermore, multi-camera systems bring users walk-through viewing experience through multiple local ray-space representation and 3-D model generation.

Unlike conventional single-view video systems, a multi-view video system allows the viewer to change viewpoint and to enjoy some special viewing experience such as View sweep and Frozen moment. It largely enhances the interactivity for users in entertainment orientated applications [1]. However, it also brings challenges to data delivery due to the huge data amounts to be transmitted. An interactive streaming system needs to make a good tradeoff between the transmission bandwidth and rendering quality [7]. Many researchers have been investigating this topic in the past few years [1, 5]. Several video formats have been developed for live or video on demand streaming, such as the multi-view video plus depth (MVD) format, in which the depth and texture information is provided to generate visual view for stereo or multi-view display [2]. The European project ATTEST has developed auto-stereoscopic 3D display with the video streaming in MVD format for the left view and right view. Compared with the conventional 2DTV, less than 20% bandwidth is increased for auto-stereoscopic 3D display with the MVD format [6]. For multi-view streaming, the bandwidth can be further reduced through view synthesis with the MVD format, since the system can just transmit selected viewpoint videos rather than all. It also means view synthesis computation can be proceeded in the user's side, and the effectiveness to generate visual views greatly affects the rendering quality. Also, computation complexity and bandwidth adaptivity need to be considered for online interactive applications. As such an interactive multi-view streaming system has following demands.

1. *Rendering Quality.* A visual view is interpolated between transmitted views to reduce disparity of interview and smooth the view sweeping process;

2. *Efficiency.* The computation complexity should be reduced to guarantee the availability of interactive data;

3. *Bandwidth Scalability.* Given the different bandwidth

conditions, it should allow users to enjoy different view quality levels adaptive to their available bandwidth.

In this paper, we present a collaborative view synthesis strategy for online interactive multi-view video streaming system. To reduce the transmission bandwidth, selected views are transmitted to users as reference views, which are utilized to generate the visual views to smooth view sweeping application. Specifically, a Shift DIBR (S-DIBR) algorithm is proposed to guarantee the rendering quality and efficiency. According to the available bandwidth, the users can also enjoy improved viewing experience with a scalable layer. The remainder of the paper is organized as follows. We first review the related work in Section II. In Section III, we outline the main structure of the interactive multi-view streaming system. The collaborative view synthesis strategy is presented in Section IV. Then we will describe the traditional DIBR algorithm and the new S-DIBR algorithm which we proposed to reduce computation complexity for a range of visual views synthesis in Section V. The experimental results are presented in Section VI. Finally, we conclude our work in Section VII.

2. RELATED WORK

In the DIBR research, effective view synthesis remains an open problem given different conditions. Xue et al. [11] proposed a visual view rendering method based on depth image, which makes a tradeoff between the image quality and computation complexity. Unfortunately the pre-process depth map by expanding object edge results in depth distortion, especially in complicated background environment. Daribo and Saito [3] improved the rendering quality through a bilateral filter by taking into account the strength of the depth discontinuity. Meanwhile, the computation complexity is increased as a tradeoff. Schmeing and Jiang [10] designed a faithful approach specially for the disocclusion problem, which provides realistic texture rather than mixture of nearby pixels. However, it is not appropriate for online interactive application, since the dissoclution area in transformed background is corrected manually. In [4] an inpainting-based layered depth view generation method was developed to reduce the amount of residual data to complete missing pixels from the main layer. These previous works considered the single view synthesis only. We on the other hand consider an efficient view synthesis method with low computation complexity to generate a group of visual views for the interactive application of multi-view streaming systems. To our knowledge, the collaborative view synthesis for the streaming system has been largely unexplored.

3. SYSTEM DESCRIPTION

In Fig.1, we outline the streaming structure of a multi-view interactive application system. The system is mainly based on the DIBR algorithm, which can generate visual view with the depth and texture information of reference views on both sides. A *depth map* records the depth value of each point on the frame, which represents the distance from the viewer to the object. A *texture map* records the pixel value of each point accordingly, which provides the color information of the object. The points in the reference views are projected to a 3D space, and then projected to the coordinates of the target visual view. From Fig.1, we can see the cameras with different colors, and each one stands

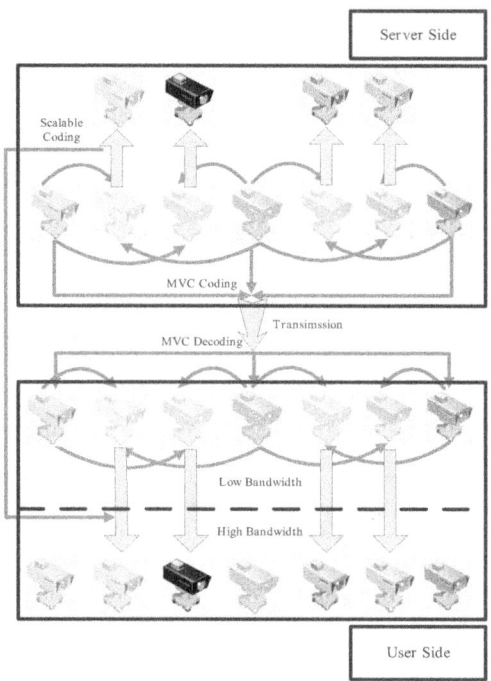

Figure 1: Multi view streaming structure

for a unique viewpoint. The opaque cameras are *reference views*, capturing depth and texture information, while the translucent cameras are *visual views* to be generated by the reference views. Actually, the streaming videos of these viewpoints are still captured in our system. They are used for scalable coding with synthesized views. A scalable layer is then transmitted to the users with high bandwidth.

The system includes both the server side and the user side. According to the bandwidth level, the users can be divided into a *high bandwidth group* and a *low bandwidth group*. After the server receives the videos captured by multi-camera, the reference view videos are chosen from these original videos. Then the streaming process provides the service with two layers, the *base layer* and the *scalable layer*. The base layer is prepared for all users and transmitted with multi-view coding (MVC) for further compression. When the users receive the base layer, view synthesis is proceeded with the reference views from MVC decoding. The scalable layer is then prepared for the high bandwidth group users to enjoy higher viewing quality. It is generated with visual views and original views in the server side, making use of scalable video coding (SVC). Our system utilizes both MVC and SVC for the efficiency and scalability. The two coding strategies can proceed in parallel, so the computation time does not delay the server or users for online streaming. From above description, we can see the view synthesis is utilized in both server side and user side. Therefore it is necessary to develop an efficient view synthesis strategy for the interactive streaming system.

4. VIEW SYNTHESIS COLLABORATION

Different from traditional view synthesis methods, which mainly focus on the accuracy of single visual view generation, we consider how to efficiently generate a group of visual views with different viewpoints for interactive appli-

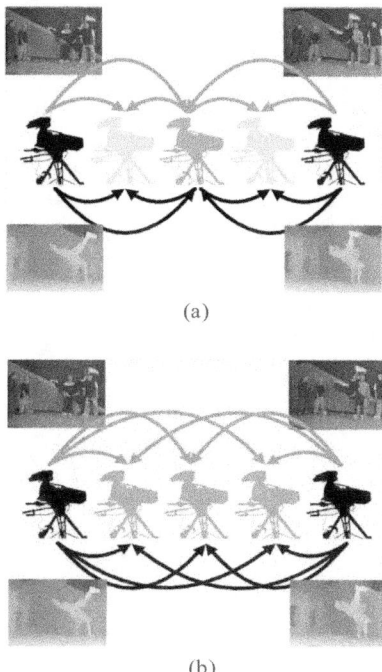

Figure 2: View Synthesis Model: (a) Middle Synthesis (b) Shift Synthesis

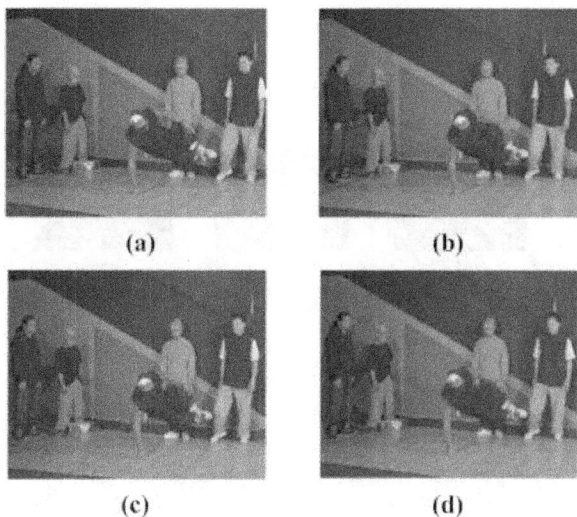

Figure 3: (a) Main reference view (b) Assistant reference view (c) Synthesized view (d) Original view

cations. Before analyzing the view synthesis algorithm, we consider two kinds of view synthesis collaboration strategies from Fig.2. The two reference views (opaque) provide texture and depth information on both sides for the generation of three visual views (translucent). The upper and lower lines show the texture and depth matching, respectively. In the middle synthesis pattern Fig.2 (a), the middle view among the visual views is generated in priority, and the remaining visual views are synthesized with the middle view and reference views. In the shift synthesis pattern Fig.2 (b), a range of visual views with different viewpoints are generated directly from the two reference views.

In our system, a shift synthesis is utilized to prepare for the texture maps of visual views for interactive applications. Comparing with the middle synthesis, there are three advantages in the aspects of efficiency, accuracy and buffer saving. (1) Given that a GPU supports the parallel computing, the shift synthesis pattern outperforms the middle synthesis pattern without waiting for the synthesized results. (2) In the middle synthesis pattern, the depth distortion during view synthesis is brought into the generation of a new visual view. The rendering quality deterioration accumulates as the number of visual view generation increases; (3) In the middle synthesis, the synthesized depth map of the visual view has to be reserved in both server side and user side for a new visual view generation. By contrast, in the shift synthesis pattern, the buffer storage space is reduced without reservation for the depth map of the visual view.

5. VIEW SYNTHESIS ALGORITHM

In this section, we first give an overview on the DIBR algorithm [6], which generates the visual view with the main reference view and the assistant reference view as shown in Fig.3. Then we will illustrate the S-DIBR to effectively generate a group of visual views between the reference views with low computational cost.

5.1 DIBR Algorithm Overview

In DIBR, Each point with a pixel in the texture map relates to a grayscale recorded by depth map. The actual depth value can be calculated as:

$$Z = \frac{1}{\frac{D}{255}(\frac{1}{MinZ} - \frac{1}{MaxZ}) + \frac{1}{MaxZ}} \quad (1)$$

where D is the grayscale of the sample point and Z is the depth value, $MinZ$ and $MaxZ$ are the depth values of the nearest and farthest points in the real world, respectively. The following steps then proceed with depth map and texture map. In the projection transform process, the points in the reference views are projected to a 3-dimensional space and then projected to the target visual view. After that, a median filter is employed as edge filter to enclose the small holes and smooth disconnections of the depth map. The texture map of the visual view is blended in the projected view and rendered according to the depth value. The remaining disocclusions generated by depth warping are inpainted by the texture map from other reference views.

5.2 Proposed S-DIBR Algorithm

From [9] we know the view projection can be described by the equation:

$$\lambda_2 p_2 = K_2 R_2 [K_1 R_1]^{-1} \lambda_1 p_1 + K_2(t_2 - t_1) \quad (2)$$

where K_n, and R_n, for $n \in [1, 2]$, are the intrinsic camera parameter and the rotation metric, respectively. The value λ_1 and λ_2 denote the depth value of the point in the target visual view and the reference view. The depth values are supposed to be the same with short horizontal shift, and the K_n and R_n are identical given that the cameras have the same setup parameters for the same scene. Equation (2) can be rewrote as follows:

$$\lambda p_2 = \lambda p_1 + K(t_2 - t_1)$$

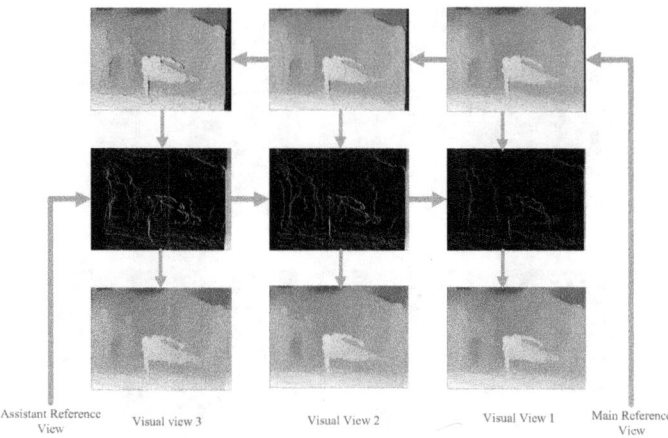

Figure 4: S-DIBR View Synthesis

which can be worked out as

$$\lambda \begin{pmatrix} x_2 \\ y_2 \\ 1 \end{pmatrix} = \lambda \begin{pmatrix} x_1 \\ y_1 \\ 1 \end{pmatrix} + \begin{pmatrix} f & 0 & x_0 \\ 0 & f & y_0 \\ 0 & 0 & 1 \end{pmatrix} \begin{pmatrix} \Delta x \\ 0 \\ 0 \end{pmatrix}$$

and it simplifies to

$$\begin{pmatrix} x_2 \\ y_2 \end{pmatrix} = \begin{pmatrix} x_1 \\ y_1 \end{pmatrix} + \begin{pmatrix} \frac{f}{\lambda} \Delta x \\ 0 \end{pmatrix} \quad (3)$$

where f is the camera's focal length and (x_0, y_0) is the offset coordinate of intrinsic parameters. Suppose that the distance between the two reference views is d, and the total number of synthesized views to be generated is N. According to Equation (3), the shift value S_0 from the main reference view to the visual view is:

$$S_0 = \frac{fdn}{\lambda N}, \text{ where } n = 1, 2, .. \frac{N}{2} \quad (4)$$

Accordingly, the shift value S_1 from the visual view to the assistant reference view is:

$$S_1 = \frac{fd}{\lambda N}(1 - \frac{n}{N}), \text{ where } n = 1, 2, .. \frac{N}{2} \quad (5)$$

From Equation (3-5), we know that the shift value S is proportional to baseline d and inversely proportional to the depth value λ. After the projecting process, some areas are disoccluded without depth or texture information. It also means the same number of pixels are occluded or projected out of boundary. Therefore the projection from other reference views is needed for inpainting disocclusion area. According to [8], the projection transform is the heaviest computation in the view synthesis process. In the traditional DIBR algorithm, each pixel from the reference view is projected to the target visual view for disocclusion area inpainting. It is necessary because the shift value of the points in the disocclusion area can not be computed without the depth information. Each pixel from the reference view has the potential to be projected in this area. However, in the view synthesis process for a group of different viewpoints, the projection transform is restricted to the hole filling area of the last transform after the first projection transform is completed. Given that $View(0)$ and $View(N+1)$ are the reference views, we take them as $R(0)$ and $R(N+1)$ for short. There are N views from $View(1)$ to $View(N)$ to be synthesized, and we denote them as $V(1), V(2), ...V(N)$ for short. In our collaborative strategy, $R(0)$ is the main reference view and $R(N+1)$ is the assistant reference view for the view synthesis of $V(1)$ to $V(N/2)$. And they exchange the roles for the view synthesis from $V(N/2+1)$ to $V(N)$. The shift value S from $V(0)$ to $R(N/2)$ is $\frac{df}{2\lambda}$. And then S decreases every $\frac{df}{N\lambda}$ until it reaches $V(1)$. Fig.4 shows the collaborative view synthesis process between the main reference view and the assistant reference view in S-DIBR. According to Equation (3), the disocclusion problem in the texture map happens when disconnections occur in the depth map. As to a pair of neighboring pixels $Pixel_a$ and $Pixel_b$ with $\lambda_b - \lambda_a \neq 0$, we have the following equation

$$S_b - S_a = \frac{fd(\lambda_a - \lambda_b)}{\lambda_a \lambda_b} \quad (6)$$

Given that the cameras shift horizontally, λ_a and λ_b keep constant after the view shift. Therefore the disocclusion area is proportional to the baseline d. When users sweep from $R(0)$ to $R(N+1)$, there are N visual views to be generated between $R(0)$ and $R(N+1)$. We have the computation latency T as follows:

$$T = N(T_p + T_m + T_t + T_h) = NT_p + \delta \quad (7)$$

where $T_p, T_m, T_t,$ and T_h are related to the time cost in pixel projection, median filtering, texture matching and hole filling process, respectively. In DIBR, all the pixels on both reference frames are required for pixel projection. Since T_p is proportional to the frame size P, the time cost in pixel projection is $T_p(D) = 2NKP$, where K is the time coefficient for pixel projection of a single frame.

In S-DIBR, only the projected pixels rather than all the pixels of the reference views are utilized for the next visual view generation. The disocclusion area reduces as the shift value between the main reference view and visual view decreases. Suppose P_i^M and P_i^A are the sets of projected pixels for $V(i)$ in warping process from the main reference view and the assistant reference view respectively, then we have the following relation:

$$\begin{cases} P_i \subset P_{i+1}, & P = P^A \\ P_{i+1} \subset P_i, & P = P^M \end{cases} \quad \text{where } i \in 1, 2, ... \frac{N}{2} \quad (8)$$

Let α_i be the possibility of the pixels projected from P_{i+1} to P_i, and from Equation (8) $P_i^M = \prod_{i=1}^{N/2} \alpha_i^M$, $P_i^A = \prod_{i=1}^{N/2-i+1} \alpha_i^A$. So we have $T_p(S)$ for S-DIBR as follows:

$$\begin{aligned} T_p(S) &= \sum_{j=1}^{N} T_{j,p} \\ &= 2K[(P_1^M + P_1^A) + (P_2^M + P_2^A)...(P_{N/2}^M + P_{N/2}^A)] \\ &= 2KP[(\alpha_1^M + \prod_{i=1}^{N/2} \alpha_i^A)... + (\prod_{i=1}^{N/2} \alpha_i^M + \alpha_1^A)] \\ &= 2KP(\sum_{j=1}^{N/2} \prod_{i=1}^{j} \alpha_i^M + \sum_{j=1}^{N/2} \prod_{i=1}^{j} \alpha_i^A) \end{aligned} \quad (9)$$

Where $T_{j,p}$ is the time cost in pixel projection process for $V(j)$. Since $T_p \gg T_m + T_t + T_h$ and $\delta^M \approx \delta^A$, we have the computation latency reduction ratio φ as follows:

$$\varphi = \frac{T(D) - T(S)}{T} = 1 - \frac{\sum_{j=1}^{N/2}(\prod_{i=1}^{j} \alpha_i^M + \prod_{i=1}^{j} \alpha_i^A)}{N} \quad (10)$$

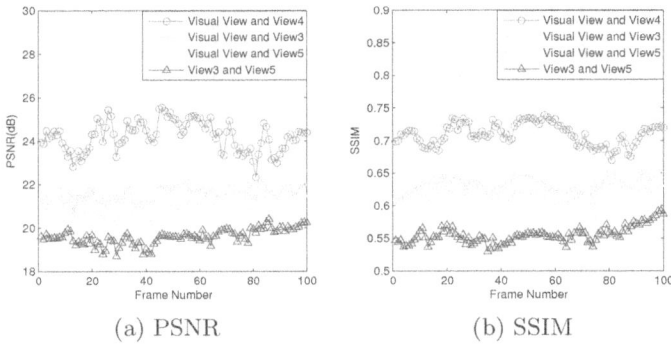

Figure 5: Different view comparison

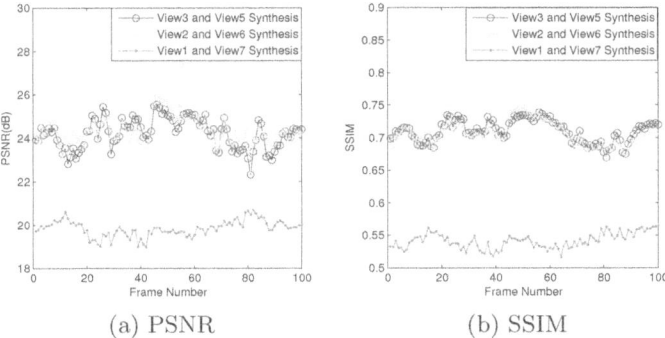

Figure 6: Synthesized with different reference view

6. EVALUATION

In the following experiments, our multi-view video data comes from the "Breakdancing" of Microsoft visual interactive group including 8 cameras setup in a horizontal line to capture the same scene from different viewpoints. The resolution for each frame is $1024*768$, and there are 100 frames to be rendered at $15fps$. The experiments are proceeded in the computer with $Pentium(R)D$ CPU 3.4 GHz and 2.00 GB of RAM.

6.1 View Synthesis Analysis

Our system is developed to provide interactive applications for users to enjoy multi-view videos. When the users sweep the views, the disparity between the views would corrupt the rendering quality. From Fig.5. we can see the great disparity between the original views ($O(i)$ for short) $O(3)$ and $O(5)$. In order to sweep the view smoothly, the visual view ($V(i)$ for short) is generated by $O(3)$ and $O(5)$. From the PSNR and Structural Similarity (SSIM), the $V(4)$ is rendered close to $O(4)$. When the user sweeps the views from $O(3)$ to $O(5)$, it will first arrive to $V(4)$ as the transitional view and then reaches the destination view. Therefore it shows that the interpolation of the visual view is helpful to smooth the view sweeping. As the distance between the two reference views increases, the view synthesis quality decreases. We perform the view synthesis for $V(4)$ with different pairs of reference views, $R(3)$ and $R(5)$, $R(2)$ and $R(6)$, $R(1)$ and $R(7)$ respectively. From Fig.6, we can see that the quality of view synthesis with reference views $R(2)$ and $R(6)$

Table 1: Rendering Quality and Efficiency

Visual View	W-DIBR	S-DIBR
$V(4)$	26.5dB/0.73	25.9dB/0.71
$V(4,5)$	25.6dB/0.72	25.8dB/0.7
$V(3,4,5)$	22dB/0.63	24.7dB/0.68
$V(2,3,4,5,6)$	20.2dB/0.62	20dB/0.6

are generally the same to that with $R(3)$ and $R(5)$. The view synthesis quality degrades sharply when the shift distance is increased to 6 views (5 visual views included). There are two reasons for this. First, from Equation (4), the shift value is proportional to the depth value. The depth distortion accumulates gradually, and it leads to mismatch during the hole filling process. Second, in S-DIBR, it is supposed that the parallel cameras are arranged in horizontal line and the depth value is constant during the view shift process. Actually, the cameras usually make a circle with an appropriate radian to capture the same scene. (e.g. in "Break Dancer" the radian is about 30 degree between the camera on the left end and the one on the right end.) And the depth value changes as the view angle changes. If the radian change can not be ignored, the depth value will not keep constant. These two reasons prevent S-DIBR from the application of long distance shift, which we expect to address in the future.

6.2 Performance Comparisons

We next compare the collaborative view synthesis algorithm S-DIBR with conventional warping DIBR (W-DIBR for short) on rendering quality and computing efficiency. The $V(4)$ is taken as the median visual view. The reference views are the neighboring views (e.g. $R(2)$ and $R(6)$ are the reference views for visual view $V(3,4,5)$, and in S-DIBR $R(2)$ and $R(6)$ are the main reference views for $V(3)$ and $V(5)$, respectively.) We generate the visual view with W-DIBR and S-DIBR and compute the average PSNR and SSIM, respectively. As the shift value increases, more visual views are generated for view interpolation to reduce the disparity during view changes. From Tab.1, we can see S-DIBR have the similar PSNR and SSIM with W-DIBR when just one single visual view is synthesized. The rendering quality of both W-DIBR and S-DIBR is maintained when the number of visual views are increased to 2. The rendering quality of W-DIBR decreases sharply when 3 visual views need to be generated. Meanwhile, S-DIBR still keeps the performance since the main reference views provide the major texture. The S-DIBR rendering quality begins to deteriorate for 5 visual views generation, due to the accumulation of depth distortion and radian expansion.

In order to compare the efficiency of W-DIBR and S-DIBR, we measure the average synthesis time over 100 frames. From Fig.7, we compare the computation latency of view synthesis, which includes the pixel projection, rendering, and hole filling.[1] For one visual view synthesis, the W-DIBR and S-DIBR have the similar time cost. In 2 visual view generation, about 15% of synthesis time is saved in S-DIBR. The gap between W-DIBR and S-DIBR keeps expanding and finally reaches 30% in 6 visual view generation. Therefore, as the visual view number increases, the efficiency of collaborative view synthesis becomes more obvious.

---

[1]Note that median filtering is not included, but it is compatible to our S-DIBR algorithm.

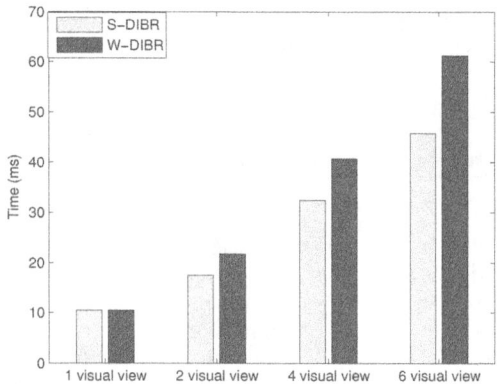

Figure 7: Computation Latency

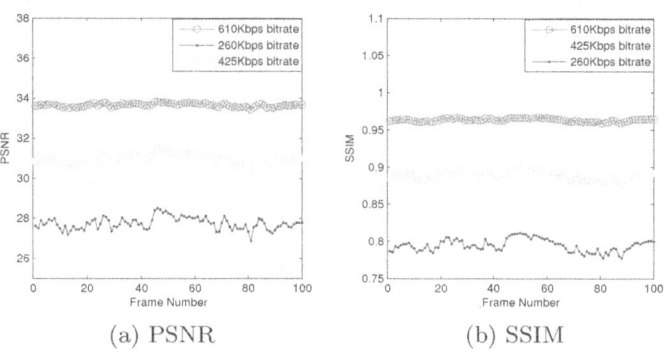

(a) PSNR (b) SSIM

Figure 8: Different bit rates comparison

6.3 Scalable Rendering

The resolution of the frames in the view video is $256*192$ compressed from $1024*768$ and the frame rate of streaming is $15fps$. The original texture map is $144K$ and the corresponding depth map is $30K$ before compression. We now measure the PSNR and SSIM value for each frame of the video with the bitrate of $260Kbps$, $425Kbps$ and $610Kbps$. In Fig.8, the different bitrates respectively stand for 3 reference views streaming, 5 reference views streaming, and 5 reference views plus scalable layer streaming. We can see that the rendering quality in bitrate of $260Kbps$ is low, with the trading off of bandwidth saving. The rendering quality is improved greatly with bitrate of $425Kbps$, because more reference views are provided and the view shift distance is reduced by about 50%. As to the bitrate of $610Kbps$, the view synthesis strategy and scalable layer cooperate to yield high rendering quality. The rendering quality with high bandwidth is also stable, because the impact of the depth distortion in view synthesis is alleviated.

7. CONCLUSION

In this paper, we have developed a collaborative view synthesis strategy for multi-view streaming system. Making use of DIBR, it has effectively reduced the amount of data transmission in traditional multi-view streaming systems, and has realized the scalable rendering according to different bandwidth levels. The proposed S-DIBR algorithm has reduced the computing complexity in pixel projection transform, which is the heaviest computation task in the traditional DIBR algorithm. The results from experiments have shown that our view synthesis for interpolation is helpful to smooth the view sweeping application. The evaluation between S-DIBR and W-DIBR has demonstrated significant performance improvement with respect to view synthesis quality and computation complexity. Furthermore the streaming quality in our streaming system has been analyzed with different bandwidth levels. However, the depth distortion and radian expansion problem still prevents S-DIBR from effectively serving long distance cameras, which will be addressed in our future work.

8. REFERENCES

[1] A. Boukerche, R. Jarrar, and R. W. Pazzi. A novel interactive streaming protocol for image-based 3d virtual environment navigation. In *Proc. IEEEICC'09*, pages 1 – 6, Dresden, June 2009.

[2] G. Bravo, D. Luat, S. Zinger, and P. With. Real-time free-viewpoint DIBR on GPUs for 3DTV systems. In *Proc. IEEE International Conference on Consumer Electronics ICCE'11*, pages 1–4, Berlin, Germany, Sept. 2011.

[3] I. Daribo and H. Saito. Bilateral depth-discontinuity filter for novel view synthesis. In *Proc. IEEE International Workshop on Multimedia Signal Processing MMSP'10*, pages 145 – 149, Oct. 2010.

[4] I. Daribo and H. Saito. A novel inpainting-based layered depth video for 3DTV. *IEEE Trans. Broadcast.*, 20:533 – 541, June 2011.

[5] Y. Ding and J. Liu. Efficient stereo segment scheduling in peer-to-peer 3d/multi-view video streaming. In *Proc. IEEE P2P'11*, Kyoto, Japan, Aug. 2011.

[6] C. Fehn. Depth-image-based rendering (DIBR), compression and transmission for a new approach on 3d-tv. In *Proc. SPIE Stereoscopic Displays and Virtual Reality Systems XI*, pages 93–104, 2004.

[7] E. Kurutepe and T. Sikora. Feasibility of multi-view video streaming over P2P networks. In *Proc. IEEE 3DTV Conference*, pages 157–160, Istanbul, May 2008.

[8] J. Lai, C. Chen, and S. Chien. Architecture design and analysis of image-based rendering engine. In *Proc. IEEE International Conference on Multimedia and Expo ICME'11*, pages 1–6, Barcelona, Spain, July 2011.

[9] D. Luat, S. Zinger, and P. Dewith. Conversion of free-viewpoint 3d multi-view video for stereoscopic displays. In *Proc. IEEE International Conference on Multimedia and Expo ICME'10*, pages 730–1734, Singapore, July 2010.

[10] M. Schmeing and X. Jiang. Depth image based rendering: A faithful approach for the disocclusion problem. In *Proc. IEEE 3DTV-CON'10*, pages 1–4, June 2010.

[11] J. Xue, M. Xi, D. Li, and M. Zhang. A new virtual view rendering method based on depth image. In *Proc. IEEE Asia-Pacific Conference on Wearable Computing Systems APWCS'10*, pages 147 – 150, Kaohsiung, Taiwan, May 2010.

Keynote

Streaming Media Evolution: Where to now?

Wu-chi Feng
Portland State University
Portland, OR 97207
wuchi@cs.pdx.edu

ABSTRACT

The notion of streaming media has been around for nearly two decades. From a research novelty to now consuming over half of all Internet bandwidth, streaming media is now much more commonplace. This keynote address will give my perspective on the history and evolution of streaming media and lessons learnt. Since the introduction of digital video in the early 1990s, our community has spent significant effort focused on the development of scalable and adaptive mechanisms for streaming media. We have witnessed techniques ranging from interactive multimedia streaming, stored video streaming, peer-to-peer streaming, and remote tele-presence. Several common themes have emerged in these technologies and as we move forward as a community, this keynote will offer some thought and observations on applying lessons learnt to future technologies and a handful of areas where streaming media can make significant impact beyond where we are today.

Categories and Subject Descriptors

H.3.4 Information Systems -- INFORMATION STORAGE AND RETRIEVAL: Systems and Software

Keywords: Streaming media evolution, Video streaming

SPEAKER BIO

Wu-chi Feng received his Ph.D. in Computer Science and Engineering from the University of Michigan in 1996. He is currently Professor of Computer Science at Portland State University. His research interests currently include video-based sensor networking, stereoscopic video systems, and adaptive streaming. He is currently serving as the steering committee chair for the ACM Multimedia Systems conference, and an editor for the ACM Multimedia Systems Journal. He has also served as a program co-chair for the ACM Multimedia 2011 conference, program chair for the 31st IEEE International Conference on Distributed Computing Systems, and numerous other program committees in the multimedia computing and networking area. He was awarded an NSF CAREER award in 1998 for his work on video-on-demand systems.

On Tile Assignment for Region-of-Interest Video Streaming in a Wireless LAN

Guntur Ravindra and Wei Tsang Ooi
Department of Computer Science
National University of Singapore
ravindra@comp.nus.edu.sg, ooiwt@comp.nus.edu.sg

ABSTRACT

We consider the following problem in this paper: A video is encoded as a set of tiles T and is streamed to multiple users via a one-hop wireless LAN. Each user selects a region-of-interest (RoI), represented as a subset of T, in the video to watch. The RoI selected by the users may overlap. Each tile may be multicast or unicast. We define the tile assignment problem as: which subset of tiles should be multicast such that every user receives, within a transmission deadline, the subset of tiles pertaining to the RoI the user selected, while minimizing the number of unwanted tiles received by users. We present and evaluate five tile assignment methods. We show that: (i) minimizing transmission delay can lead to significant wasteful reception in the multicast group, (ii) using tile access probability to assign tiles frequently leads to assignments that violate the deadline, and (iii) a fast, greedy, heuristic works well: it performs close to the optimal method and can always find an assignment within the deadline (as long as such assignment exists).

Categories and Subject Descriptors

H.5.1 [**Multimedia Information Systems**]: Video

General Terms

Algorithms, Performance

Keywords

Zoomable Video, Region-of-Interest Video Streaming

1. INTRODUCTION

Region-of-interest (RoI) streaming is a popular approach for streaming large format images [4] and high-resolution video [7, 8]. Users select a RoI of choice, and the server streams all the data required to render the RoI at the client end. In the case of video streaming, frames may be encoded at multiple resolutions, with the lowest resolution served to the users by default. A user may select a RoI from the lower resolution video to zoom in on and view in higher resolution. The RoI is then cropped from a higher resolution compressed

Permission to make digital or hard copies of all or part of this work for personal or classroom use is granted without fee provided that copies are not made or distributed for profit or commercial advantage and that copies bear this notice and the full citation on the first page. To copy otherwise, to republish, to post on servers or to redistribute to lists, requires prior specific permission and/or a fee.
NOSSDAV'12, June 7–8, 2012, Toronto, Ontario, Canada.
Copyright 2012 ACM 978-1-4503-1430-5/12/06 ...$10.00.

video and sent to the user for display. To support such functionality, the video frames may be encoded as a grid of non-overlapping tiles [13, 5]. Another method is to use overlapping tiles [6] and encode each tile area as a separate video stream. All tiles intersecting with the RoI are cropped and streamed by the server. Representing a video as tiles reduces temporal dependency across frames and allows some degree of random access into RoI.

In this paper, we consider the problem of efficient RoI streaming in a wireless LAN, exploiting the fact that many users may select overlapping RoIs. This scenario arises in a system we are developing, where we want to stream live HD videos to many users equipped with our video player that supports RoI viewing.

While attempts have been made to improve bandwidth efficiency by encoding video based on RoI access pattern [12], reducing bandwidth alone would not suffice as there is a limit to the extent to which bandwidth may be reduced without degrading the video quality. In a one-hop wireless LAN, one could exploit an optimal combination of multicast and unicast capabilities of the access point, in order to transmit overlapping and non-overlapping regions of users' RoIs.

Figure 1 depicts a case where three users have partially overlapping RoIs. The video frame is shown as a grid of tiles with some tiles marked with the different users requiring those tiles. The two tiles required by all the three users (marked "1,2,3") could be multicast. If they are unicast, then these tiles are transmitted three times separately to each of the three users. The figure also shows that two tiles (marked "1,3") are required by only two users. If these two tiles are multicast, then User 2 also receive these two tiles although they are not part of this user's RoI. We term such an unwanted reception as *wasteful reception*. Issue of unwanted reception can be eliminated with users subscribing to advertised multicast groups and the server transmitting chosen tiles over these multicast groups. In the example of Figure 1, tiles marked "1,2,3" could be multicast on one multicast group and tiles marked "1,3" could be multicast on a different multicast group. Although such an approach would improve transmission efficiency, this approach is impractical in a setting where users can frequently change their RoI. The multicast groups would frequently change, new multicast groups would have to be created, and new groups have to be advertised. The ensuing protocol nightmare may be avoided if there is only one predefined multicast group to which all users subscribe, in addition to the unicast port over which video tiles are transmitted by the server. The onus is then on the server to assign the tiles into multicast and unicast groups, transmit all the multicast tiles on the multicast port, and unicast tiles separately to each user requiring these tiles.

The key is to address the assignment of the tiles into either multicast or unicast. The multicast transmission rate is typically lower than the unicast rate. As a result, a tile transmitted over multicast

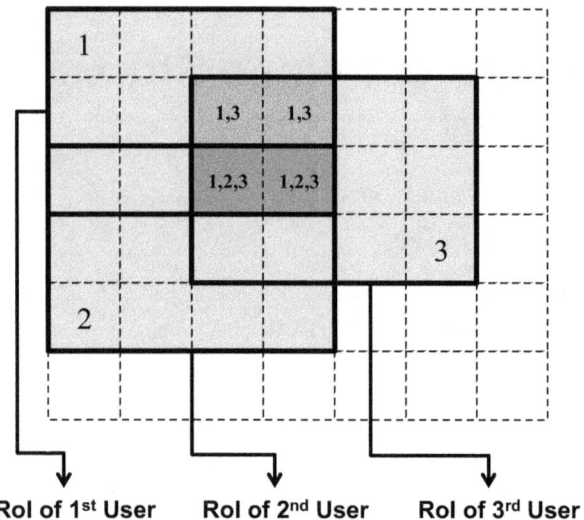

Figure 1: A depiction of RoI overlap

f	frame rate (frames per second)
T	the set of tiles
b	average tile size
R_i	set of tiles selected by user u_i
T_m	set of tiles selected for multicast
n	number of users
n_t	number of users requiring a tile t
m_t	set of users requiring the tile t
B_m	multicast data rate
B_u^i	unicast data rate for User u_i
p	probability that a multicast tile will reach all users
$\psi_u(t)$	utility of a tile t being unicast
$\psi_m(t)$	utility of a tile t being multicast

Table 1: Table of Notations

will arrive after a delay that is greater than when the tile is transmitted over unicast. Firstly, as a rule, a tile that is needed by all users in the system should be sent via multicast. If the tile is sent via unicast then the bandwidth utilized is as many times as the number of users in the system. Secondly, all the tiles in a frame should reach all the users before the tiles of the next frame can be transmitted. Hence a transmission deadline has to be met.

In this paper, we describe five methods to assign tiles into either the multicast and the unicast channel such that (i) the transmission deadline may be met, and (ii) wasteful reception of tiles is minimized.

The rest of the paper is organized as follows: in Section 2, a brief introduction to related work is mentioned. In Section 3, the problem of tile assignment is formulated. Section 4 describes five tile assignment methods. Section 5 is dedicated to an evaluation of the methods, followed by a conclusion in Section 6.

2. RELATED WORK

Partitioning data into multiple groups for transmission over different access channels is well studied as a channelization problem in a publish-subscribe paradigm. The solution invariably involves some form of resource allocation meeting a constraint. Adler et al. studied how to assign a published resource to different multicast groups with resource duplication [1]. The Hyper project uses a hybrid approach [14] where a multicast distribution tree may be bypassed in order to establish a unicast channel between the publisher and subscriber. Bickson et al. investigated the mapping of flows into multicast and unicast sets in a quantitative manner [2] with heuristic solutions such as, random assignment with flow merges, use of k-means clustering, and use of binary matrix decomposition. In all these approaches a generic data type is assumed. In this paper, we propose a solution for a specific video streaming case over a single hop wireless network. Although our framework fits the publish-subscribe paradigm, the need for the tiles constituting a region-of-interest reaching all the subscribers within a deadline is unique to the problem being solved. Further we explore a situation where the multicast grouping may change every second during streaming of a video. The goal that the video player should be simple in design restricts the number of multicast channels that it can subscribe to.

The problem of assigning tiles into unicast and multicast groups can be formalized as an optimization problem involving a transmission deadline, the multicast and unicast rates, the number of users in the system, and their RoI access patterns. Hence, before we embark on strategies for tile assignment, the problem at hand is formalized.

3. PROBLEM DEFINITION

Let the video rate be f frames per second. We assume that every second consists of one GoP of encoded video. Let each video frame be partitioned into a set T of equal sized tiles, each of size b bits (average tile size). Let $U = \{u_1, u_2, ..u_n\}$ be the set of users. User u_i selects a RoI $R_i \subseteq T$ comprising of a subset of tiles to view. The RoIs for all the n users, i.e., $\cup_{i=1}^{n} R_i$, must be delivered within $\frac{1}{f}$ seconds. Note that, as RoIs can overlap, a tile may be needed by multiple users.

In a setting described so far, it is prudent to assign tiles optimally to the multicast and unicast connections of the wireless network. As discussed in the previous section, we assume that all users subscribe to a single multicast channel (IP address and port number). The channel is known a priori, is subscribed to when the session starts, and does not change during the streaming session. Let m_t be the set of users requiring tile t. If a tile t is sent via multicast, then t is also received by users who do not require the tile, as all users have subscribed to a single pre-determined multicast group. This unnecessary reception is termed as a wasteful reception. Receiving unwanted tiles would impact the client side performance in terms of CPU utilization and battery consumption as a result of processing these tiles. Hence the goal of the assignment should be to minimize wasteful reception while honoring the deadline of $\frac{1}{f}$ seconds.

To quantify the "wasteful" reception we define a utility function ψ. Consider a system where there are n clients, and $n_t = |m_t|$ clients need a tile t. If t is transmitted via unicast, then it has to be transmitted n_t times, once to each user. Hence the utility is defined as

$$\psi_u(t) = \frac{n_t}{n}.$$

If t is transmitted via multicast, then n_t users that needs t receive the tile, but the other $n - n_t$ users also receive the tile even though it is not required by them. The utility is now defined as

$$\psi_m(t) = \frac{n_t p - (np - n_t)}{n} = \frac{(1+p)n_t - np}{n},$$

where p is the probability that a multicast packet reaches all the users. The term $\frac{np - n_t}{n}$ is a penalty term for the wasteful reception.

Further, define the supported multicast data rate as B_m and the unicast data rate for user u_i be B_u^i. Hence a tile t when transmitted over the multicast channel would complete transmission in $\frac{b}{B_m}$ seconds, while it takes $\frac{b}{B_u^i}$ seconds on the unicast channel for user u_i.

Now, let T_m be the set of tiles being multicast, and $R_i - T_m$ be the set of tiles being unicast to user u_i in the system, The transmission deadline can be expressed as

$$\frac{|T_m|b}{B_m} + \sum_{i=1}^{n} \left(\frac{|R_i - T_m|b}{B_u^i} \right) \leq \frac{1}{f}. \quad (1)$$

A tile assignment is said to be *valid* if it satisfies the Inequality (1). Our goal is to find the valid tile assignment such that the total utility in the system (over all tiles) is maximized. Note that a valid tile assignment may not exist.

4. TILE ASSIGNMENT ALGORITHMS

We now describe several possible algorithms to assign the tiles, starting with two simple algorithms that serves as the baseline for comparisons.

4.1 Minimizing Transmission Delay

We begin with a naive tile assignment algorithm that compares the time to send a tile t over the unicast channel and the multicast channel. If t has a shorter transmission delay over the multicast channel, we transmit t via multicast. Otherwise, we send t via unicast. This algorithm leads to the minimum total delay for sending the tiles. We call this algorithm MIN-DELAY.

If the minimum delay produced by MIN-DELAY is larger than $1/f$, then there is no valid assignment. Note that MIN-DELAY does not consider utility when deciding the tile assignment. It, however, can support the most number of users while keeping within the deadline.

4.2 Maximizing Utility

The next baseline algorithm is one that finds the valid assignment that maximizes the utility. We can formulate the problem of finding maximum utility recursively as follows.

Let $T_k = \{t_1, t_2, ..., t_k\}$ be the subset of tiles (with $T_0 = \{\}$). Define $\Psi(T_k, D)$ as the maximum utility over all possible tile assignments for T_k that satisfy the deadline D. We therefore are interested in finding $\Psi(T, 1/f)$.

We can define $\Psi(T_k, D)$ recursively by considering whether to multicast t_k (for $k \geq 1$). If t_k is sent via multicast, then deadline D reduces by b/B_m. The total utility is

$$\Psi_k^m = \Psi\left(T_{k-1}, D - \frac{b}{B_m}\right) + \psi_m(t_k).$$

Otherwise, if t_k is sent via unicast, D reduces by $\sum_{i \in m_{t_k}} b/B_u^i$, and

$$\Psi_k^u = \Psi\left(T_{k-1}, D - \sum_{i \in m_{t_k}} \frac{b}{B_u^i}\right) + \psi_u(t_k).$$

The maximum utility is then:

$$\Psi(T_k, D) = \begin{cases} \max\{\Psi_k^u, \Psi_k^m\} & \text{if } k \geq 1 \text{ and } D \geq 0 \\ 0 & \text{if } k = 0 \text{ and } D \geq 0 \\ -\infty & \text{if } D < 0 \end{cases}$$

Implementing the above recursion leads to an exponential time search algorithm. To keep the running time tractable, we quantize the deadline D and use dynamic programming, which caches the intermediate results. The resulting algorithm is pseudo polynomial. We denote this algorithm as MAX-UTIL. While MAX-UTIL has a tractable running time (in the order of minutes for our implementation), it is still too slow for our deployment where the running time is required to be within a few milliseconds. We therefore explore other methods below.

4.3 Threshold Algorithm

The first heuristic is called THRESHOLD, and decides the tile assignment based on utility alone. It works as follows: For each tile t, if $\psi_m(t) > 0$ then t is multicast, otherwise t is unicast. THRESHOLD simply ensures that the utility is always positive.

Since THRESHOLD does not consider delay when assigning tiles, the resulting assignment from THRESHOLD is not always valid. It is, however, a fast, linear time, algorithm.

4.4 Greedy Algorithm

We now discuss a greedy heuristic (GREEDY) to assign the tiles. The greedy algorithm begins with the solution from MIN-DELAY and repeatedly converts a multicast tile to unicast until the deadline is violated.

Consider what happens when we convert a multicast tile t to unicast. Tile t will be transmitted via unicast to every user in m_t. Let $T_m' = T_m - \{t\}$ be the new set of multicast tiles. Then Inequality (1) is changed to:

$$|T_m'|\frac{b}{B_m} + \sum_{i=1}^n |R_i - T_m'|\frac{b}{B_u^i} \leq \frac{1}{f}$$

$$(|T_m|-1)\frac{b}{B_m} + \sum_{i=1}^n |R_i - T_m|\frac{b}{B_u^i} + \sum_{l \in m_t} \frac{b}{B_u^l} \leq \frac{1}{f}. \quad (2)$$

The time to transmit all the tiles changes by

$$\Delta T = \left(\sum_{l \in m_t} \frac{b}{B_u^l}\right) - \frac{b}{B_m}. \quad (3)$$

If ΔT is negative (when $B_m \ll B_u^l$ and n_t is small), then we have reduced the time to transmit the tiles. On the other hand, the total utility changes by

$$\Delta \psi = \frac{n_t}{n} - \frac{n_t p - (np - n_t)}{n}$$
$$= (n - n_t)\frac{p}{n}. \quad (4)$$

Since $\Delta \psi$ is always non-negative, the total utility never decreases by reassigning a multicast tile t to unicast.

Equations (3) and (4) lead to the following greedy algorithm: repeatedly find a tile $t \in T_m$ with smallest n_t (to maximize the increase in utility) to unicast, until such operation would have violated the deadline constraint.

Note that if the unicast bandwidth B_u^i is the same for all users, the selected tile will also give the smallest ΔT. GREEDY is therefore optimal in this case.

4.5 Expectation

The four methods presented so far are run-time algorithms that rely on the current tile access pattern. We have also considered an offline algorithm that relies only on the probability of access to a tile in the frame. We call this offline algorithm EXPECTATION.

In many videos, the RoI has a locality of reference that may be predicted [11] and exploited [10, 12]. The probability that users would select a region is dependent on the content in the video and changes for every GoP. EXPECTATION uses the tile access probability to assign tiles into unicast and multicast groups, and does not depend on the actual access pattern. This algorithm can therefore be run offline and the tile assignment can simply be looked up during run time.

The tile assignment computed by EXPECTATION relies on the number of users n. The algorithm therefore would need to pre-compute the tile assignment for different values n.

Let $P(t)$ be the probability of accessing a tile t. The unicast utility can be written as $\psi_u(t) = P(t)$ and the multicast utility is $\psi_m(t) = (1+p)P(t) - p$ (where $pP(t)$ is the reward and $p - P(t)$ is the penalty).

The optimal tile assignment in this case can be computed recursively in a manner similar to MAX-UTIL. We replace n_t in MAX-UTIL with $nP(t)$, and $\sum_{i \in m_t} \frac{b}{B_u^i}$ with $\frac{nb}{B_u}$, where B_u is the average unicast bandwidth to a user, and obtain the following:

$$\Psi_k^m = \Psi\left(T_{k-1}, D - \frac{b}{B_m}\right) + (1+p)P(t_k) - p$$
$$\Psi_k^u = \Psi\left(T_{k-1}, D - \frac{nbP(t_k)}{B_u}\right) + P(t_k)$$

Since EXPECTATION is an offline algorithm, we can afford the extensive computation time needed to run the algorithm.

5. EVALUATION

In the previous section, five methods to manage tile assignment over the multicast and unicast channels was detailed. In this section, we compare the methods in terms of their ability to meet the transmission deadline and the resulting utility of the system.

The experiment is simulation based. We set the multicast channel rate B_m to 2 Mbps, and the unicast rate B_u^i varies between 18 to 30 Mbps for the users. The video has a resolution of 1920×1088, with tile size of 32×32, at 25 frames per second ($f = 25$). The decoder plays the video by fetching all tiles of the RoI, before decoding for playback. The video rate is assumed to be 0.99 Mbps at 352×288 and the RoI dimension is 352×288. There are 99 tiles in each RoI. We assume that the RoI has an average data rate of 0.99 Mbps irrespective of which frame dimension it is cropped from. The bitrate of each tile b is thus 0.01 Mbps.

To compute $\psi_m(t)$, we set the probability that a multicast transmission reaches all the users, p, to 1 and 0.6386, for multicast rate of 2 Mbps and 5.5 Mbps respectively. These valeus are based on the throughput rate as measured by Khayam et al. [9].

We use the RoI traces of 70 users who accessed a zoomable video system described in Carlier et al. [3], and use these traces to compute tile access probabilities for each of the four video resolutions. The zoomable video system relies on multiple resolution videos with compressed domain RoI cropping in order to create a virtual zoom and pan effect. Hence traces from such a system are ideal for our evaluation.

We use four different RoI patterns to evaluate the assignment methods and present the average results from these patterns below. In the case of EXPECTATION, we need a training set and a testing set. The training set is the four RoI patterns mentioned earlier, from which the probability $P(t)$ is obtained. Once the tile positions have been marked for unicast/multicast, we use the test set of RoI patterns to validate the usefulness of EXPECTATION. The test set represents the run-time pattern that needs to be handled by the server and is generated randomly following the same distribution as the training set.

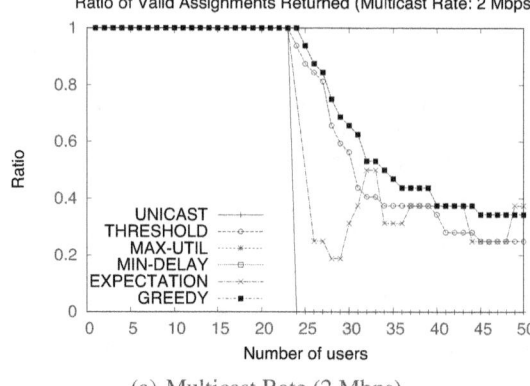

(a) Multicast Rate (2 Mbps)

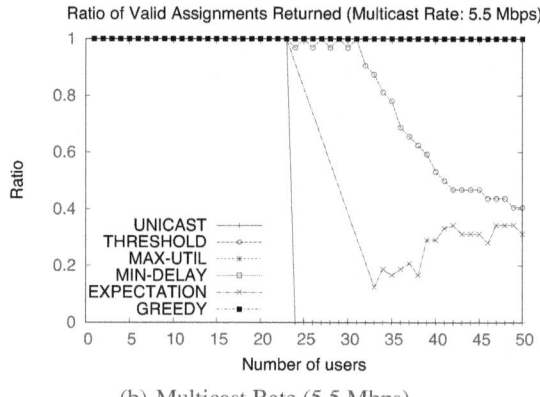

(b) Multicast Rate (5.5 Mbps)

Figure 2: Ratio of Times a Given Algorithm Yields a Valid Assignment

With the parameters and inputs as described above, we simulate the different methods for different number of users, n, ranging from 1 to 50. For each n, we simulate 32 times (8 times for each pattern) and average the results.

5.1 Results

Number of Users Supported. Figure 2 shows the percentage of instances where a given method yields a valid assignment that meets the deadline. The line labeled UNICAST is a naive method where every tile is sent via the unicast channel. This method cannot meet the target deadline when n is larger than 23.

The figure shows that GREEDY, MIN-DELAY, and MAX-UTIL give a valid assignment in more instances than the other algorithms (the three lines coincide with each other). At multicast rate of 5.5 Mbps, these three methods give a valid assignment in all cases simulated. Recall that GREEDY reassigns tiles based on the assignment from MIN-DELAY, while keeping the assignment within the deadline. Therefore, GREEDY yields a valid assignment if and only if MIN-DELAY has an assignment. MAX-UTIL is also able to yield a valid assignment if one exists, since it exhaustively searches for all possible assignments.

Figure 2 also shows that EXPECTATION and THRESHOLD produce more assignments that are not valid. The result for THRESHOLD is expected, since it does not consider deadline in assigning the tiles. The result for EXPECTATION, however, is unexpectedly low. Recall that EXPECTATION maximizes for utility offline using access probability and average unicast bandwidth as input. As a result, it tends to yield an assignment whose *expected* total transmission time is close to the deadline. Variations in the actual access pattern and unicast bandwidth, however, would lead to violation of deadline, invalidating the chosen assignment. Due to the low success rate of EXPECTATION, we will not discuss it further in the following paragraphs.

Transmission Time. Figure 3 shows the average transmission time for the tile assignment computed by the different methods. Only valid assignments are included in the averages. The horizontal line at 0.04s indicates the deadline $1/f$.

The GREEDY and MAX-UTIL methods have the highest transmission time among the existing methods, while keeping the transmission time within the deadline. This result is expected due to the following reasons: GREEDY repeatedly reassigns multicast tiles to unicast until the deadline is violated, and therefore bumps the transmission time to as close to the deadline as possible; MAX-UTIL explores all possible solutions within the deadline, and naturally finds an assignment close to the deadline.

The figure also indicates that THRESHOLD has a lower transmission time than GREEDY and MAX-UTIL for larger n, but a higher transmission time for small n. The condition for multicasting a tile can be expressed as $n_t > np/(1+p)$. Thus, in the case of 2 Mbps multicast rate, only tiles that are needed by more than half of the users are multicast, resulting in potentially large number of unicast tiles, and therefore a larger transmission time than the other methods for small n. As n increases, many of the inputs result in an invalid assignment when we use THRESHOLD to compute the assignment. The inputs that still yield a valid assignment are those where the RoIs are highly concentrated (high n_t) and benefit from multicast.

Figure 3(b) shows that the total transmission time of MIN-DELAY is significantly lower at 5.5 Mbps than all the other methods as it now has the opportunity to assign tiles to the multicast channel that has a lower transmission time (higher bandwidth). It also supports as many users as GREEDY or MAX-UTIL but at a lower transmission time (Figure 2). This result clearly indicates that many more users can be supported in the system (but at a higher channel error rate).

Note that in the case of a multicast rate of 2 Mbps, for some values of n, the average transmission time for THRESHOLD is even lower than MIN-DELAY. This lower value is due to some instances where THRESHOLD fails to give a valid assignment even when one exists. Since we only show the average results for valid assignments, the average value for THRESHOLD becomes lower than MIN-DELAY.

Utility. Figure 4 shows the total utility of all tiles (average over all instances that give a valid assignment) for different methods. For $n \leq 23$, there is a trivial solution that gives the highest utility (unicast every tile). The THRESHOLD method, however, chooses to multicast the popular tiles and pays the penalty for delivering unwanted tiles to some users, resulting in lower utility.

For larger n, THRESHOLD results in largest total utility (even larger than MAX-UTIL). This result is, again, due to failure of THRESHOLD to return a valid assignment. Since MAX-UTIL always finds a valid assignment as long as one exists, it sometimes returns an assignment that gives a low utility value, leading to lower average utility overall.

The figure also indicates that GREEDY is doing as good as MAX-UTIL in terms of utility in our experiments. GREEDY always converts a multicast tile to unicast in a way that maximizes utility (lowest n_t), and if this operation also always leads to smallest increase

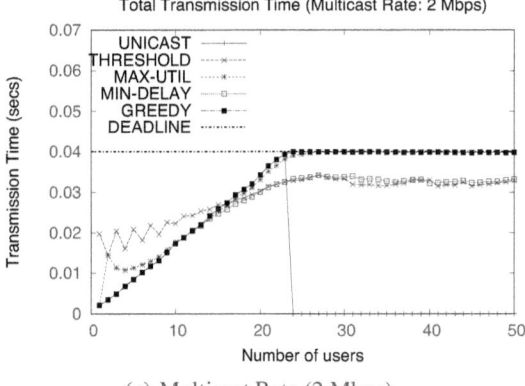

(a) Multicast Rate (2 Mbps)

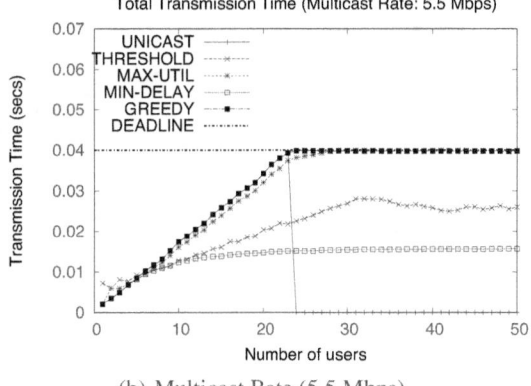

(b) Multicast Rate (5.5 Mbps)

Figure 3: Total Transmission Time

in transmission time, then GREEDY is also optimal. We found that this condition holds in our simulation.

Finally, we note that MIN-DELAY gives low utility than GREEDY and MAX-UTIL for most cases. This is expected, since it does not optimize for utility. The impact is more severe at multicast rate of 5.5 Mbps as MIN-DELAY assigns more tiles to the multicast channel in order to reduce the total transmission time, leading to very low utility. For large n, the utility becomes negative for MIN-DELAY, indicating that more useless tiles are received than useful tiles. Hence, even though MIN-DELAY can support more users than other methods we studied, it is not suitable in scenarios with many users.

Discussion. Our simulation results show that GREEDY is a reasonable method to use. It results in a valid assignment that meets the deadline as long as one exists, and is optimal (in terms of utility) under some conditions. It is fast: requiring an $O(|T|)$ step to find the minimum delay assignment, an $O(|T| \log |T|)$ step to sort the multicast tiles in increasing order of n_t, and finally another $O(|T|)$ step to convert the multicast tiles to unicast tiles.

6. CONCLUSION

We present five methods to efficiently transmit tiled regions of a video supporting region-of-interest (RoI) streaming in a wireless LAN. Each method decides to multicast or unicast a set of tiles based on how many users require these tiles and the supported data rates. A utility function that quantifies wasteful reception of

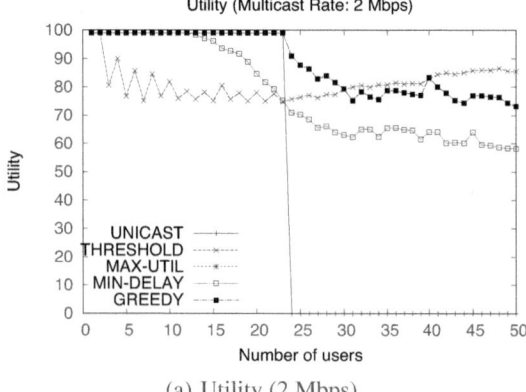

(a) Utility (2 Mbps)

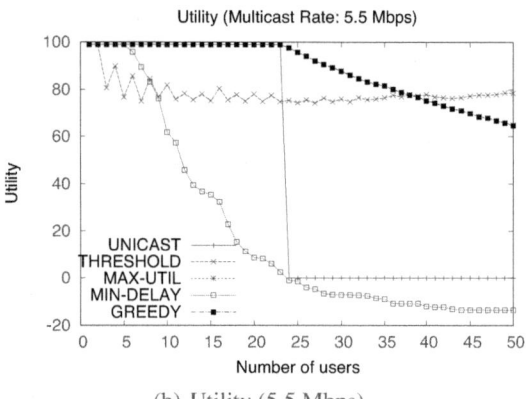

(b) Utility (5.5 Mbps)

Figure 4: Total Utility

tiles as a result of multicasting was suggested. We showed that the GREEDY method always meets the transmission deadline (as long as a solution exists) and leads to larger utility than other methods.

In this paper, only a simple, abstract, model of the problem is considered. We plan to extend our model to include more realistic settings, such as varying b based on estimated encoding rate of each tile. We also plan to implement the assignment methods into our system and measure their performance in practice.

Acknowledgement

This research is conducted under the NExT Search Center, supported by the Singapore National Research Foundation and the Interactive Digital Media R&D Program Office of Media Development Authority under research grant WBS:R-252-300-001-490.

7. REFERENCES

[1] M. Adler, Z. Ge, J. F. Kurose, D. Towsley, and S. Zabele. Channelization problem in large scale data dissemination. In *Proceedings of the Ninth International Conference on Network Protocols*, ICNP '01, pages 100–109, Washington, DC, USA, 2001.

[2] D. Bickson, E. N. Hoch, N. Naaman, and Y. Tock. A hybrid multicast-unicast infrastructure for efficient publish-subscribe in enterprise networks. In *Proceedings of the 3rd Annual Haifa Experimental Systems Conference*, SYSTOR '10, pages 1–7, Haifa, Israel, 2010.

[3] A. Carlier, R. Guntur, V. Charvillat, and W. T. Ooi. Combining content-based analysis and crowdsourcing to improve user interaction with zoomable video. In *Proceedings of the 19th ACM International Conference on Multimedia*, MM '11, pages 43–52, Scottsdale, AZ, USA, 2011. ACM.

[4] S. Deshpande and W. Zeng. Scalable streaming of JPEG2000 images using hypertext transfer protocol. In *Proceedings of the 9th ACM International Conference on Multimedia*, MM '01, pages 372–381, Ottawa, Canada, 2001.

[5] W. Feng, T. Dang, J. Kassebaum, and T. Bauman. Supporting region-of-interest cropping through constrained compression. In *Proceedings of the 16th ACM International Conference on Multimedia*, MM '08, pages 745–748, Vancouver, Canada, 2008.

[6] S. Halawa, D. Pang, N.-M. Cheung, and B. Girod. ClassX: an open source interactive lecture streaming system. In *Proceedings of the 19th ACM International Conference on Multimedia*, MM '11, pages 719–722, Scottsdale, AZ, USA, 2011.

[7] S. Heymann, A. Smolic, K. Mueller, Y. Guo, J. Rurainsky, P. Eisert, and T. Wiegand. Representation, coding and interactive rendering of high-resolution panoramic images and video using MPEG-4. In *Proceedings of the Panoramic Photogrammetry Workshop*, PPW '05, 2005.

[8] M. Inoue, H. Kimata, K. Fukazawa, and N. Matsuura. Interactive panoramic video streaming system over restricted bandwidth network. In *Proceedings of the 18th ACM International Conference on Multimedia*, MM '10, pages 1191–1194, Firenze, Italy, 2010.

[9] S. Khayam, S. Karande, H. Radha, and D. Loguinov. Performance analysis and modeling of errors and losses over 802.11b LANs for high-bit-rate real-time multimedia. *Signal Processing: Image Communication*, 18:575–595, 2003.

[10] A. Mavlankar and B. Girod. Pre-fetching based on video analysis for interactive region-of-interest streaming of soccer sequences. In *Proceedings of the 16th IEEE International Conference on Image Processing*, ICIP '09, pages 3061–3064, Cairo, Egypt, 2009.

[11] A. Mavlankar, D. Varodayan, and B. Girod. Region-of-Interest prediction for interactively streaming regions of high resolution video. In *Proceedings of International Packet Video Workshop*, PV '07, pages 68–77, Lausanne, Switzerland, 2007.

[12] K. Q. M. Ngo, R. Guntur, and W. T. Ooi. Adaptive encoding of zoomable video streams based on user access pattern. In *Proceedings of the 2nd ACM Multimedia Systems Conference*, MMSYS '11, pages 211–222, San Jose, CA, USA, 2011.

[13] K. Q. M. Ngo, R. Guntur, A. Carlier, and W. T. Ooi. Supporting zoomable video streams with dynamic region-of-interest cropping. In *Proceedings of the 1st ACM Multimedia Systems Conference*, MMSYS '10, pages 259–270, Phoenix, AZ, USA, 2010.

[14] R. Zhang and Y. C. Hu. Hyper: A hybrid approach to efficient content-based publish/subscribe. In *Proceedings of the 25th IEEE International Conference on Distributed Computing Systems*, ICDCS '05, pages 427–436, Washington, DC, USA, 2005.

Minimizing Server Throughput for Low-Delay Live Streaming in Content Delivery Networks

Fen Zhou
Telecom Bretagne
Brest, France
fen.zhou@telecom-bretagne.eu

Shakeel Ahmad
De Montfort University
Leicester, United Kingdom
sahmad@dmu.ac.uk

Eliya Buyukkaya
Telecom Bretagne
Brest, France
eliya.buyukka@telecom-bretagne.eu

Raouf Hamzaoui
De Montfort University
Leicester, United Kingdom
rhamzaoui@dmu.ac.uk

Gwendal Simon
Telecom Bretagne
Brest, France
gwendal.simon@telecom-bretagne.eu

ABSTRACT

Large-scale live streaming systems can experience bottlenecks within the infrastructure of the underlying Content Delivery Network. In particular, the "equipment bottleneck" occurs when the fan-out of a machine does not enable the concurrent transmission of a stream to multiple other equipments. In this paper, we aim to deliver a live stream to a set of destination nodes with minimum throughput at the source and limited increase of the streaming delay. We leverage on rateless codes and cooperation among destination nodes. With rateless codes, a node is able to decode a video block of k information symbols after receiving slightly more than k encoded symbols. To deliver the encoded symbols, we use multiple trees where inner nodes forward all received symbols. Our goal is to build a diffusion forest that minimizes the transmission rate at the source while guaranteeing on-time delivery and reliability at the nodes. When the network is assumed to be lossless and the constraint on delivery delay is relaxed, we give an algorithm that computes a diffusion forest resulting in the minimum source transmission rate. We also propose an effective heuristic algorithm for the general case where packet loss occurs and the delivery delay is bounded. Simulation results for realistic settings show that with our solution the source requires only slightly more than the video bit rate to reliably feed all nodes.

Categories and Subject Descriptors

C.2.1 [**Computer-Communication Networks**]: Network Architecture and Design; G.2.2 [**Discrete Mathematics**]: Graph Theory—*network problems, trees*

General Terms

Algorithms, Design, Performance

Keywords

Rateless Codes, Live Streaming, Delivery Trees, CDN

1. INTRODUCTION

As illustrated by the recent decision from Korea Telecom to block Samsung's Smart TVs from accessing the Internet [7], *over-the-top live streaming* represents a major challenge for Internet Service Providers (ISPs) and Content Delivery Networks (CDNs). The bottleneck of large-scale live streaming delivery platforms is no longer in the *last-mile* since rate-adaptive streaming enables a match between video bit-rate and available bandwidth [8]. It is not in the *peering link* either because ISPs and CDNs develop more friendly relationships, including co-location of edge servers. Today, the bottleneck is likely located *within the CDN infrastructure*, which has to cope with the tremendous growth of video traffic and the multiplication of video encodings per TV channel. The (relative) failure of the latest SuperBowl streaming confirms this trend [13].

For live streaming, the infrastructure of a CDN comprises three distinct elements. The role of the *origin server* is to forward the original stream to *edge servers*. However the origin server has a limited fan-out, *i.e.*, the number of streams it can concurrently emit is limited. The CDN thus uses some *intermediate nodes*, which are called reflectors [3] or shield caches [5]. While these intermediate nodes have to serve a subset of the thousands of edge-servers, they have a limited upload capacity. The bottleneck in the CDN infrastructure comes either from the origin server that cannot serve the intermediates nodes, or from the intermediate node that cannot serve the edge servers.

In this paper, we introduce the generic problem of one source (either origin server or intermediate node) that has to serve a small set of nodes (respectively intermediate nodes or edge servers) in such a way that the throughput of the source is minimized and the streaming delay stays reasonable. We explore a solution based on rateless codes and data exchanges among the nodes. Since the latest rate-adaptive streaming protocols rely on a segmentation of streams into independent chunks, the use of *rateless codes* on every video chunk appears as an attractive idea. With rateless codes (*e.g.*, Raptor codes [12] and LT codes [9]), a video chunk of k information symbols can be recovered with high probability if slightly more than k encoded symbols are received. The idea is that the source applies rateless codes to every video chunk and delivers each created symbol to only one node, which then uses an application-level multicast tree to deliver this symbol to some other nodes.

1.1 Related Work

The first publications about live streaming in CDNs are ten years old (*e.g.*, [2, 4, 11]). Most of these publications emphasized the fan-out limitations of intermediate equipments. The focus of these papers was to build on top of large overlays a set of low-delay application-level multicast trees, subject to the constraints of the capacity of nodes. We revisit this objective through more recent delivery techniques, including rateless codes and video chunks. Moreover, we restrict our study to a specific local part of the whole overlay, where the bottleneck lies.

After five years without much academic activity, the delivery of a live stream in CDNs has become hot again with a series of recent publications [1, 3, 8]. These works consider the equipment bottleneck as well. They aim at creating delivery trees but their optimization purpose is generally to save bandwidth cost. Since we are within the CDN infrastructure, we neglect bandwidth cost.

Previous works related to rateless codes focus on peer-to-peer systems (*e.g.*, [6, 14, 15]). These works address problems related to scalability and management of churn. These issues are not major in CDN infrastructures, where the number of nodes is typically less than one hundred, and machines are rarely faulty.

1.2 Our Contributions

Our contributions are twofold:

- theoretical contribution: we aim at building a multi-tree structure that minimizes the source transmission rate. When we do not take into account the constraints of delay and packet loss, we give in §3.1 an exact algorithm (minimum source transmission rate). When we consider the joint height constraint of the delay and the reliability, we give in §3.2 an effective heuristic algorithm.

- practical contribution: our evaluation in §4 highlights that when the nodes can reserve an upload bandwidth that is larger than the video bit-rate, the source needs slightly more than the video bit-rate to transmit a video block to up to 25 nodes in a short delay and in a reliable way.

Our paper makes a first step toward addressing the problem of *equipment bottleneck* within CDN networks.

The rest of this paper is organized as follows. In §2, we present the system model and formulate the problem of minimizing the throughput for live streaming in CDNs. To this end, we propose two diffusion forest construction algorithms in §3. Then we evaluate the performance of our heuristic algorithm with simulations in §4. Finally, we conclude this paper and mention future work in §5.

2. SYSTEM MODEL

The source is the equipment that is the bottleneck of the CDN infrastructure. We suppose that the CDN is able to identify it. We denote it by s. This source is expected to deliver a flow of video chunks to some other equipments within the CDN networks. We denote by V this set of equipments ($|V| = n$), and we denote by $G = (V, E)$ the connected symmetric digraph modeling the small part of the whole CDN network that we consider in this paper. This is the network that is affected by the lack of upload capacity of the source. Our goal is to prevent the bottleneck to affect the whole CDN, thus we propose that these nodes cooperate in order to fix the bottleneck issue. We refer to this network as the *support network*. As usual, E is the set of links between nodes ($|E| = m$). The source s does not belong to V. An arc from u to v is denoted by (u, v). We assume that the support network is fully connected.

Every node $v \in V$ is associated with a *support capacity* (or capacity for short), denoted by c_v, which is the number of packets the node v can relay in the support network. It is important to understand that the equipments are not expected to re-transmit data to their sibling equipments in a hierarchical infrastructure like today's CDN networks. That is, intermediate nodes do usually not transmit data to intermediate nodes, and edge servers do not communicate with other edge servers. But there is not a lot of options for addressing the equipment bottleneck. We thus consider that the CDN has "reserved" a small fraction of the overall upload capacity in every equipment for the support network.

The *transmission delay* over the link (u, v) is d_{uv}. We assume that the transmission delay is a real value in $(0, 1]$, for example a fraction of the maximum Round-Trip Time (RTT) experienced in the CDN network.

The *transmission reliability* over the link (u, v), which corresponds to the probability that a packet sent by u is successfully received by v, is denoted by p_{uv}. It is also in $(0, 1]$. Note that the delay is additive while the reliability is multiplicative over arcs.

In the support network, we use a multi-tree structure for the diffusion of each video chunk. Each tree is the support for the transmission of *one* packet of encoded symbols from the source to nodes. To recover the video chunk, a node should receive at least K packets of encoded symbols. In other words, a node should belong to at least K trees. We illustrate our proposal in Figure 1. On the left, in the gray box, we represent the support network. On the right, we represent the four trees that allow each node to receive $K = 3$ packets of encoded symbols.

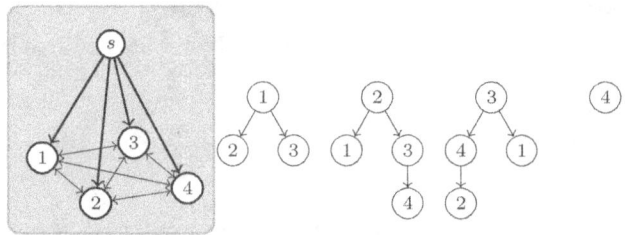

Figure 1: Multi-tree structure for the diffusion of each video chunk (four nodes and $K = 3$)

As the capacity of each node is limited, it may be impossible to use one tree to relay a packet to all nodes. In addition, to guarantee on-time delivery and reliability at the nodes, the end-to-end delay and transmission reliability on the path from the source to each node should be bounded to a reasonable value.

Our objective is to minimize the transmission rate for the source. The more trees are used in order to ensure that all nodes receive at least K packets, the higher is the source transmission rate. Thus, minimizing the source transmission rate is equivalent to minimizing the number of trees. In light of this, we formulate the video diffusion problem in the support network as a *Height-Bounded Spanning Forest problem with Capacity constraint* (HBSFC). The goal of HBSFC is to find a forest F with minimum cardinality such that

- each tree $T \subseteq G$ is rooted on a node, which directly receives a packet from s. For simplicity, we assume no packet loss between s and a root.

- for each node $v \in V$, the sum of its out-degrees in all trees of F is not greater than its capacity c_v. Let $deg_T^+(v)$ be the out-degree of v in $T \in F$,

$$\forall v \in V, \sum_{T \in F} deg_T^+(v) \leq c_v \quad (1)$$

- each node $v \in V$ is spanned in at least K trees of F. Let $F(v)$ be the set of trees in which v is included. Then $|F(v)| \geq K, \forall v \in V$.

- for each tree $T \in F$, the transmission delay from the root to each node in T is no bigger than a given threshold $D_h > 0$. That is, the *delay height* of each tree is bounded by D_h.

- for each tree $T \in F$, each node $v \in T$ receives a packet from the root with a reliability no smaller than a reliability bound $P_h \in (0, 1]$. Let $SP_T(v)$ be the list of arcs in the path from the root to v in tree T. Then

$$\forall T \in F, \forall v \in T, \prod_{e \in SP_T(v)} p_e \geq P_h \quad (2)$$

By applying logarithms on both sides, we obtain:

$$\forall T \in F, \forall v \in T, \sum_{e \in SP_T(v)} \log(p_e) \geq \log(P_h) \quad (3)$$

which means that the *logarithmic reliability height* of each tree is bounded by $\log(P_h)$.

3. DIFFUSION FOREST CONSTRUCTION ALGORITHMS

We propose two *polynomial-time* algorithms to optimize the diffusion forest in two models: unbounded height model and bounded height model.

3.1 Unbounded Height Model

We first assume an unbounded height model: (*i*) the transmission reliability is $p_e = 1$ for all $e \in E$, and (*ii*) the delay threshold D_h satisfies $D_h \geq n - 1$, so that no tree will violate this constraint. Please refer to Algorithm 1 for the pseudocode of our algorithm. Note that notation $\overline{V_k}$ stands for $V \setminus V_k$ and (V_k, E_k) represents tree T_k. We use c_v' to denote the available capacity of a node v.

This algorithm consists of two phases. First, we construct K trees, and maximize the number of nodes that are spanned

---

Algorithm 1: Unbounded Height Model

Input : Complete graph $G = (V, E)$, capacity c_v of $v \in V$, number of packets K
Output: A forest F

1 $k \leftarrow 1$;
2 $F \leftarrow \emptyset$;
3 **for** $v \in V$ **do** $c_v' = c_v$;
4 $V_c \leftarrow \{v : c_v' > 0, v \in V\}$;
5 **while** $k \leq K$ **and** $V_c \neq \emptyset$ **do**
6   find node $r \in V_c$ **s.t.** $c_r' = \max\{c_v' : v \in V_c\}$;
7      $V_k \leftarrow \{r\}$;
8      $E_k \leftarrow \emptyset$;
9      $T_k \leftarrow (V_k, E_k)$;
10   **while** $V_k \neq V$ **and** $V_c \neq \emptyset$ **do**
11   find node $u \in \overline{V_k}$ **s.t.** $c_u' = \max\{c_v' : v \in \overline{V_k}\}$;
12   pick any node $w \in V_k \cap V_c$;
13         $V_k \leftarrow V_k \cup \{u\}$;
14         $E_k \leftarrow E_k \cup \{(w, u)\}$;
15         $T_k \leftarrow (V_k, E_k)$;
16         $c_w' \leftarrow c_w' - 1$;
17   **if** $c_w' = 0$ **then**
18             $V_c \leftarrow V_c \setminus \{w\}$
19     $F \leftarrow F \cup \{T_k\}$;
20     $k \leftarrow k + 1$;
21 **for** $v \in V$ **do**
22     $k_v \leftarrow$ number of trees v belongs to;
23   **if** $k_v < K$ **then**
24   add $(K - k_v)$ trees $(\{v\}, \emptyset)$ to F

---

in these trees. For each tree, the root r is selected as the node having the biggest available capacity. Then, we attach nodes to this tree starting from the nodes with biggest available capacity until either all nodes are spanned or no node has available capacity. Second, we take care of nodes that are not spanned in the K trees. As all nodes have exhausted their capacities, we span them by building *shallow trees* containing only one node. For example, the tree on the right in Fig. 1 is a shallow tree as it contains only the node 4.

THEOREM 1. *In the unbounded height model, the optimal forest has cardinality*

$$|F| = \begin{cases} K & \text{if } \sum_{v \in V} c_v \geq K(n-1) \\ K \times n - \sum_{v \in V} c_v & \text{otherwise} \end{cases} \quad (4)$$

PROOF. Let c_v^F be the sum of the out-degrees of node v in F. Then the number of nodes in F is equal to $\sum_{v \in V} c_v^F + |F|$. In an optimal solution, exactly $K \times n$ nodes belong to F. We have

$$|F| + \sum_{v \in V} c_v \geq |F| + \sum_{v \in V} c_v^F = K \times n \quad (5)$$

When $|F| = K$, the sum of capacities should thus verify:

$$\sum_{v \in V} c_v \geq K(n-1) \quad (6)$$

Otherwise, the total capacity is not enough to span $K \times n$ nodes in K trees. To minimize $|F|$, we should use all the nodal capacities, i.e., $\forall v \in V, c_v^F = c_v$. Thus, we obtain a forest cardinality of $|F| = K \times n - \sum_{v \in V} c_v$. □

THEOREM 2. *Algorithm 1 computes an optimal solution*

PROOF. At step (5) of Algorithm 1, the first loop terminates when one of the following conditions is satisfied:

- All nodes are spanned K times in the K trees. Thus only K trees are required, $|F| = K$. Every tree in F contains n nodes, so exactly $K(n-1)$ out degree is needed. Thus we have $\sum_{v \in V} c_v \geq K(n-1)$.

- All nodes have exhausted their capacity ($V_c = \emptyset$) before finishing K trees. Let $\bar{k} \leq K$ be the number of constructed trees. These trees contain $\bar{k} + \sum_{v \in V} c_v$ nodes. As no node has available capacity, all remaining trees in the resulting forest are shallow trees, and $K \times n - (\bar{k} + \sum_{v \in V} c_v)$ shallow trees are needed. Thus,

$$|F| = \bar{k} + K \times n - (\bar{k} + \sum_{v \in V} c_v) = K \times n - \sum_{v \in V} c_v \quad (7)$$

In short, the forest built by Algorithm 1 has minimum cardinality and spans each node exactly K times. □

At each step of Algorithm 1, it takes $\mathcal{O}(n)$ time to find the node with the biggest capacity and there are at most $K \times n$ steps, thus the overall time complexity is $\mathcal{O}(Kn^2)$.

3.2 Bounded Height Model

We now take into account both the delay and the reliability constraints. We suppose that the delay and reliability are identical over all links, i.e., $\forall e \in E, d_e = d > 0, p_e = p < 1$. Let $h(T)$ be the height of T, the delay height constraint and the reliability constraint in equation (3) are thus simplified into one joint tree height constraint, i.e.

$$\forall T \in F, h(T) \leq H = \min\{\lfloor \frac{D_h}{d} \rfloor, \lfloor \frac{\log(P_h)}{\log(p)} \rfloor\} \quad (8)$$

This is to say that the number of hop counts from the root to each node is bounded by H in any tree. When $H = 0$, each tree contains only a node, and thus Kn trees are required. When H is bigger than $n-1$, the unbounded height algorithm that we previously presented can be used. For all other heights, we propose a time-efficient heuristic algorithm, detailed in Algorithm 2. We use $h(T_k)$ for the height of tree T_k and $h_{T_k}(w)$ for the depth of a node w in T_k. In the pseudocode, V_K stores the set of nodes not yet spanned in K trees, and V_k^+ stores the nodes via which a node can be added to T_k without violating the height and capacity constraint.

Following the same idea as in Algorithm 1, our algorithm consists of two phases. The first one exhausts node capacity and the second one creates additional shallow trees if necessary. For every tree, we select the root as the node having the biggest available capacity, then we attach other nodes to the tree in a breadth-first manner starting from the nodes having biggest capacity until either the height of the tree reaches $H - 1$ or no more unattached node has capacity. Note that a node can be attached although it has already been spanned K times. At the end of each tree, we add the nodes that are still in V_K starting from the nodes with the smallest capacity until until either all nodes are spanned, or all capacities of nodes with height smaller than H are exhausted, i.e., $V_k^+ = \emptyset$. In the second phase, we build the remaining shallow trees if V_K is not empty. At most $K \times n$

Algorithm 2: Bounded height model

Input : Complete graph $G = (V, E)$, capacity c_v of $v \in V$, number of packets K, and height H
Output: A height-bounded forest F

1. $k \leftarrow 1$;
2. $F \leftarrow \emptyset$;
3. $V_K \leftarrow V$;
4. **for** $v \in V$ **do** $c'_v = c_v$;
5. $V_c \leftarrow \{v : c'_v > 0, v \in V\}$;
6. **while** $V_c \neq \emptyset$ **and** $V_K \neq \emptyset$ **do**
7.   find node $r \in V_c$ s.t. $c'_r = \max\{c'_v : v \in V_c\}$;
8. $V_k \leftarrow \{r\}$;
9. $E_k \leftarrow \emptyset$;
10. $T_k \leftarrow (V_k, E_k)$;
11.   **if** $r \in V_K$ **and** r is spanned K times **then**
12. $V_K \leftarrow V_K \setminus \{r\}$;
13. $V_k^+ \leftarrow \{v : v \in V_k \cap V_c \text{ and } h_{T_k}(v) < H\}$;
14.   **while** $\overline{V_k} \cap V_K \neq \emptyset$ **and** $V_k^+ \neq \emptyset$ **do**
15.   find $w \in V_k^+$ s.t. $h_{T_k}(w) = \min\{h_{T_k}(v) : v \in V_k^+\}$;
16.   **if** $h_{T_k}(w) < H - 1$ **and** $\overline{V_k} \cap V_c \neq \emptyset$ **then**
17.   find $u \in \overline{V_k}$ s.t. $c'_u = \max\{c'_v : v \in \overline{V_k}\}$;
18.   **else**
19.   find $u \in \overline{V_k} \cap V_K$ s.t. $c'_u = \min\{c'_v : v \in \overline{V_k} \cap V_K\}$;
20. $V_k \leftarrow V_k \cup \{u\}$;
21. $E_k \leftarrow E_k \cup \{(w, u)\}$;
22. $T_k \leftarrow (V_k, E_k)$;
23. $c'_w \leftarrow c'_w - 1$;
24.   **if** $c'_w = 0$ **then**
25. $V_c \leftarrow V_c \setminus \{w\}$;
26. $V_k^+ \leftarrow \{v : v \in V_k \cap V_c \text{ and } h_{T_k}(v) < H\}$;
27.   **if** $u \in V_K$ **and** u is spanned K times **then**
28. $V_K \leftarrow V_K \setminus \{u\}$;
29. $F \leftarrow F \cup \{T_k\}$;
30. $k \leftarrow k + 1$;
31. **for** $v \in V_K$ **do**
32. $k_v \leftarrow$ the number of trees v belongs to;
33.   add $K - k_v$ trees $(\{v\}, \emptyset)$ to F

trees may be computed and each tree contains at most n nodes. It also takes $O(n)$ time to find the node with the maximum or minimum capacity. Thus the time complexity is $O(Kn^3)$.

4. SIMULATIONS

We use the ns-2 network simulator to evaluate the performance of our heuristic algorithm (Algorithm 2).

4.1 Video and Rateless Code Settings

The video was compressed with the H.264 coder at various bitrates ranging from 320 kbps to 3.2 Mbps. The resulting bitstream was partitioned into chunks where each chunk corresponded to one Group of Pictures (GOP). Each chunk had a playback duration of 0.5 s. The source applies rateless coding on each chunk and sends the encoded symbols in successive UDP packets of size 1,000 bytes. The size of

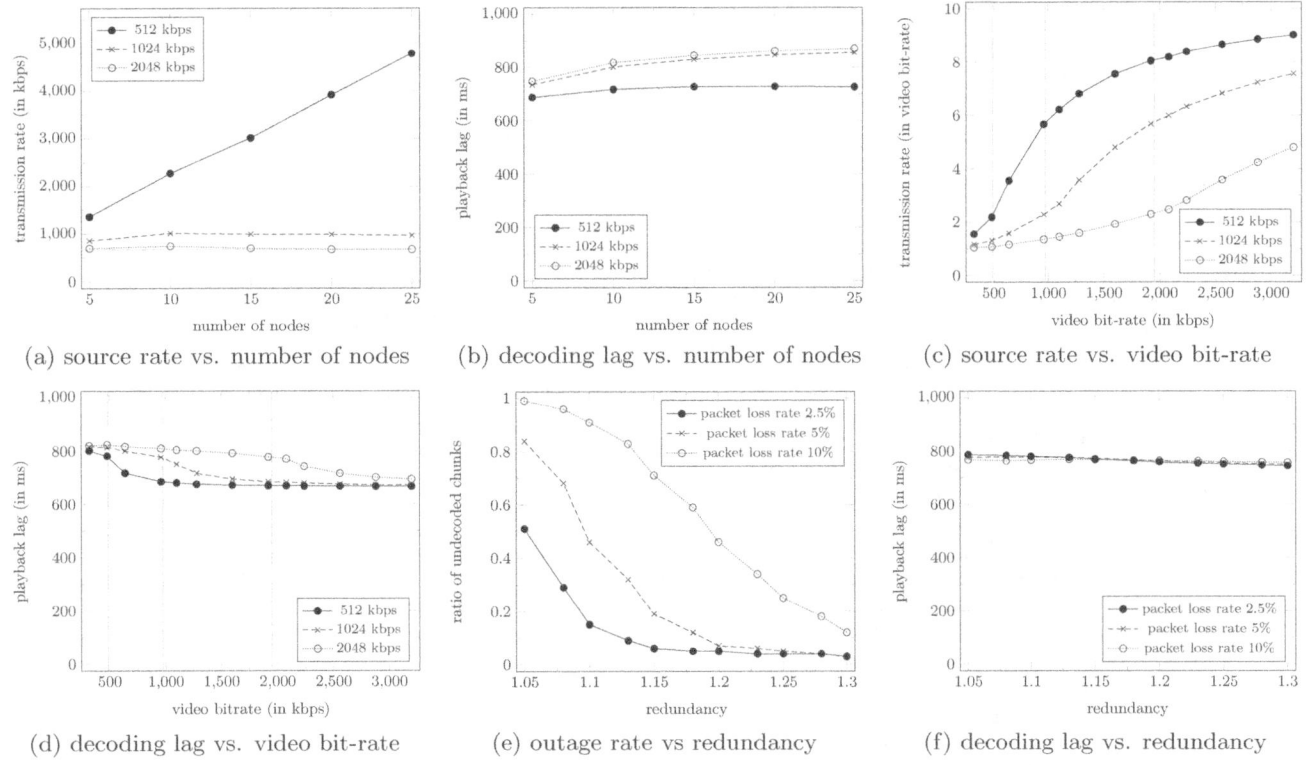

Figure 2: Results of our evaluation

an encoded symbol was one byte. For rateless coding, the Raptor code model proposed in [10] was used. With this model, a redundancy of 5%, gives a very high probability of successful decoding [10]. Thus, for a default video bitrate of 640 kbps, a node needs about 672 kbps to recover the original chunk.

4.2 Nodes Settings

The number of nodes varied from 5 to 25 (by default 10). Since there is no existing solution like the one we propose, it is hard to set the support capacity of the node. Our goal is to explore various capacity distributions and to observe the impact on the performance. Thus, our simulations can guide CDNs to set the support capacity. We used a log-normal distribution. The first parameter is the mean upload capacity, which was chosen in the set {512 kbps, 1,024 kbps, 2,048 kbps}. The second parameter is σ, which we abusively call *capacity heterogeneity*. We used three values for σ: $\{0.1, 0.8, 1.5\}$. The first value $\sigma = 0.1$ corresponds to a homogeneous configuration where the capacity of all nodes is close to the mean. At the other end, the value $\sigma = 1.5$ generates heterogeneous configurations where a few nodes have a high capacity while the remaining ones have a low capacity. As we have observed a low impact of the capacity heterogeneity, we do not present curves with distinct heterogeneities.

4.3 Network and Algorithm Settings

The core network of the CDN is a homogeneous network where most equipments and links are standard. Thus, we assume that both RTT and the packet loss probability are identical on every link (respectively set to 50 ms, and, for the packet loss probability to zero in Figs. 2(a) to 2(d) and 0.025, 0.05, or 0.1 in Fig. 2(e) and 2(f)). The Raptor code redundancy was set to 5% in Figs. 2(a) to 2(d). We used three different height bounds, $H \in \{1, 2, 3\}$. As for the capacity heterogeneity, we do not present results for each tree height bound separately because this parameter had a low impact on the overall performance. Therefore, every point on a curve corresponds to the average value of ten runs for three different tree height bounds and three different capacity heterogeneities.

4.4 Discussion

Figs. 2(a) and 2(c) show the required transmission rate at the source to guarantee that all nodes are able to decode the video chunk for various numbers of nodes and video bit-rates, respectively. Figs. 2(b) and 2(d) show the average lag between the time at which the source sends the first packet of a video chunk and the time at which a node is able to decode the video chunk again for various numbers of nodes and video bit-rates, respectively. Gray vertical lines in Figs. 2(c) and 2(d) indicate the video bit-rate for which the support network is just-provisioned for our different mean upload capacities. In the following, we use these four figures to highlight that our proposal has two distinct behaviors regarding the provisioning of the support network.

When the support network is under-provisioned, upload resources are exhausted before all nodes are spanned K times, so the source has to compensate for the lack of upload capacity by directly sending the last packets of the video chunk in shallow trees. On one hand, these shallow trees are costly in terms of source transmission rate because each one transmits one packet to only one node. On the other hand, as no relay is necessary, the decoding lag is lower. The more under-provisioned is the support network, the larger is the number of shallow trees in the forest. Therefore in the extreme case (video bit-rate 3.2 Mbps for mean capacity 512 kbps), the playback delay is stable around the minimum transmission delay, and the source transmission rate is roughly equal to the number of nodes times the video bit-rate.

When the support network is over-provisioned, the source does not need to build shallow trees. Our algorithm ensures that the forest contains compact and well-balanced trees. The decoding lag is less than 400 milliseconds, even when 25 nodes should be served. Our algorithm also succeeds in fully utilizing the resources of the nodes, as demonstrated by the source transmission rate, which is stable around the optimal lower bound in Fig. 2(a) for a mean capacity 2,048 kbps and never requires the transmission of more than 2.5 times the video bit-rate in every over-provisioned configuration. Our ability to serve a large number of nodes in a short delay makes the case for our proposal.

We then evaluate the performances of our algorithm when UDP packets can be lost during transmission. Rateless codes allow the diffusion of a potentially infinite number of distinct symbols until all nodes can decode the chunk. In our context, we fix a redundancy index, which indicates the bit-rate of the encoded stream including the redundancy in comparison to the video bit-rate (*e.g.*, a redundancy of 1.05 for a video bit-rate of 1,000 kbps means a stream bit-rate of 1,050 kbps). Fig. 2(e) shows the *outage rate*, which is the ratio of chunks that are not decoded to the overall number of transmitted chunks. Fig. 2(f) shows the decoding lag of the successfully decoded chunks.

Since the packets may be relayed many times before reaching a node, packet loss has a dramatic impact on successful chunk decoding. With low redundancy (less than 1.10), the outage rate is intolerable when the network is faulty (almost no chunk successfully decoded when 10% of transmissions are faulty). However, the benefits of using rateless codes become clearer for stream bit-rates that include a reasonable redundancy (between 1.15 and 1.20). Here, the outage rate falls below 0.2 in the most realistic scenarios. Finally, as shown in Fig. 2(f), neither the redundancy nor packet loss affect the decoding lag. When the redundancy increases, the number of shallow trees increases, and the decoding lag paradoxically decreases.

5. CONCLUSION AND FUTURE WORK

In this paper, we try to prevent one equipment (source) to throttle a whole CDN infrastructure in the context of live stream delivery. We propose the notion of support network where the equipments that receive the video chunks from the source cooperate in order to compensate for its missing capacity. We study one solution for this support network, which consists in leveraging on rateless codes. We modeled the problem as finding a diffusion forest with guaranteed end-to-end delay and bounded packet loss probability such that the total number of trees in the forest is minimized. We presented an optimal solution when both the delay and packet loss rate are not bounded. When the delay and the reliability are bounded and identical over all links, we proposed a heuristic algorithm.

The numerical results demonstrate the performance of the heuristic algorithm in diverse system configurations. Future work will include a real implementation in a real CDN infrastructure in order to validate the practical interest of our solution on the overall CDN.

Acknowledgment

The research leading to these results has received funding from the European Commission's Seventh Framework Programme (FP7, 2007-2013) under the grant agreement no. ICT-248175 (CNG project).

6. REFERENCES

[1] M. Adler, R. K. Sitaraman, and H. Venkataramani. Algorithms for optimizing the bandwidth cost of content delivery. *Computer Networks*, 55(18):4007–4020, 2011.

[2] J. M. Almeida, D. L. Eager, M. K. Vernon, and S. J. Wright. Minimizing delivery cost in scalable streaming content distribution systems. *IEEE Trans. Multimedia*, 6(2):356–365, 2004.

[3] K. Andreev, B. Maggs, A. Meyerson, J. Saks, and R. Sitaraman. Algorithms for constructing overlay networks for live streaming. *CoRR 1109.4114*, 2011.

[4] K. Andreev, B. M. Maggs, A. Meyerson, and R. K. Sitaraman. Designing overlay multicast networks for streaming. In *Proc. ACM SPAA*, pages 149–158, 2003.

[5] R. Gibbs. A new approach to publishing and caching video. Technical report, Alcatel-Lucent, Jan. 2012.

[6] M. Grangetto, R. Gaeta, and M. Sereno. Rateless codes network coding for simple and efficient P2P video streaming. In *Proc. of ICME*, pages 1500–1503, Jul. 2009.

[7] S. Higginbotham. Smart TVs cause a net neutrality debate in S. Korea. Giga OM, Feb. 2012.

[8] C. Liu, I. Bouazizi, M. M. Hannuksela, and M. Gabbouj. Rate adaptation for dynamic adaptive streaming over HTTP in content distribution network. *Signal Processing: Image Communication*, 27(4):288–311, 2012.

[9] M. Luby. LT Codes. In *Proc. of FOCS*, pages 271–280, 2002.

[10] M. Luby, T. Gasiba, T. Stockhammer, and M. Watson. Reliable multimedia download delivery in cellular broadcast networks. *IEEE Trans. Broadcast.*, 53(1):235–246, 2007.

[11] J. Ni and D. H. K. Tsang. Large-scale cooperative caching and application-level multicast in multimedia content delivery networks. *IEEE Commun. Mag.*, 43(5):98–105, May 2005.

[12] A. Shokrollahi. Raptor codes. *IEEE Trans. Inf. Theory*, 52(6):2551–2567, 2006.

[13] T. Siglin. Super Bowl Streaming Fail. Streaming Media, Feb. 2012.

[14] N. Thomos and P. Frossard. Network coding of rateless video in streaming overlays. *IEEE Trans. Circuits Syst. Video Technol.*, 20(12):1834–1847, 2010.

[15] C. Wu and B. Li. rstream: Resilient and optimal peer-to-peer streaming with rateless codes. *IEEE Trans. Parallel Distrib. Syst.*, 19(1):77–92, 2008.

SmartTransfer: Transferring Your Mobile Multimedia Contents at the "Right" Time

Yichuan Wang, Xin Liu
Dept. of Computer Science
University of California, Davis
Davis, CA 95616
yicwang@ucdavis.edu,
xinliu@ucdavis.edu

Angela Nicoara
Deutsche Telekom Innovation
Laboratories
Silicon Valley Innovation
Center
Mountain View CA 94043
angela.nicoara@telekom.com

Ting-An Lin, Cheng-Hsin Hsu
Dept. of Computer Science
National Tsing Hua University
Hsin Chu, Taiwan
tim19890901@gmail.com,
chsu@cs.nthu.edu.tw

ABSTRACT

Today's mobile Internet is heavily overloaded by the increasing demand and capability of mobile devices, in particular, multimedia traffic. However, not all traffic is created equal, and a large portion of multimedia contents on the mobile Internet is delay tolerant. We study the problem of capitalizing the content transfer opportunities under better network conditions via postponing the transfers without violating the user-specified deadlines. We propose a new framework called SmartTransfer, which offers a unified content transfer interface to mobile applications. We also develop two scheduling algorithms to opportunistically schedule the content transfers. Via extensive trace-driven simulations, we show that our algorithms outperform a baseline scheduling algorithm by far: up to 17 times improvement in upload throughput and/or at most 20 dBm boost in signal strength. The simulation results also reveal various tradeoff between the two proposed scheduling algorithms. We have implemented our framework and one of the scheduling algorithms on Android, to demonstrate their practicality and efficiency.

Categories and Subject Descriptors

C.2.4 [**Distributed Systems**]: Distributed Applications

General Terms

Performance

Keywords

Opportunistic transfers, scheduling, resource conservation, user profiling

1. INTRODUCTION

Recent mobile devices can generate and render multimedia contents, such as audios, images, and videos. These mobile devices, however, are resource-constrained and have to frequently transfer the multimedia contents from/to some back-end servers or clouds. Cisco reports that mobile data is expected to increase almost 40 times by 2015 and 66% of this increase is due to mobile video [1]. In fact, the service providers have moved away from unlimited dataplans to tiered services [2] and may even consider time-dependent pricing [9], which could increase the bills on the mobile users. Therefore, modern mobile devices must regulate their network resource consumption, i.e., become more *network-friendly*.

To achieve this goal, we study an innovative approach of regulating the network resource consumed by each mobile user. A key observation is that *not all traffic is created equal*: (i) Many popular mobile applications are *delay tolerant*. The delay tolerance of such traffic varies from sub-seconds to hours; and (ii) Data from a large cellular network shows that there exists *a significant lag between content generation and user-initiated upload time,* more than 55% multimedia contents uploaded from mobile network is at least 1 day old [17]. We call such traffic *elastic*, which can be leveraged to opportunistically schedule content transfers when the network condition is more favorable in terms of, e.g., signal strength, network throughput, energy consumption, and access price. In other words, since mobile users perceive time-varying channel condition and network load, choosing the "right" time to transfer each multimedia content is critical to system performance.

In this paper, we study how to capitalize the content transfer opportunities under better network conditions via postponing the transfers without violating the user-specified deadlines. More specifically, when delay-tolerant content is generated at a mobile device, one can opportunistically schedule the transfer to minimize network/device resource utilization, such as network air time or battery consumption. Making such a decision (throughout the paper) is challenging for two reasons. First, implementing the decision making logics in individual mobile applications is time consuming, expensive, and error-prone. Hence, such optimization techniques are unlikely to be adopted by mobile application developers; many of them are freelance programmers. We address this challenge by adding a new module called *SmartTransfer* in mobile operating systems, which provides a unified content transfer interface to applications. We present the SmartTransfer framework in Sec. 2.

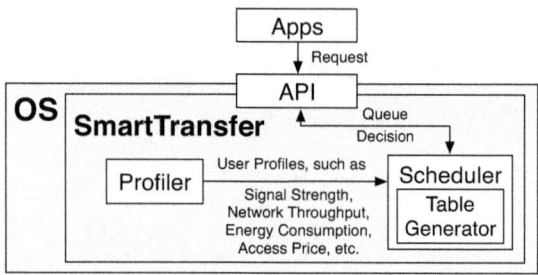

Figure 1: The proposed SmartTransfer framework.

Second, making such decisions requires prediction on future network conditions, e.g., how soon and likely a mobile device will enter a region with strong cellular network signals. A simple approach is to use the moving average of past few samples [4, 13]. While this approach may work for small time scales (e.g., in a few minutes), it is less applicable to large time scales because a mobile user may visit several different locations and experience diverse network conditions. We address this challenge by collecting longer, say 30 days, historical data on mobile devices, which are referred to as user *profiles* throughout this paper. Individual human mobility in large time scales is highly predictable [7, 16], therefore profiles allow us to make more accurate predictions because mobile user's future network conditions are time and location dependent. We present how we leverage user profiles to design content transfer scheduling algorithms in Sec. 3.

We evaluate the proposed framework and scheduling algorithms in Sec. 4 via extensive trace-driven simulations. The simulation results reveal that the proposed algorithms outperform a baseline algorithm by up to 17 times in terms of upload throughput and/or 20 dBm in terms of signal strength. One of our proposed algorithms employs a more comprehensive statistical model, and demands for more resources. The other proposed algorithm employs a lightweight model, and always terminates in 560 msecs throughout all simulations. In Sec. 5, we implement the SmartTransfer framework and OSS_L algorithm on Android and deploy a delay-tolerant application via the Android Market, which demonstrate the practicality of the proposed solution.

2. SMARTTRANSFER FRAMEWORK

Fig. 1 presents the SmartTransfer framework, which runs on mobile devices and consists of three components: *profiler*, *scheduler*, and *API* (Application Programming Interface). The profiler collects user profiles, which are essentially timestamped log files. The profiler itself can be general that collects the network conditions in various performance metrics, including signal strength, network throughput, energy consumption, and access price. Some of these metrics can be retrieved from the network interfaces, such as the signal strength and network throughput, some of them may be measured by on-board instruments, such as energy consumption, and some of them could be provided by the cellular service providers, such as the access price. The profiler monitors the profile size to avoid filling up the storage space. It also keeps the updated profile, and provides the most recent, e.g., last three-month, profile to the scheduler. The profile provides input to the scheduler that runs the scheduling algorithms to make decisions on when to start content transfer. For scheduling algorithms that cannot run in real-time, we may pre-process the user profiles while the mobile devices are charging and idling, in order to eliminate the negative impacts on the user experience. The output of the pre-processing step is typically a lookup table, and thus is referred to as *table generator* as illustrated in Fig. 1. In extreme cases, where the scheduling algorithms are too complicated for mobile devices, we may even offload the table generator to the cloud. Mobile applications connect to the framework via the API and submit content transfer requests, including the content size and delay requirement. The SmartTransfer then helps the mobile applications to schedule the user-generated multimedia contents to upload them under good network conditions; they may also help mobile applications to prefetch certain contents for later usage, perhaps chosen by a content recommender [3], under good network conditions. The SmartTransfer framework supports different optimization criteria, such as minimizing: (i) network resource consumption, (ii) transfer duration, (iii) energy consumption, and (iv) access cost. This is achieved by choosing the corresponding user profiles and scheduling algorithms.

3. SCHEDULING ALGORITHMS

3.1 Scheduling Model

In this section, we present a slotted scheduling model. We consider a transfer request from the application layer, which is available at time zero. There exists a hard deadline called *horizon* N, by which the data transfer must be completed otherwise user experience will be disrupted. N is a system parameter, which may be derived via experimental studies on user tolerance on delay, and could be application-dependent. To maximize user experience, a user can request an instantaneous data transfer, via a user interface, at any time slot. We model the time slot in which such instantaneous transfer request occurs by a random variable M called *freeze time*. The realization of M is unknown a priori. For simplicity, we consider a content transfer that can be finished in a time slot, while it is our future work to generalizing our analysis to multiple and heterogeneous content transfers. If user did not request an instantaneous data transfer at time slot t ($M > t$), the scheduler makes a decision $D_t \in \{\text{Wait}, \text{Transfer}\}$.

Fig. 2 summarizes the considered scheduling model. A content is transferred at time slot t if (i) $t = N$, or (ii) $M = t$, or (iii) $D_t = \text{Transfer}$. If $D_t = \text{Wait}$, the content is delayed to time slot $t + 1$.

Let X_t ($t \in [1, N]$) be the *transfer cost* at slot t. Waiting costs nothing. Let V_t be the *optimal cost* to transfer a content between time slot t and N, assuming the optimal schedule is applied. V_t can be calculated using the statistics of X_t and M, which are derived from the user profile. In Secs. 3.2 and 3.3, we develop two scheduling algorithms, which employ different statistical models for the transfer costs X_t, under different assumptions.

3.2 Optimal Stopping Scheduling (OSS)

We propose a scheduling algorithm that minimizes the expected cost. Our algorithm is inspired by earlier work on

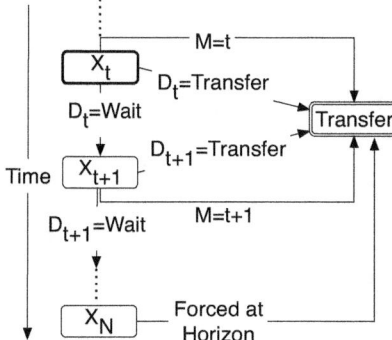

Figure 2: The considered scheduling model.

classic optimal stopping problems [6, 14] that try to maximize the probability of finding the best candidate in a job interview. To the best of our knowledge, the optimal stopping problem for minimizing the expected cost with random freeze time has not been rigorously studied. We refer to our algorithm as optimal stopping scheduling (OSS).

The OSS algorithm employs a Markovian model to capture the transfer costs. In this model, the transfer cost X_t depends on time, and previous transfer cost X_{t-1}. Statistics for M and X are derived from user profiles.

The principle of optimality is as follows. If transfer cost X_t is less or equal to the expect optimal cost $E(V_{t+1})$, transfer at the time slot t, otherwise wait until time slot $t+1$. With the above notations, the optimal schedule is written as:

$$D_t = \begin{cases} \text{Transfer,} & M = t; \\ \text{Transfer,} & M > t, X_t \leq E(V_{t+1}|X_t); \\ \text{Wait,} & M > t, X_t > E(V_{t+1}|X_t). \end{cases} \quad (1)$$

Due to its Markovian property, $E(V_t|X_{t-1})$ can be obtained by backward induction:

$$\begin{aligned} E(V_N|X_{N-1}) &= E(X_N|X_{N-1}); \\ E(V_t|X_{t-1}) &= P(M=t|M\geq t) \cdot E(X_t|X_{t-1}) \\ &\quad + P(M>t|M\geq t) \cdot \\ &\quad \sum_c \{P(X_t=c|X_{t-1}) \cdot \min(c, E(V_{t+1}|X_t=c))\}. \end{aligned} \quad (2)$$

On mobile devices, at charging time, the optimal decision D_t for all time and previous cost X_{t-1} can be pre-calculated and saved as a table. At runtime, we simply look up the table using previous cost and time to find the optimal decision. We call this pre-calculated data as the *decision* table.

The model presented in Eq. (1) and (2) are general, but may come with some limitations. First, we need to accumulate enough samples to accurately derive $E(X_t|X_{t-1})$ for all t and X_{t-1}. Hence, the OSS algorithm requires a long user profile for deriving model parameters. Second, let T be the number of total time slot, and $|X|$ be the number of all possible transfer costs. The decision table has $|X| \cdot T \cdot N$ elements, which is huge in the time scale that we are interested in implementing the algorithm, e.g., one day. Computing and storing the optimal schedule may be too demanding for mobile devices. For example, consider 1 minute time slot in 1 day, 1 hour horizon, 30 different cost values, the decision table is as large as 2.6 MB, which is significant to mobile devices.

3.3 Lightweight Optimal Stopping Scheduling (OSS_L)

To alleviate the limitation of the OSS algorithm, we propose a simplified optimal stopping algorithm. The Lightweight Optimal Stopping Scheduling (OSS_L) algorithm leverages the same principle of optimality as the OSS algorithm, but has a more relaxed assumption on the statistical model of the transfer costs. In particular, OSS_L assumes that X_t are independent over time.

Following similar derivations of the OSS algorithm, we write the optimal decision as:

$$D_t = \begin{cases} \text{Transfer,} & M = t; \\ \text{Transfer,} & M > t, X_t \leq E(V_{t+1}); \\ \text{Wait,} & M > t, X_t > E(V_{t+1}). \end{cases} \quad (3)$$

where

$$\begin{aligned} E(V_N) &= E(X_N); \\ E(V_t) &= P(M=t|M\geq t) \cdot E(X_t) \\ &\quad + P(M>t|M\geq t) \\ &\quad \cdot [P(X_t \leq E(V_{t+1})) \cdot E(X_t|X_t \leq E(V_{t+1})) \\ &\quad + P(X_t > E(V_{t+1})) \cdot E(V_{t+1})]. \end{aligned} \quad (4)$$

Note that the $E(V_t)$ ($1 \leq t \leq N$) can also be derived using backward induction, which starts from $V_N = E(X_N)$ as the transfer must be done by time slot N regardless the cost. Then, the rest of $E(V_t)$ can be computed using the user profile, which reveals various statistics of X_t such as $P(X_t \leq E(V_{t+1}))$ and $E(X_t|X_t \leq E(V_{t+1}))$. We precompute all $E(V_t)$ ($1 \leq t \leq N$) using Eq. (4), and refer to it as the *threshold* table. Upon optimum $E(V_t)$ ($1 \leq t \leq N$) are derived, the proposed scheduler computes optimal schedule using Eq. (3). Compared the OSS algorithm, the OSS_L algorithm employs a simpler underneath model. Hence, OSS_L can be trained with shorter user profiles, at the expense of potentially higher inaccuracy.

4. TRACE-DRIVEN SIMULATION

4.1 Simulation Setup

For fair comparisons, we adopt a set of 3-month long traces collected from 12 North American Android users, who are heterogeneous in terms of demography, sex, and age. The traces were collected and used in another project [11], and we process the raw trace files to extract the relevant measurements: Received Signal Strength Indication (RSSI), and upload/download throughput. A higher value in RSSI or throughput reduces the transmission time of data, in turn reduces network resource and battery consumption. In the current work, we only consider data collected from the cellular network; data from WiFi is excluded. The resulting traces are used to drive the simulator.

The simulator is developed in Matlab and run on a Linux PC with a 2.8 GHz Intel CPU. The simulator implements a time slotted system. Contents arrive to the system follows a Poisson process. Four algorithms are implemented to schedule the content transfers. The first one is a baseline algorithm Instant transfer (INS). INS schedules a content to

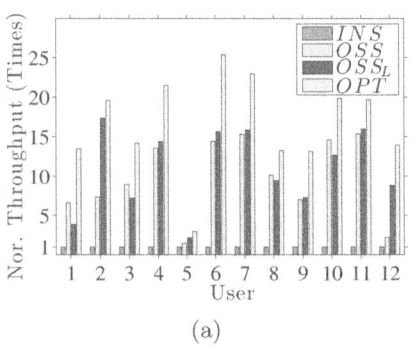 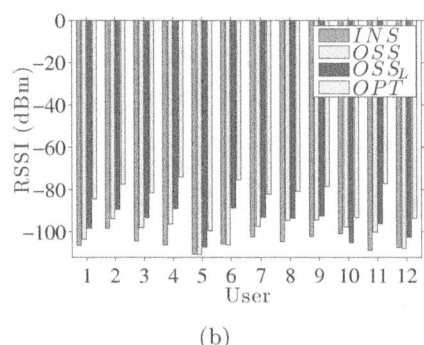 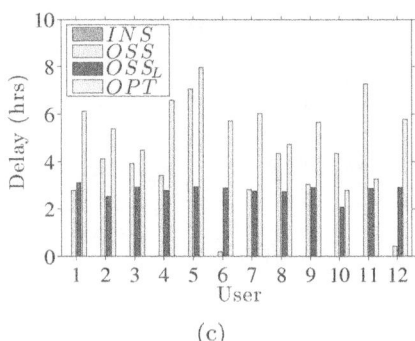

Figure 3: (a) Normalized throughput achieved by the scheduling algorithms, (b) signal strength achieved by the scheduling algorithms, and (c) delay due to the scheduling algorithms, INS leads to no delay.

transfer right after it becomes available. The second algorithm is the OSS algorithm introduced in Section 3.2. Part of the traces are passed to OSS algorithm as user profile. With user profile, OSS generates a decision table for each user. After a content becomes available, each time slot, the current optimization criteria, either RSSI or upload throughput, and current time is used to look up the decision table and find the current action (Transfer or Wait). The third algorithm is the OSS_L algorithm presented in Section 3.3. OSS_L also employs traces as user profile, however OSS_L generates a threshold for each time slot using a simplified model. Each time slot, OSS_L compares the current optimization criteria with the corresponding threshold. OSS_L transfer the content if the current value is better than the threshold. Finally, an offline algorithm OPT is implemented as an upper bound for scheduling algorithms. We assume that OPT knows all the future RSSI or throughput at the beginning. After each content becomes available, OPT will choose the time slot with the highest RSSI or throughput to transfer the content, which is of course not realistic.

If not otherwise specified, we let the user profile be half of the trace length, time horizon be 8 hours, use the upload throughput as the optimization criterion, and schedule on average 32 content transfers per day. We also study the implications of varying user profile length and time horizon. Each content is scheduled by all four algorithms, the resulting RSSI or throughput, along with incurred delay are collected. The decision table or threshold table size and the time taken to generate these tables are also collected.

4.2 Simulation Results

We first report the simulation results with default parameters. We then study the implications of the parameters. We also present computation time and memory consumption of the proposed algorithms.

Throughput optimized scheduling. We use the results from INS as the baseline, and compute the relative upload throughput of the proposed algorithms. We plot the throughput results in Fig. 3(a). This figure shows that the proposed OSS and OSS_L algorithms always outperform the INS algorithm, and in the extreme case by up to 17 times. This demonstrate the benefits of the proposed algorithms.

Signal strength optimized scheduling. We plot the RSSI values in Fig. 3(b). This figure reveals that the SmartTransfer framework supports various optimization criteria. Moreover, the proposed OSS and OSS_L algorithms outperform the INS algorithm for most users, except for users 5, 10, and 12, in which the RSSI values resulting from the OSS and OSS_L may be slightly worse than that of the INS algorithm. We took a closer look at the traces, and found that these users tend to spend a very long time, e.g., a day, at a single location. Therefore, their RSSI values over each day are rather static, and thus our proposed algorithms may not result in too much improvement. We also plot the delay of content transfers in Fig. 3(c).

Implications of profile length. For individual users, we plot the average upload throughput achieved by each algorithm under various profile lengths, between 1 and 32 days. The figures are not shown due to the space limitations. We found that the OSS and OSS_L significantly outperform the INS algorithm. Moreover, the resulting throughput is generally higher with longer profile length. Next, we report the overhead of the proposed algorithms. The decision table of the OSS algorithm contains 15256 elements, while the threshold table of the OSS_L algorithm only has 4920 elements. As a consequence, the OSS_L algorithm runs much faster than OSS: less than 200 msecs versus up to 44 secs. This shows that OSS_L is preferable when the computational resources are scarce.

Implications of time horizon. Fig. 4 reports the sample results from user 3 with various time horizons. Fig. 4(a) indicates that the OSS algorithm outperforms the OSS_L algorithm when the time horizon is shorter than 12.5 hrs, while the OSS_L performs better when time horizon is longer. This means that OSS_L is more suitable to content transfers that are tolerant to longer delays. Fig. 4(b) plots the running time of the two algorithms. We make two observations. First, the OSS algorithm does not scale well with the time horizon, the running time is 100 secs when time horizon is 32 hrs. Second, the OSS_L algorithm runs efficiently, at most 560 msecs running time is observed (not visible in this figure due to the Y-axis scale). Figs. 4(a) and 4(b) show that OSS_L is preferable when time horizon is large.

5. REAL IMPLEMENTATION AND EXPERIMENTS

5.1 SmartTransfer on Android

SmartTransfer can be implemented entirely as a user-space library. However we choose to integrate it into Android framework, so all Android applications can readily use

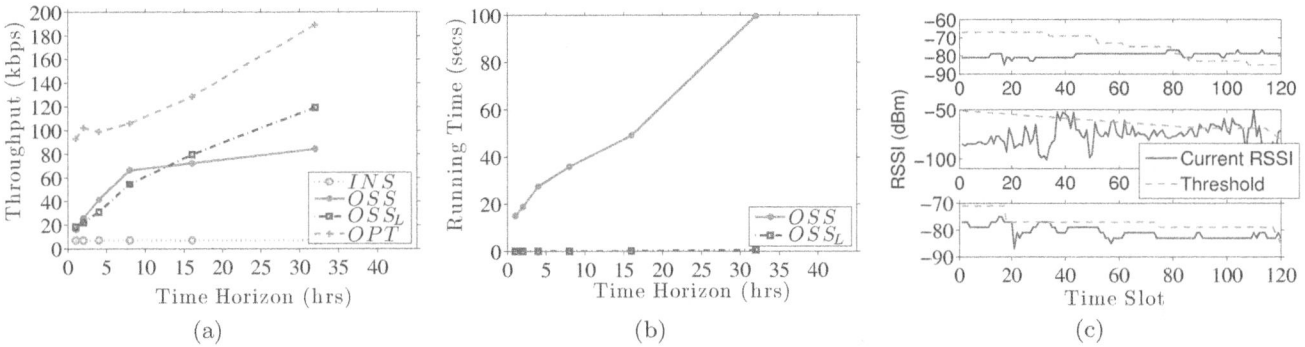

Figure 4: (a) Implications of the time horizon on throughput, (b) OSS does not scale to longer time horizon, and (c) sample scheduling decisions from the real experiments.

our content transfer service without reinventing the wheel. We have patched the Android 2.2 source tree of the Android Open Source Project (AOSP) with the proposed Smart-Transfer framework. The SmartTransfer framework is realized as a service on Android. As a proof-of-concept, our current implementation supports the OSS_L algorithm; we are integrating the OSS algorithm into it. We collect user profiles in the background with a time slot of 30 seconds. The user profiles, up to 60 days, are used to generate the threshold table whenever the phone is being charged. Once there exists a pending content transfer request, we use the pre-computed threshold table to pick the best time for data transfer.

5.2 Application: VideoBlogger

We have implemented a sample Android application, called VideoBlogger, which emulates a smartphone user who regularly records videos and uploads them to a web site using the SmartTransfer API over the 3G network. The VideoBlogger generates realistic video uploads as follows. We develop a crawler to retrieve the metadata of YouTube videos. We use the crawler to get the sizes of 500 random videos, and built an empirical Cumulative Distribution Function (CDF). The VideoBlogger periodically generates video uploads with the sizes following this CDF, and employs a Poisson process with a mean of 10 minutes to determine the inter-arrival time of video uploads. Poisson process is often used to describe nature events in the real world. After each video update, the VideoBlogger sends the measurement results, including the start/end time, video size, and network throughput, to a backend ftp server. We run both the web and ftp servers on a Windows PC connected to the Internet over a Gigabit Ethernet link.

The VideoBlogger is implemented for large-scale experiments. It is implemented as a background service on Android, and has been deployed to experimental subjects over the Android Market since late February 2012. The recurring video uploads allow us to collect statistically-meaningful results without any subject intervention. We name all the log files using an one-way hash function of the mobile device IDs (IMEI numbers) to maintain subjects' privacy. We deployed VideoBlogger to subjects of diverse occupations, age, sex, and even in different time-zone. By choosing heterogeneous subjects, we show that the SmartTransfer automatically adapts to different users.

5.3 Preliminary Experimental Results

Due to the time and space limitations, we only report preliminary results in this section. Fig. 4(c) shows sample transfers from three subjects chosen from a total of 12 subjects. The solid lines show the RSSI values measured during the experiment, and the dashed lines show the thresholds generated by OSS_L. The first time RSSI falls below the current threshold, OSS_L will transfer the content. Using the experiments, we demonstrate the practicality of the proposed solution.

6. RELATED WORK

The idea of leveraging delay tolerant content transfer has been studied in the literature. For example, Hao et al. [8] proposed to selectively postpone less critical user-generated multimedia uploads to save energy on mobile devices. Their smartphone application first uploads the geographical metadata of each video at the capture time, and only uploads the video itself when there are explicit interests from other users. Their work in [8] is complementary to ours, as they consider on-demand user requests, while we concentrate on content transfer scheduling. In [17], the authors proposed to add drop zones for efficiently offloading upload traffic. In [4], the authors used WiFi network whenever possible to offload data from 3G connections, which is achieved by analyzing recent WiFi availability to predict the future availability. Schulman et al. [15] used location service to derive the user paths, which are then leveraged to predict future network condition. In comparison to [17], our solution does not require additional network infrastructure. On the other hand, in [4, 15], short history (e.g., last several measurements in a few minutes) is used to predict future network condition, which is valid for a short time scale, say minutes. In comparison, we have used much larger time-scale history profile, which enables us to provide longer time scale prediction, say in the time horizon of one hour. Because of the large time scale, we cannot use simple average to estimate future time condition, this "non-stationarity" introduces technical challenges which are addressed in this paper.

A different approach of capitalizing delay tolerant content transfers is to batch several requests together. Balasubramanian et al. [5] proposed a heuristic batching algorithm, based on the measurements of tail energy in the various networks. Kononen and Paakkonen [10] tackled the tail behavior of networks using a timer alignment technique. Qian et al. [12] proposed to optimize the UMTS radio resource management state machine in order to balance energy saving and performance. We are working on including batching into the proposed opportunistic scheduling algorithms.

7. CONCLUSION AND FUTURE WORK

We propose SmartTransfer framework and two scheduling algorithms to intelligently schedule delay tolerant data to more favorable network conditions in order to potentially reduce network resource consumption, alleviate network congestion, and improve battery lifetime. In this preliminary work, we show that user network profile is an indispensable component to accurately predict future network condition, which is crucial for efficiently leveraging delay tolerance to save network resource. Our proposed solution is simple yet effective, and can be implemented on mobile platforms. We have discussed in details the implementation of SmartTransfer, as well as its practical applications. Using both real traces and experimental study, we have demonstrated the desirability of the proposed SmartTransfer.

We are extending the current study in several directions. First, we will consider the scenario where multiple transmissions with various sizes. Some of the transmissions could be combined/batched. The main benefit of batching is to reduce overhead induced by network setup, link setup, and tail effect of network interfaces. Second, we would like to further investigate machine learning technique to achieve a good balance between model complexity and profile data availability. We would like to also study the benefit of non-parametric learning. Furthermore, our proposed solution, in principle, can be used to alleviate network congestion, i.e., using the congestion level as the cost. The main challenge in studying network congestion alleviation is to achieve a good estimate of network congestion without imposing heavy probing overhead on both the device and the network.

8. ACKNOWLEDGEMENTS

This work is supported by HTC Magic Labs. C. Hsu and T. Lin are partially supported by National Science Council (NSC) of Taiwan (#100-2218-E-007-015-MY2).

9. REFERENCES

[1] Cisco visual networking index: Forecast and methodology, 2010–2015. http://www.cisco.com/en/US/solutions/collateral/ns341/ns525/ns537/ns705/ns827/white_paper_c11-481360.pdf, 2011.

[2] Why Verizon dropped its unlimited data plan (and what you can do about it). http://moneyland.time.com/2011/06/23/why-verizon-dropped-its-unlimited-data-plan/, 2011.

[3] M. Albanese, A. d'Acierno, V. Moscato, F. Persia, and A. Picariello. A ranking method for multimedia recommenders. In *Proc. of ACM International Conference on Image and Video Retrieval (CIVR'10)*, pages 311–318, Xian, China, 2010.

[4] A. Balasubramanian, R. Mahajan, and A. Venkataramani. Augmenting mobile 3G using WiFi. In *Proc. of ACM International Conference on Mobile Systems, Applications, and Services (MobiSys'10)*, pages 209–222, San Francisco, CA, 2010.

[5] N. Balasubramanian, A. Balasubramanian, and A. Venkataramani. Energy consumption in mobile phones: A measurement study and implications for network applications. In *Proc. of ACM SIGCOMM Conference on Internet Measurement (IMC'09)*, pages 280–293, Chicago, IL, 2009.

[6] J. P. Gilbert and F. Mosteller. Recognizing the Maximum of a Sequence. *Journal of the American Statistical Association*, 61(313):35–73, 1966.

[7] M. C. Gonzalez, C. A. Hidalgo, and A.-L. Barabasi. Understanding individual human mobility patterns. *Nature*, 453(7196):779–782, 2008.

[8] J. Hao, S. Kim, S. Ay, and R. Zimmermann. Energy-efficient mobile video management using smartphones. In *Proc. of ACM Conference on Multimedia Systems (MMSys'11)*, pages 11–22, San Jose, CA, 2011.

[9] C. Joe-Wong, S. Ha, and M. Chiang. Time-dependent broadband pricing: Feasibility and benefits. In *Proc. of IEEE International Conference on Distributed Computing Systems (ICDCS'11)*, pages 288–298, Minneapolis, MN, 2011.

[10] V. KoÌLnoÌLnen and P. Paakkonen. Optimizing power consumption of always-on applications based on timer alignment. In *Proc. of International Conference on Communication Systems and Networks (COMSNETS'11)*, pages 1–8, Bangalore, India, 2011.

[11] S. Nirjon, A. Nicoara, C. Hsu, J. Singh, and J. Stankovic. MultiNets: Policy oriented real-time switching of wireless interfaces on mobile devices. In *Proc. of IEEE Real-Time and Embedded Technology and Applications Symposium (RTAS'12)*, Beijing, China, 2012.

[12] F. Qian, Z. Wang, A. Gerber, and Z. Mao. Characterizing radio resource allocation for 3G networks. pages 137–150, 2010.

[13] M. Ra, J. Paek, A. Sharma, R. Govindan, M. Krieger, and M. Neely. Energy-delay tradeoffs in smartphone applications. In *Proc. of ACM International Conference on Mobile Systems, Applications, and Services (MobiSys'10)*, pages 255–270, San Francisco, CA, 2010.

[14] E. Samuel-Cahn. Optimal Stopping With Random Horizon With Application to the Full-Information Best-Choice Problem With Random Freeze. *Journal of the American Statistical Association*, 91(433):357–364, 1996.

[15] A. Schulman, V. Navda, R. Ramjee, N. Spring, P. Deshpande, C. Grunewald, K. Jain, and V. Padmanabhan. Bartendr: A practical approach to energy-aware cellular data scheduling. In *Proc. of ACM Annual International Conference on Mobile Computing and Networking (MobiCom'10)*, pages 85–96, Chicago, IL, 2010.

[16] C. Song, Z. Qu, N. Blumm, and A.-L. BarabÃạsi. Limits of predictability in human mobility. *Science*, 327(5968):1018–1021, 2010.

[17] I. Trestian, S. Ranjan, A. Kuzmanovic, and A. Nucci. Taming user-generated content in mobile networks via drop zones. In *Proc. of IEEE INFOCOM'11*, pages 2040–2048, Shanghai, China, 2011.

Content and Geographical Locality in User-Generated Content Sharing Systems

Kévin Huguenin
EPFL
Lausanne, Switzerland
kevin.huguenin@epfl.ch

Anne-Marie Kermarrec
INRIA
Rennes, France
anne-marie.kermarrec@inria.fr

Konstantinos Kloudas
INRIA
Rennes, France
konstantinos.kloudas@inria.fr

François Taïani
Lancaster University
Lancaster, UK
f.taiani@lancs.ac.uk

ABSTRACT

User Generated Content (UGC), such as YouTube videos, accounts for a substantial fraction of the Internet traffic. To optimize their performance, UGC services usually rely on both proactive and reactive approaches that exploit spatial and temporal locality in access patterns. Alternative types of locality are also relevant and hardly ever considered together. In this paper, we show on a large (more than 650,000 videos) YouTube dataset that *content locality* (induced by the related videos feature) and *geographic locality*, are in fact correlated. More specifically, we show how the geographic view distribution of a video can be inferred to a large extent from that of its related videos. We leverage these findings to propose a UGC storage system that *proactively* places videos close to the *expected* requests. Compared to a caching-based solution, our system decreases by 16% the number of requests served from a different country than that of the requesting user, and even in this case, the distance between the user and the server is 29% shorter on average.

Categories and Subject Descriptors

H.3.2 [**Information Systems**]: Information Storage and Retrieval—*Information Storage*

General Terms

Measurement, Algorithm, Design

Keywords

User-generated content, content distribution

Permission to make digital or hard copies of all or part of this work for personal or classroom use is granted without fee provided that copies are not made or distributed for profit or commercial advantage and that copies bear this notice and the full citation on the first page. To copy otherwise, to republish, to post on servers or to redistribute to lists, requires prior specific permission and/or a fee.
NOSSDAV'12, June 7–8, 2012, Toronto, Ontario, Canada.
Copyright 2012 ACM 978-1-4503-1430-5/12/06 ...$10.00.

1. INTRODUCTION

Over the last few years, users have become the most prolific content generators on the Web, prompting the phenomenal success of user-generated content (UGC) sharing sites such as YouTube [3, 6]. This rapid growth combined with the never fulfilled user demand for better quality, makes serving UGC to an increasing number of users all around the world a daily engineering feat [13]. To this end, UGC sharing sites rely on Content Delivery Networks (CDNs) to place content close to consumers. To achieve this goal, CDNs employ both *proactive* approaches that rely on *a priori* knowledge (e.g., it is likely that a French-speaking video will be accessed mostly from French-speaking countries) and *reactive* ones where the history of a given video is analyzed to predict its future requests [8, 4, 17].

Interestingly, beyond traditional forms of locality that account for each content item independently, recent studies have shown that UGC viewing patterns are significantly influenced by the fact that content in these sites is no longer independent but is organized in a *content graph*. In YouTube, this *content graph* is embodied by the lists of "related videos" present on each video's page, and its influence on the viewing behavior of users has been clearly documented [10, 18].

In this paper we study the geographic viewing patterns of UGC and how they are affected by the content graph. Our analysis on a novel YouTube dataset shows that (i) related videos tend to have correlated geographic viewing patterns, with most of their views coming from the same countries, and (ii) popular videos tend to have their views more uniformly spread across more countries than less popular ones. The latter category accounts for the vast majority of YouTube's content and have their views coming from a small number of countries.

Building on these insights, we propose DTUBE, a system that accurately predicts the origins of a video's *future* views by looking at its position in the *content graph* and *proactively* places its replicas close to its *expected* consumers. Although the impact of *content locality*, i.e. proximity in the *content graph*, on a video's views and *geographically concentrated* viewing patterns have been studied independently [14, 18, 2], to the best of our knowledge, this is the first work that considers both aspects to optimize the placement of UGC.

We show that our system manages to deliver videos over

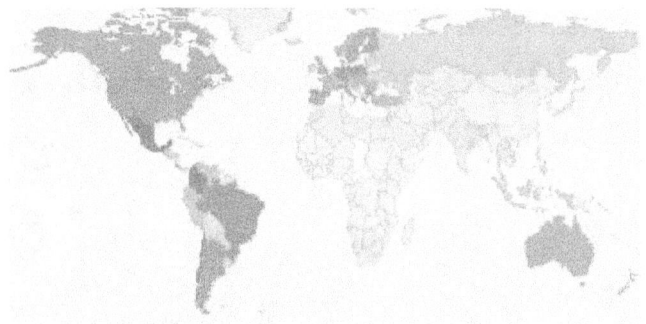

Figure 1: Geographic distribution of the origin of views for a sample YouTube video.

Country	US	CA	GB	BR	JP	DE	PL	AU
Prop. of views (%)	6.6	3.1	3.0	3.0	2.6	2.5	2.2	2.2

Table 1: Geographic distribution of views at the granularity of a country (top 8 countries).

contained in the VSVs to analyze the geographic distribution of views in our dataset. Our goal is to explore the feasibility of a geographically-driven *proactive* placement mechanism that places videos in countries where they are likely to be viewed.

Category	# views	% of videos	% of total views
C_1	$[0, 10^4]$	42.0	0.49
C_2	$(10^4, 10^5]$	33.5	5.10
C_3	$(10^5, 10^6]$	19.7	25.18
C_4	$(10^6, 10^7]$	4.4	45.02
C_5	$(10^7, 10^8]$	0.3	21.10
C_6	$(10^8, \infty)$	0.04	3.10

Table 2: Popularity categories and statistics

shorter distances than a standard caching-based solution, thus reducing network latencies and improving user experience. In particular, DTUBE can decrease the proportion of remote requests, i.e., that cannot be served by a node in the same country as the requesting users, by as much as 16%. We also show that DTUBE can decrease the average distance between users and stored videos by up to 29% for remote requests.

The rest of this paper is organized as follows. In Section 2 we show that content and geographic locality are correlated in YouTube. In Section 3 we present DTUBE's *replica placement* algorithm and we report on its evaluation in Section 4. We survey related work in Section 5 and conclude in Section 6.

2. LOCALITY IN UGC

Using a YouTube dataset we crawled in March 2011, we show that there is a strong correlation between *the geographic distribution* of a video's views and that of its related videos. We then explore how this correlation can be used to predict the geographic distribution of a video's future views.

2.1 Dataset Description

We crawled our own dataset from YouTube, during the first three weeks of March 2011, using snowball sampling with an initial set consisting of the 10 most popular videos for 25 different countries. For each video, we collected three attributes: (i) its list of related videos as provided by YouTube, (ii) its total number of views, and (iii) its *View Source Vector* (VSV). The VSV of a video represents how many views this video received from each country in the world. For most of the videos, the VSV is available, on the statistics page, as a color map (Fig. 1) generated by a specific URL (charts.apis.google.com) containing (country, #views) couples encoded in Google's *Simple Encoding Format*. In our experiments, we extracted the actual VSVs from these URLs. Tab. 1 shows the distribution of the views (top 8 countries) at the granularity of a country, over the whole dataset. The original dataset contained 1,063,844 videos. We removed the videos with no VSV, and filtered out non-crawled videos from the related video lists. This left us with 689,265 videos, each having 8 related videos on average, for a maximum of 25 related videos allowed in YouTube.[1]

In the following, we use the view-per-country information

[1] Because the geographic information in our dataset is given

2.2 Popularity vs. Geographic Distribution

We first investigate the link between a video's overall popularity and the geographical distribution of its views. To this end, we partition our dataset into six categories based on a video's number of views. The distribution of videos shown on Tab. 2 confirms earlier analysis [2, 3], highlighting a long-tail distribution of views. Very popular videos (categories C_5 and C_6) represent less than 1% of videos while accounting for almost 25% of all views. Because of the long tail, the bandwidth cost of "unpopular" videos is however far from being negligible: The 3 least popular categories (C_1, C_2, C_3, or 95.2% of all videos) still represent more than 30% of the views.

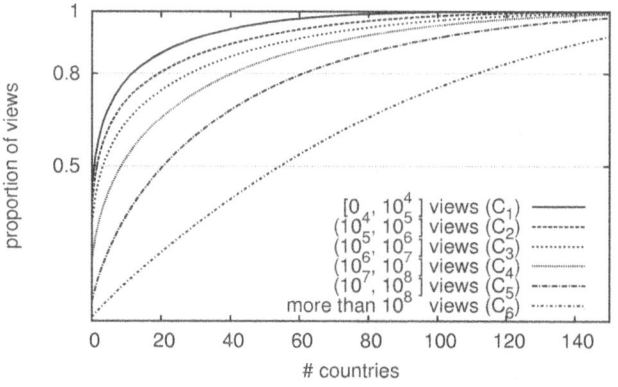

Figure 2: Geographic cumulative distribution of views for various popularity categories

To analyze the geographic distribution of views for each category, we compute the average geographic spread of video views as follows. For a given video, we sort the countries of its VSV in decreasing order according to the proportion of views originating from each country. We then compute the cumulative distribution of views of each video and plot

at the granularity of a country, we conduct our analysis at the same granularity throughout the paper.

the average over each popularity category (Fig. 2). A point (n, m) on the graph means that the n top countries for videos in this category account for $m\%$ of the total number of views.

Fig. 2 clearly shows that the views of niche videos (C_1, less than 10,000 views) are geographically highly concentrated: 80% of all views for videos in C_1 come from less than 15 countries. This phenomenon fades out as the popularity of videos increases, to reach an almost uniform global distribution for extremely popular videos (C_6).

Yet, this concentration effect remains relatively strong for all videos up to 100M views (categories C_1–C_5, 96.9% of all views). This shows that a proactive placement mechanism could gain from accurately predicting the top n countries from which a video's views originate. For instance, for videos in C_3 (between 100,000 and 1M views, 25.18% of all views), proactively placing video replicas in (or close to) the top 25 countries would cover 80% of all views.

We further study the geographic spread of the origins of the views by taking into account the distances between the main sources of views. The motivation behind this experiment is that it is easier to serve a video with low latency, with a single replica, for users in France and in Switzerland than for users in the UK and in India. For each video, we compute the average of the pairwise distance between the main sources of views (i.e., the top country covering 80% of the views), weighted by the proportion of views each country is responsible for. For instance, for a video viewed 1,000 times, whose three main sources are US (500 views), UK (200 views), and Japan (100 views), our metric is:

$$\frac{(0.5 + 0.2)d(\mathsf{us}, \mathsf{uk}) + (0.2 + 0.1)d(\mathsf{uk}, \mathsf{jp}) + (0.1 + 0.5)d(\mathsf{jp}, \mathsf{us})}{(0.5 + 0.2) + (0.2 + 0.1) + (0.1 + 0.5)},$$

In our dataset, we observed this average distance to be 26% less for unpopular videos ($\sim 5{,}200$ km) than for popular ones ($\sim 7{,}000$ km).

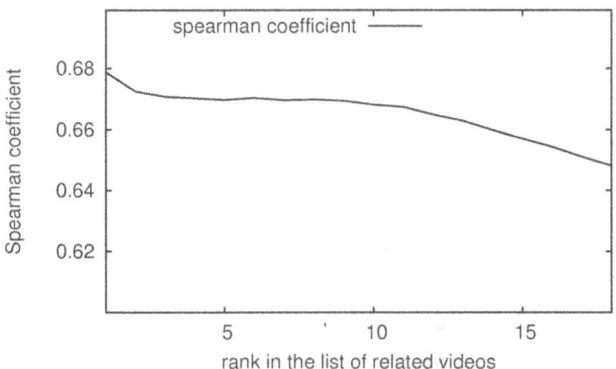

Figure 3: Spearman correlation coefficient between a video's geographic distribution of views and that of its related videos, as a function of their rank in the list of related videos

2.3 Geographic vs. Content Locality

To explore how the top n countries of a video might be predicted, we now turn to the relation between *content locality* and *geographic locality*. For each video, we compute the Spearman correlation coefficient between its sorted VSV (i.e., the list of all countries sorted by decreasing number of views) and that of each of its related videos, and plot it as a function of the rank in the list of related videos (see Fig. 3). The Spearman coefficient captures the correlation between the rank of countries in two sorted VSVs, taking into account the permutations of ranks. The closer the absolute value of the coefficient to 1, the more correlated the lists. In our dataset, this correlation is relatively high for all related videos (in 0.64-0.68, Fig. 3) and decreases with the rank. This means that a video's VSV can be inferred from that of its related videos, and that the first related videos are the best candidates.

In order to see if the above finding can be translated into an efficient mechanism for proactively placing video replicas, we conduct the following experiment. For a given video V and its first related $Rel(V)[1]$, we compute for a given number m of replicas, the percentage of views covered by placing them on the first m countries of the VSV of $Rel(V)[1]$, normalized by the percentage of views covered by placing the replicas on the first m countries of the actual VSV of V. The later corresponds to an ideal case where the placement mechanism knows in advance where the views will come from. The results are presented in Fig. 4: even for a small number of replicas, this simple prediction mechanism can accurately follow the actual geographic distribution of the views of a given video. For instance, 85% of the views covered by the first 5 countries of V's VSV are covered by the first 5 countries of $Rel(V)[1]$'s VSV.

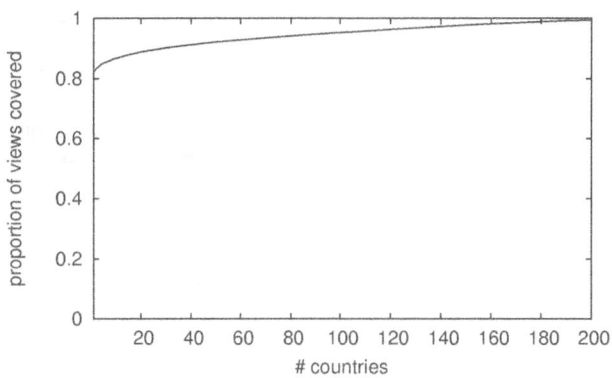

Figure 4: Views covered by placing replicas of a video V in top-countries of the VSV of V's first related video, normalized by the number of views covered when using V's actual VSV.

In summary, unpopular videos, which represent a large proportion of the YouTube dataset, have (i) most of their views originating from a few countries which (ii) spread in a limited region, thus foreseeing a great potential for geographic locality-aware data placement. Furthermore, the geographic distribution of views of a video is strongly correlated with that of its related videos. This implies that the geographic distribution of views of a video can be predicted, but most importantly, it makes the case for a placement mechanism in which videos close in the content graph are stored geographically close to one another.

3. DTUBE

Building on the insight from the previous section, we propose DTUBE, a proactive placement mechanism that places videos close to their future requests, extracting geographical patterns from the content graph.

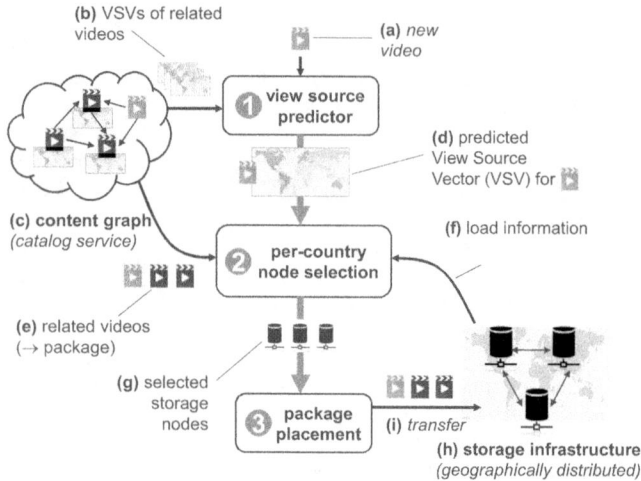

Figure 5: Overview of DTube's placement strategy.

3.1 System model

We consider a UGC sharing system that uses geographically-distributed nodes as its storage infrastructure. Our findings hold for both residential gateways [7, 11], and peer-assisted CDN systems [8].

DTUBE assumes the existence of a *catalog service* that holds, for each video, the location of its replicas, its current View Source Vector and its meta-data including the list of its related videos. This service is used to retrieve up-to-date meta-data about videos. We further assume the existence of a recommendation algorithm that dynamically computes videos' lists of related videos and updates the catalog accordingly.

3.2 Video placement

The key steps of DTUBE's placement mechanism are depicted in Fig. 5. When a new video V is uploaded to the system (a), YouTube's recommendation mechanism computes the related videos list, thus making it part of the content graph (c). DTUBE then estimates V's main future view sources, $\widehat{\mathsf{VSV}}(V)$ (d) which is later used to place replicas of V on $\Re$ storage nodes. $\Re$ is a system parameter called *replication factor* and corresponds to the minimum number of replicas a video must have to ensure *durability* in case of storage node failure. In Section 2 we showed that the higher the position of a video in V's related videos list, the higher the correlation between its VSV and the one of V. Applying this finding, we compute $\widehat{\mathsf{VSV}}(V) = \mathsf{VSV}(Rel(V)[1])$ (d) by obtaining the VSV of its first related video (b) from the catalog (d). One may envision a more sophisticated prediction strategy that combines the VSV of several related videos. Yet simple, our strategy performs well (see Section 4).

Each of the $\Re$ replicas of V attracts a replica of each of V's related videos $Rel(V)$ (e). We call this bundle of $|Rel(V)|+1$ videos a *package*, with V being a *primary* replica and the others, *secondary* replicas. This *package* mechanism creates a coupling between *content* and *geographic* locality, as related videos are placed on the same node. In addition, a coupling is established between a video's *number of replicas* (primary and secondary) and its *in-degree* in the content graph. This is a desirable property as it is shown in [18] that there is a strong correlation between the view count of a video and those of its top referrer videos, i.e., its in-degree.

Each *package* of a video V is placed on a node in each of the $\Re$ first countries of $\widehat{\mathsf{VSV}}(V)$ (d) as most views are expected to come from these countries. To minimize transfer and storage costs, only replicas of the videos that *do not* exist in the country are transferred. In addition, to evenly balance the load among the nodes in the system, for a node to be eligible to store a new *package*, the number of videos it already stores must be lower than the average storage load over all nodes (this value can be computed with a standard averaging gossip protocol). Finally, copies of the package are transferred (i) to the selected nodes (g).

4. EVALUATION

In this section, we evaluate through simulations the performance of DTUBE with respect to the geographic distance between users and the storage nodes serving the videos and compare it against a system that employs *reactive* caching on top of persistent storage.

4.1 Evaluation Setup

We distribute the storage nodes in countries according to the proportion of views originating from this country as observed in our dataset (see Tab. 1). We set the number of storage nodes to 10,000 and we consider the videos from our dataset, with the corresponding popularity and the content-graph induced by the related video feature.

We generate synthetic view traffic based on individual users' behavior, using the model proposed in [18], with the popularity values from our dataset: We consider a number of users (50,000 in our experiments), distributed across all countries as storage nodes according to the geographic distribution of views observed in our dataset (see Tab. 1). The number of videos a user watches during a session is picked at random, with an average value of 10. The first video V a user watches is selected from the whole set of videos according to the probability of this video being watched in her country, i.e., the number of views for V originating from her country divided by the total number of views originating from her country (for all videos). Each subsequent video she watches is selected among the related videos of the previous video, excluding already viewed ones. The probability of a video being picked is set to be inversely proportional to the video's rank in V's list of related videos, following a Zipf distribution.

4.2 DTube and Alternatives

We compare DTUBE against standard caching. For DTUBE, we use the placement algorithm as described in Section 3. In addition, we implement and evaluate several variations of DTUBE to identify the performance gains conveyed by the different mechanisms involved, namely without the use of packages (Partial DTUBE) and using the actual VSV of the video (Ideal DTUBE) instead of that of its first related video. Ideal DTUBE can be thought of as an upper bound on DTUBE's performance and reflects how the efficiency of the VSV prediction mechanism (evaluated in Section 2) translates in practice with respect to the viewer experience. In our experiments, videos are served from the node closest to the user.

As for caching, we consider a storage infrastructure composed of *persistent* storage nodes (e.g., YouTube servers)

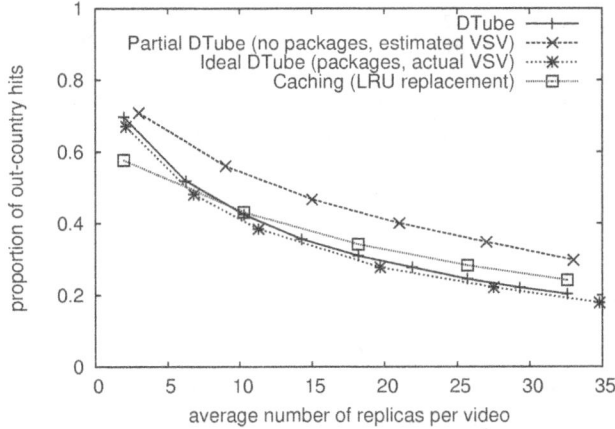

Figure 6: Proportion of out-country requests with DTube and caching.

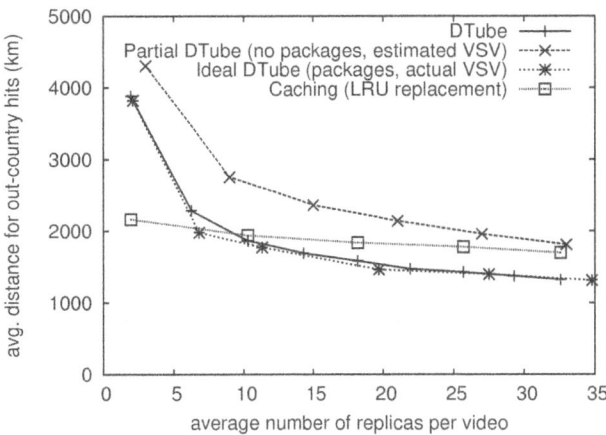

Figure 7: Average distance to storage node for out-country requests with DTube and caching.

and CDN *caching* nodes (e.g., Akamai servers). The persistent storage nodes hold a complete copy of the YouTube dataset, thus ensuring durability. Videos are only served by CDN nodes, the caches of which are populated in a reactive fashion, based on the users' view traffic: Consider a user located in a given country who requests a given video. If the video is stored on a CDN node in this country, it is served from this node to the user. If not, the video is first fetched from a persistent node to a random CDN node (with free storage space) in the country and then served. If none of the CDN nodes in the country has sufficient free storage space to store the video, we apply LRU cache replacement: the least recently used video is replaced by the new entry.

4.3 Evaluation Results

We evaluate and compare the performance of all placement strategies with respect to the geographic distance between the user and the node serving the video. More specifically, we look at (i) the out-country hit-rate, that is the proportion of requests that are served from a storage node (i.e., a gateway or a CDN node) located in a different country than the user, and (ii) the distance between the user and the storage node when the video is served from a different country. We assume that networking infrastructure is usually well integrated in each country, thus in-country hits are likely to encounter better network quality and that geographic distance is a good indicator of transfer latency.

In order for DTUBE and caching to be comparable, we use the same storage space in both. More specifically, for a given replication factor $\Re$, we first run simulations with DTUBE. Because it makes use of packages, the average number of replicas R per video is larger than $\Re$. We therefore run simulations with caching, for a system composed of $\Re$ persistent storage nodes and CDN nodes with a storage space of $(R-\Re) \times$ (total number of videos)/(number of CDN nodes), which corresponds to the same total storage space as for DTUBE. We evaluate our metrics at steady state, i.e., when all the caches of all CDN nodes are full.

Fig. 6 depicts the out-country hit-rate for the different versions of DTUBE and caching. It can be observed that for larger values of the average number of replicas per videos, DTUBE outperforms the caching-based solution. For instance, for an average number of 30 replicas per video, DTUBE decreases the proportion of out-country request from 0.25 to 0.21, that is a 16% improvement. By comparing DTUBE to Ideal DTUBE and Partial DTUBE, we observe that (i) the use of packages accounts for a significant part of DTUBE's performance, (ii) the estimation of a video's VSV from that of its related videos (i.e., based on the content graph) incurs only a little decrease in performance compared to an omniscient solution in which the actual VSV is known in advance. This illustrates the synergy between our geographic prediction and the use of packages. Similar results can be observed in Fig. 7, which depicts the average distance between the user and the storage node serving the video for out-country requests. For instance, with an average of 30 replicas per videos, DTUBE reduces the average distance by 29%. Note that the distance remains relatively high as the distance to the closest country can be large, e.g., ∼2000km between the US and Canada which are the two main sources of views.

5. RELATED WORK

YouTube has generated numerous studies on user behavior and video characteristics: Cha *et al.* propose to use a video's history to predict its future demand [3], while Zhou *et al.* in [18] study the impact of a video's position in the content graph on its popularity. In [2], Brodersen *et al.* analyze the correlation between popularity and geographical locality. Finally, Torres *et al.* [16] evaluated YouTube's CDN performance.

In [11], the authors show the feasibility of building a system like YouTube, using residential gateways. The concept of CDNs composed of gateways has been investigated for decentralized video storage and delivery in [7]. Peer-assisted CDNs also received a great deal of attention lately [8, 4, 17]. However, none of the proposed systems leverages the content graph.

In [14], monitoring social cascades in online social networks is proposed to predict a video's future view pattern. Kangasharju *et al.* [9] investigate optimal placement strategies in P2P content networks to maximize availability in content communities. Tan *et al.* [15] investigate the same problem for VoD but focus on upload bandwidth.

Volley [1] leverages the content graph to place the data so that the perceived latency is decreased. But contrary to

DTUBE, there is only one copy of each content item as data durability is not considered. NetTube [5] is a peer-assisted VoD system that leverages the content graph of UGC videos through social-aware pre-fetching and overlays to optimize swarming and decrease start-up delays. Finally, SPAR [12] is a social partitioning and replication system that achieves *one-hop replication* of user profiles in social networks.

6. CONCLUSION

In this paper we have highlighted the correlation between content locality and geographic locality in User Generated Content (UGC). More precisely, we have shown using a large YouTube dataset that related videos present similar geographic viewing patterns and that, except for extremely popular videos, video views are concentrated in a limited number of countries.

This coupling between content and geographic locality in UGC system has led us to propose DTUBE, a decentralized storage infrastructure which *proactively* places content close to their future requests leveraging on the videos' positions in the content graph.

In the future, we plan to investigate the serving part of our UGC system: more specifically, how to adapt the number of replicas and bandwidth allocation to the popularity of the videos and how to efficiently prefetch and serve videos from multiple storage nodes. We also plan to consider how caching and geographic view prediction can be combined, e.g., by exploring how predicted views might be used in the cache's replacement strategy.

Acknowledgment

This work has been partially funded by the ERC Starting Grant GOSSPLE number 204742.

7. REFERENCES

[1] AGARWAL, S., DUNAGAN, J., JAIN, N., SAROIU, S., WOLMAN, A., AND BHOGAN, H. Volley: Automated Data Placement for Geo-Distributed Cloud Services. In *NSDI* (2010).

[2] BRODERSEN, A., SCELLATO, S., AND WATTENHOFER, M. YouTube Around the World: Geographic Popularity of Videos. In *WWW* (2012).

[3] CHA, M., KWAK, H., RODRIGUEZ, P., AHN, Y.-Y., AND MOON, S. I Tube, You Tube, Everybody Tubes: Analyzing the World's Largest User Generated Content Video System. In *IMC* (2007).

[4] CHEN, Z., LIN, C., YIN, H., AND LI, B. On the Server Placement Problem of P2P Live Media Streaming System. In *PCM* (2008).

[5] CHENG, X., AND LIU, J. NetTube: Exploring Social Networks for Peer-to-Peer Short Video Sharing. In *INFOCOM* (2009).

[6] GILL, P., ARLITT, M., LI, Z., AND MAHANTI, A. YouTube Traffic Characterization: A View From The Edge. In *IMC* (2007).

[7] HE, J., CHAINTREAU, A., AND DIOT, C. A Performance Evaluation of Scalable Live Video Streaming with Nano Data Centers. *Computer Networks 53* (2009), 153–167.

[8] HUANG, C., WANG, A., LI, J., AND ROSS, K. W. Understanding Hybrid CDN-P2P: Why Limelight Needs its Own Red Swoosh. In *NOSSDAV* (2008).

[9] KANGASHARJU, J., ROSS, K. W., AND TURNER, D. A. Optimizing File Availability in Peer-to-Peer Content Distribution. In *INFOCOM* (2007).

[10] KHEMMARAT, S., ZHOU, R., GAO, L., AND ZINK, M. Watching User Generated Videos with Prefetching. In *MMSys* (2011).

[11] MARCON, M., VISWANATH, B., CHA, M., AND GUMMADI, K. P. Sharing Social Content from Home: A Measurement-driven Feasibility Study. In *NOSSDAV* (2011).

[12] PUJOL, J. M., ERRAMILLI, V., SIGANOS, G., YANG, X., LAOUTARIS, N., CHHABRA, P., AND RODRIGUEZ, P. The Little Engine(s) That Could: Scaling Online Social Networks. In *SIGCOMM* (2010).

[13] SAXENA, M., SHARAN, U., AND FAHMY, S. Analyzing Video Services in Web 2.0: A Global Perspective. In *NOSSDAV* (2008).

[14] SCELLATO, S., MASCOLO, C., MUSOLESI, M., AND CROWCROFT, J. Track Globally, Deliver Locally: Improving Content Delivery Networks by Tracking Geographic Social Cascades. In *WWW* (2011).

[15] TAN, B. R., AND MASSOULIÉ, L. Adaptive Content Placement for Peer-to-Peer Video-on-Demand Systems. *CoRR abs/1004.4709* (2010).

[16] TORRES, R., FINAMORE, A., KIM, J. R., MELLIA, M., MUNAFÒ, M., AND RAO, S. Dissecting Video Server Selection Strategies in the YouTube CDN. In *ICDCS* (2011).

[17] YIN, H., LIU, X., ZHAN, T., SEKAR, V., QIU, F., LIN, C., ZHANG, H., AND LI, B. LiveSky: Enhancing CDN with P2P. *ACM TOMCCAP 6* (2010), 16:1–16:19.

[18] ZHOU, R., KHEMMARAT, S., AND GAO, L. The Impact of YouTube Recommendation System on Video Views. In *IMC* (2010).

Video Sharing in Online Social Networks: Measurement and Analysis

Haitao Li, Haiyang Wang, Jiangchuan Liu
School of Computing Science
Simon Fraser University, Vancouver, BC, Canada
Email: {haitaol, hwa17, jcliu}@sfu.ca

Ke Xu
Department of Computer Science & Technology
Tsinghua University, Beijing, China
Email: xuke@mail.tsinghua.edu.cn

ABSTRACT

Online social networks (OSNs) have become popular destinations for connecting friends and sharing information. Recent statistics suggest that OSN users regularly share contents from video sites, and a significant amount of requests of the video sites are indeed from them nowadays. These behaviors have substantially changed the workload of online video services. To better understand this paradigm shift, we conduct a long-term and extensive measurement of video sharing in RenRen, the largest Facebook-like OSN in China. In this paper, we focus on the video popularity distribution and evolution. In particular, we find that the video popularity distribution exhibits perfect power-law feature (while videos in YouTube exhibit a power-law waist with a long truncated tail). Moreover, we observe that the requests for the new published videos generally experience two or three days latency to reach the peak value, and then change dynamically with a series of unpredictable bursts (while in YouTube, videos reach the global peak immediately after introduction to the system, and then the accesses generally decrease overtime, except possibly on some special days). These differences can raise new challenges to content providers. For example, the video popularity is now hard to predict based on their historical requests. We further develop a simple yet effective model to simulate user requests process across videos in OSNs. Trace-based simulation shows that it can well capture the observed features.

Categories and Subject Descriptors

J.4 [**Social and Behavioral Sciences**]: Sociology; H.3.5 [**Information Storage and Retrieval**]: Online Information Services—*Web-based services*

General Terms

Measurement, Performance

Permission to make digital or hard copies of all or part of this work for personal or classroom use is granted without fee provided that copies are not made or distributed for profit or commercial advantage and that copies bear this notice and the full citation on the first page. To copy otherwise, to republish, to post on servers or to redistribute to lists, requires prior specific permission and/or a fee.
NOSSDAV'12, June 7–8, 2012, Toronto, Ontario, Canada.
Copyright 2012 ACM 978-1-4503-1430-5/12/06 ...$10.00.

Keywords

Social network, video sharing, popularity distribution, popularity evolution, power-law

1. INTRODUCTION

Traditionally, users have discovered videos on the Web by browsing or searching [5]. Recently, word-of-mouth has emerged as a popular way of discovering the videos, particularly on social network sites such as Facebook and Twitter [11]. On these sites, users discover video contents by following their friends' shares. Such word-of-mouth based content discovery has become a major driver of traffic to many video sharing sites. YouTube statistics [2] reported that as of January 2011 more than 500 tweets per minute containing a YouTube link, and over 150 years worth of YouTube video is watched on Facebook every day. Besides Facebook(Twitter)/YouTube, we have seen similar trends in other OSNs/VSSes, for example, between RenRen [3], the biggest Facebook-like OSN in China, and Youku [4], one of the most popular video sharing sites in China. Our measurement shows that, as of July 2011, more than 54 million unique RenRen users have participated in video viewing and 20 million participated in sharing, generating 12.4 million views, and 1.64 million shares every day. 80% of these videos are hosted by Youku.

However, such characteristics have not yet been explored in real online social networks at large scales due to a number of challenges. First, privacy protection generally prevents crawling video viewing information as easily in OSNs (e.g., Facebook/RenRen) as in VSSes (e.g., YouTube/Youku); Second, unlike dedicated video sites, OSNs can rarely provide rich statistics about shared videos; Finally, given the wide distribution of OSN users, tracing traffic from a small set of network routers/switches can hardly reveal the geographic evolution of video sharing, not to mention the sheer volume of the mixed network traffic to be analyzed.

To understand video sharing in OSNs, we closely collaborate with RenRen to analyze its server access logs. Starting from March 24th, 2011, we recorded the detailed user video viewing and sharing behaviors over three months. When a user started to view a video shared by her/his friend or further shares the video, a separate record was sent to the log server. The trace data records such information as the time, viewer, sharer, and video URL, which enable us to extract rich statistics. Our measurement unveils many distinctive features of video sharing through OSNs as compared to VSSes, especially on the video popularity distribution and evolution. For popularity distribution, we find that the plot of requests and video ranks exhibits perfect power-law feature (while previous study [9] showed that in VSSes, it exhibits a power-law waist with a long truncated tail). We also find the user requests are much more skewed across the videos in OSNs (top-0.5% videos account for 80% requests) than that in VSSes (10%-80%). To further understand these unique features, we design a model to simulate the user requests process in OSNs, and analyze whether the OSN-based spreading mechanism can result in the observed distribution. For popularity evolution, we observe that the requests for the new published videos generally experience two or three days latency to reach the peak value, and then change dynamically with a series of unpredictable bursts (while in YouTube, videos reach the global peak immediately, and then the accesses generally decrease overtime, except possibly on some special days).

The rest of the paper is organized as follows. We present related works in Section 2. Sections 3 gives an overview of the RenRen OSN and our measurement methodology. We present measurement results on the video popularity distribution in Sections 4. In Section 5, we further design a model to analyze how OSN-based spreading mechanism can change the user requests across videos. We make a preliminary study of the video popularity evolution in Section 6. Finally, we conclude in Section 7.

2. RELATED WORK

To our best knowledge, our work is the first one on characterizing the patterns of video requests from OSNs, by measurement and model. There are some pioneer data-driven analysis of information spreading in OSNs. Cha et al. [12] conducted a large-scale measurement study on Flickr network, one of the most popular photo sharing social networks. They found that even popular photos spread slowly through the network. By contrast, we found that the videos in an OSN spread much faster. Rorigues et al. [11] studied the propagation of URL links posted in Twitter, using large data gathered from Twitter. They presented the distribution of height, width, and size of propagation trees and found that Twitter yields propagation trees that are wider than they are deep. They did not separate the video links from their dataset to give them an individual analysis. Scellato et al. [16] pointed that given the increasing size of Twitter and other OSNs, they may generate millions of accesses to YouTube, accounting for a consistent fraction of the total number of daily requests. Instead of studying the video popularity characteristics, they focused on the geographic property of social cascades of videos by tracking social cascades of YouTube links over Twitter.

There are also plenty of works on the user access patterns from video sharing sites (e.g., YouTube) either by crawling the webpages or tracing traffic from a set of network routers/switches. Cha et al. [9] presented an in-depth study of the static popularity distribution, and dynamic popularity evolution of videos in two large-scale VSSes, YouTube and Daum. They found that the video popularity in YouTube shows a power-law waist with a long truncated tail for huge unpopular videos. Cheng et al. [10] also studied the distribution and evolution of videos in YouTube, and found similar results. They further presented other statistics of YouTube video files such the length, bitrate, and size. More recently, Figueiredo et al. [14] made an in-depth analysis on how the popularity of individual videos evolves since the video's upload time. They found that popularity growth pattern depends on the choice of the video dataset. Besides those works that focused on the global nature of YouTube traffic by crawling YouTube webpages, and there are some complementary works by collecting YouTube traffic from local networks. Gill et al. [7] characterized the YouTube traffic collected at the University of Calgary campus network, comparing its properties with those previously reported for Web and streaming media workloads. They analyzed daily and weekly patterns as well as several videos characteristics such as duration, bitrate, age, ratings, and category. Another similar study [8] by Zink et al. also analyzed network traces for YouTube traffic at a campus network to understand the benefits of alternative content distribution strategies. Our work focuses on the distinguished features for videos shared in the RenRen OSN especially regarding video popularity distribution and evolution. And we demonstrate the word-of-mouth based social sharing can dramatically affect the pattern of user requests for videos.

3. BACKGROUND AND MEASUREMENT

This section gives an overview of the RenRen online social network and our measurement methodology.

3.1 The RenRen Social Network

Launched in 2005, RenRen is the earliest and so far the largest OSN in China. RenRen can be best characterized as Facebook's Chinese twin, implementing Facebook's features, layout, and a similar user interface. Like Facebook, RenRen's users can post video links from VSSes. Unlike Facebook, RenRen has two unique features that make it an attractive platform for our study. First, while RenRen users have full privacy control over their private profiles, their shared videos are public and thus can be crawled. For example, each individual user has a page that list all shared videos with their statistics, including the number of views and shares within RenRen. Second and perhaps more importantly, RenRen provides certain proprietary information about users' viewing behaviors.

Video sharing in RenRen is based on the friend relationships. Initially, a user shares a video link from a VSS in RenRen; This link immediately appears in her/his friends' main page as a "News Feed" in chronological order; Meanwhile, this shared video is also listed in the sharer's home page, which lists all her/his ever shared contents. Then her/his friends will probably click the shared video appeared in "News Feed"; or they may regularly visit friends' home pages to watch those shared videos, though this frequency is much lower than the first way. A video can be further propagated if some viewers share the link again.

3.2 Measurement Methodology

To understand the video sharing in OSNs, we closely collaborate with RenRen to analyze its server access logs. Starting from March 24th, 2011, RenRen had been recording the detailed user video viewing and sharing behaviors over three months. When a user starts to view a video shared by her/his friend or further shares the video, a separate record will be sent to the log server. The data record of each viewing action includes: (*Starting Time, Viewer ID, Video URL, Direct Sharer ID, Original Sharer ID*). We use an example to explain the data format. Initially, $User_A$ shared $Video_1$

(denoted by URL_1) from a video sharing site; At $Time_1$, $User_B$ watched URL_1 through the share link created by $User_A$, and $User_B$ further shared URL_1 after watching it; At the $Time_2$, $User_C$ watched URL_1 through the share link created by $User_B$. For the viewing behaviors of $User_B$ and $User_C$, two records are reported: ($Time_1$, $User_B$, URL_1, $User_A$, $User_A$) and ($Time_2$, $User_C$, URL_1, $User_B$, $User_A$). Similarly, the format of sharing action is (*Creating Time, Video URL, Creating User, Direct Sharer, Original Sharer*). Table 1 summarizes our dataset with basic statics in one-day period (March 24th, 2011). In this paper, we use both short-term traces (from one day to one week) to analyze the video popularity distribution, and long-term traces (several months) to explore the video popularity evolution. Since all trace data are within 2011, we omit the year index in the later sections.

Table 1: Summary of trace in one-day period

Views	Shares	Users	Videos	NewVideos
12,432,708	1,628,852	3,514,461	201,517	71,236

4. VIDEO POPULARITY DISTRIBUTION

In this section, we present the measurement results on video popularity[1] distribution in the RenRen OSN from two perspectives: Pareto principle and Power-law behavior, and compare them with the corresponding results in VSSes, which were studied by a previous work of Cha et al. [9].

4.1 Pareto Principle

The Pareto principle [15] (also known as the 80-20 rule) is widely used to describe the skewness in distributions. For example, the analysis of YouTube shows that 10% of the most popular videos account for 80% of user requests [9]. It is interesting to see whether the social-network-based sharing amplifies or smooths this skewness. As shown in Fig. ??, we can see a dramatically skewed result that 0.5% videos account for more than 80% of the total requests (the x-axis of this figure represents the videos sorted from the most popular videos to the least popular ones, with video ranks being normalized between 0 and 1); and top-2% videos account for 90% of the total requests. This suggests that OSNs amplify the skewness of video popularity. For attractive videos, more friends would view them if some users shares them; and again with higher probability these viewers will further share them. For unattractive videos, few users want to view them and are also not likely to share them after the viewing. Such difference in videos' attractiveness[2] can be further amplified over the cascading process along friend links. Therefore, attractive videos become more popular and unattractive videos become more unpopular and fade out quickly. An immediate implication of this skewed distribution is that caching can be made very efficient since storing only a small set of objects can produce high hit ratios.

To further analyze user requests distribution, we also take a closer look at the videos that are initially shared on the

---

[1] We define a video's *popularity* as the amount of requests to this video.
[2] We use the term of *attractiveness* to reflect whether a video is likely to be watched and shared by users when they see it in their "News Feed" pages.

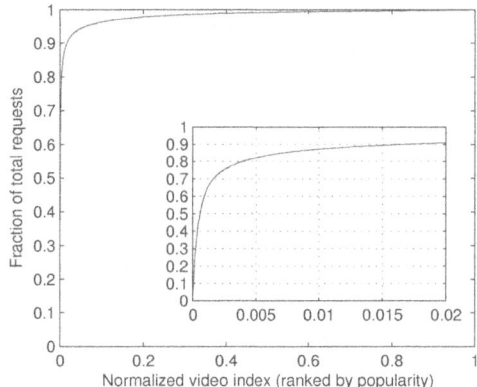

Figure 1: Skewness of requests across all videos

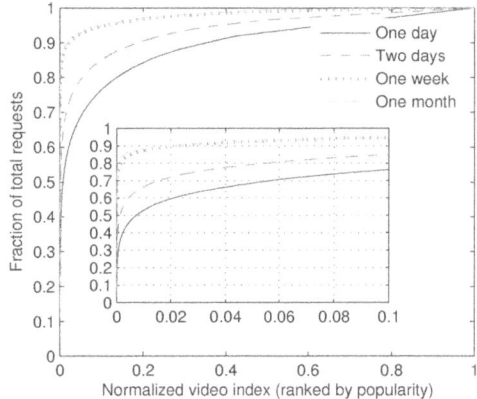

Figure 2: Requests of videos initially shared on the same day

same day (March 24th). Since mostly users are more interested in newly updated videos, this analysis will avoid the possible bias due to different video ages. We count the cumulative requests of those videos within one day, two days, one week, and one month respectively since March 24th, and plot the results in Fig. 2. Similarly, the popularity of those videos also exhibits such a high skewness that the top-2% popular videos account for 90% of the total requests. We also notice that the skewness increases as the time-window increases, and almost converges after one week.

4.2 Power-law Behavior

The Power-law model [15] has been increasingly used to explain various statistics appearing in the computer science and network systems. To check the power-law pattern for the videos in OSNs, Fig. 3 plots the requests versus video ranks of all videos initially shared on the same day. We find that the plot exhibits perfect power-law (the exponent value is also given in the figure) pattern[3], and the curves of different days are very similar except for some top videos. As a comparison, the video popularity in YouTube shows a power-law waist, with a long truncated tail for huge un-

---

[3] A distinguished feature of power-law is a straight line in the log-log plot.

popular videos and sharp decay for popular videos [9]. It indicates that OSNs provide chance for all videos (including niche videos) to become popular, and they also amplify the effect of difference in videos' attractiveness along the spreading process. Next we will propose a model to further analyze the reason under this power-law distribution.

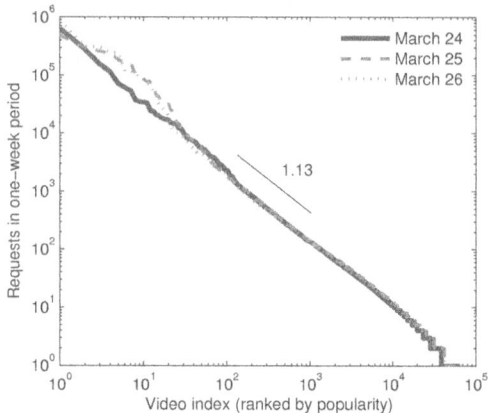

Figure 3: Requests versus video ranks (log-log)

5. MODEL ANALYSIS

Our measurement has shown distinctive popularity distribution pattern for video sharing in OSNs. To further testify whether the OSN-based spreading mechanism is the underlying reason for these features, we develop a simple yet effective model to make some preliminary analysis.

5.1 Modeling Video Spreading Process

Preferential attachment process is widely used to simulate the processes whose underlying mechanism is *rich-get-richer*. The most common example is Yule-Simon process [13], which was first introduced by Yule to study the growth in the number of species per genus. A general form of this process can be described as follows: balls are added to the system at an overall rate of m new balls for each new urn. Each newly created urn starts out with k_0 balls and further balls are added to urns at a rate proportional to the number that they already have (v_i) plus a constant $c > k_0$. In other words, when an existing entity has to be incremented by one, the ith entity is chosen with probability $P(i)$:

$$P(i) = \frac{v_i + c}{\sum_{j=1}^{n} v_j + nc} \quad (1)$$

where n is the current number of urns in the system.

It is intuitive that the videos that have gained more requests have more chance to gain more requests, and this is the reason why we choose Yule-Simon Process as the basics of of model. However, it is not enough to directly apply this process to capture the video spreading process in OSNs, because it is not precise that the rate for a new request to be assigned to a video is proportional to the number of users that have already watched this video. In fact, at a given moment the number of potential requests for a video is determined by the number of users who can find this video in their "News Feed" pages but have not yet watched it. And the number of users who can find a video is mainly determined by the number of shares of this video, because in OSNs almost all videos that a user can find come from the shares of their friends. Now we formulate the preferential attachment mechanism in video spreading process by the following equation:

$$P(i) = \frac{E_i - V_i}{\sum_{j=1}^{n}(E_i - V_i)} \quad (2)$$

where $P(i)$ indicates the probability that a new request will be assigned to video i; n is the current number of videos in the system; E_i is the expected total number of requests for current shares of video i; V_i is number of requests that have happened. Thus, the value of $E_i - V_i$ reflects the number of expected requests in the future for current shares.

Therefore, the user requests process in an OSN can be described as follows: initially, all videos have one share and zero request; when a new user request comes, the model chooses video i by Eq. 2 and adds one user access to current V_i; after that it determines whether this user will further share this video by a probability–$ShareRate(ShR)$. Then if the user shares, it uses a random variable–$BranchingFactor$ (BrF) to determine the expected number of requests for this share and add BrF to current E_i. We can find that two main inputs (BrF and ShR) determine this process. BrF reflects the number of requests that follow a share, and is determined by both the video's attractiveness and the number of the sharer's friends. ShR reflects the probability a viewer will further share the viewed video, and is simply determined by the video's attractiveness to the viewer.

5.2 Validation and Analysis

We first validate whether our model can reflect the real video spreading process in OSNs by inputting the parameters extracted from RenRen. For the number of videos and requests, we configure the same values (63,591 and 2,905,276) as those in Fig. 3. To get the distribution of BrF in Ren-Ren, we collect all 1628852 shares created on March 24th and count the followed requests separately over three months. The distribution along with the fitting function are shown in Fig. 4. We also notice that the average BrF does not have obvious correlation with the total requests of a video ($\rho_p = -0.001$ and $\rho_s = -0.15$). We thus configure all videos with the same BrF distribution. To get the distribution of ShR, we collect all 12,432,708 views on March 24th and record whether there is a following share behavior after the view. We count the average ShR for each video separately and show the distribution of ShR along with the fitting function in Fig. 5. One key observation in our measurement is that the plot of requests versus video ranks shows perfect power-law distribution. As shown in Fig. 6, we can see the simulation result and real-world data are pretty matched. We also count the skewness of the video popularity distribution, and the simulation result shows that the top-2% videos account for 85% of the total requests, which is very close to our observation (2%-90%). In summary, these results thus verify the validity of our model.

Given the video popularity distribution in a VSS, we now analyze whether the OSN-based spreading mechanism can amplify the skewness of such popularity distribution. To do this, we first collect all Youku (YouTube-like VSS) videos shared in RenRen in one-day period, and crawl the number of their requests in Youku VSS. We then translate the num-

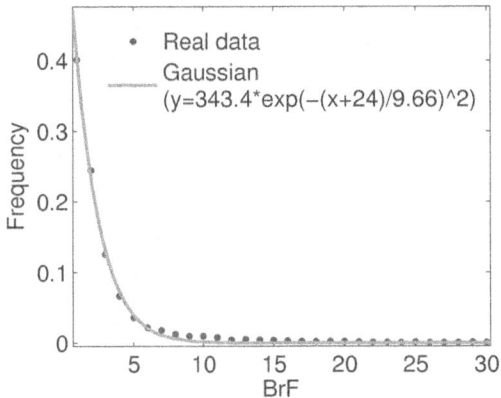

Figure 4: Distribution of BrF

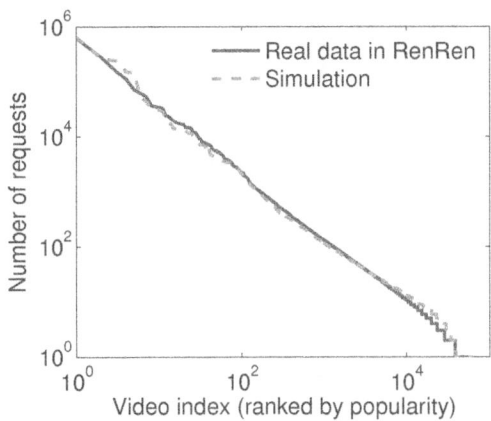

Figure 6: Model validation

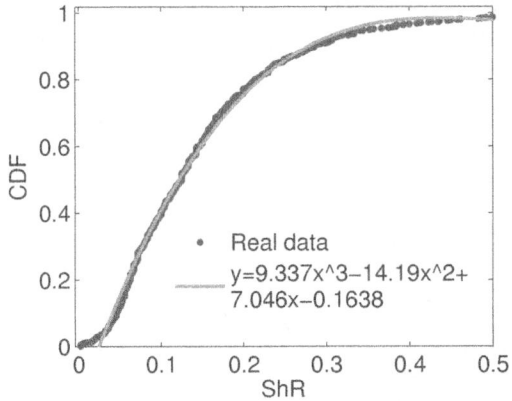

Figure 5: Distribution of ShR

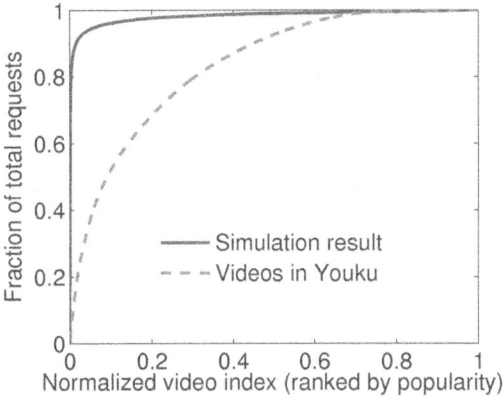

Figure 7: Popularity comparison

ber of video requests in YouTube to the value of ShR in our model by a linear function [4]. Finally, we simulate our model taking such a ShR distribution as the input parameter. For BrF, we configure the same distribution as that in Fig. 4. The comparison result is shown in Fig. 7. The result indicates that the difference in videos' attractiveness is indeed amplified over their spreading in OSNs.

6. VIDEO POPULARITY EVOLUTION

So far we have studied the static properties of video popularity. In this section, we make some preliminary analysis on video popularity evolution since they are initially shared in OSNs. When a video is shared in an OSN, it will start to attract users' attention and the number of requests will change over time. Fig. 8 shows the popularity evolution of three representative groups of videos over three months, with each group consisting of all videos with identical age (we sample three sets of videos that were initially shared on March 24th, 25th, 26th perspectively). We observe that the requests for the new published videos generally experience two or three days latency to reach the peak value, and then change dynamically with a series of unpredictable

---

[4]Actually their relationship is much more complicated and need further study. Here we choose the linear function as a simplified case.

bursts (while in YouTube, videos reach the global peak immediately after introduction to the system, and then the accesses generally decrease overtime, except possibly on some special days). An intuitive explanation for the local bursts is that, when the video is shared by a *super spreader* (the user who has a great number of friends), the video's popularity is very likely to increase again in the OSN. The fact that the local bursts for different groups do not appear on the same day also indicates the dynamic of popularity evolution. Note that the evolutions are based on the overall videos (around 0.2 million on each day). Thus the evolution for individual videos could be more dynamic.

This dynamics of popularity evolution can raise significant challenges to content providers. For example, a video's popularity is now harder to predict based on their historical requests. We compare the first few days' video requests with those after some period of time (e.g., 1, 3, and 7 days) and calculate both Pearson correlation coefficient (ρ_p) [1] and Spearman's rank correlation coefficient (ρ_s) [3] [5]. As shown in Table 2, we can see that the historical requests only have

---

[5]ρ_p has been widely used for measuring the strength of linear dependence between two variables, and ρ_s assesses how well the relationship between two variables can be described using a monotonic function. The ranges of both ρ_p and ρ_s are from -1 to 1, where a value greater than 0 indicates positive correlation, and less than 0 indicates negative correlation.

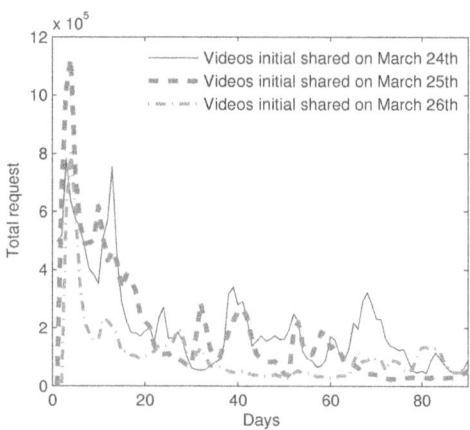

Figure 8: Popularity evolution of videos initially shared on different days

correlation with the requests in the next day, but no obvious correlation with the requests after one week. This is different from earlier study on the YouTube videos [9], where the historical requests can be effectively used to predict more distant future popularity (e.g., three months afterwards). This result suggests that some more sophisticated OSN-based models are needed to provide a better popularity prediction, which we will examine in the future work.

Table 2: Correlation (ρ_p, ρ_s) between video requests in early days and in near future

Age (x_0)	x_0+1 days	x_0+3 days	x_0+7 days
1st day	(0.48,0.53)	(0.25,0.29)	(0.13,0.21)
2nd day	(0.93,0.97)	(0.79,0.88)	(0.11,0.19)
3rd day	(0.97,0.99)	(0.80,0.89)	(0.10,0.18)

7. CONCLUSIONS AND FUTURE WORK

In this paper we presented an extensive data-driven analysis on video sharing in the RenRen OSN. Our measurement showed that videos exhibit different popularity distribution pattern compared with that in VSSes. Particularly, it shows much more popularity skewness in the OSN. We further developed a model to simulate the video spreading process in OSNs, and validated that the OSN-based spreading mechanism is the fundamental reason under such new video popularity distribution. We also made some preliminary measurement on the video popularity evolution in OSNs and revealed some distinctive features, such as the randomness, unpredictability, and multiple peaks. To capture such popularity evolution features, some enhancements are needed for our current model, and we will take this for the future work.

8. ACKNOWLEDGMENTS

Part of this work was done when Haitao Li interned at the Oak Pacific Interactive Corporation (the operator of RenRen) during the summer vacation, 2011. We want to thank the engineers from RenRen, especially Song Wen, Liang Zhang, Zhiliang Wang, Yunlong Bai, and Jing Huang. They helped us collect the data and also provided many valuable suggestions during the writing of this paper. This research was also supported by a Canada NSERC Discovery Grant, an NSERC DAS grant, a Nokia University Relation Fund, and an NSFC Major Program of International Cooperation.

9. REFERENCES

[1] J. S. Maritz. Distribution-free Statistical Methods. Chapman & Hall, 1981.

[2] YouTube Statistics. http://www.youtube.com/t/press_statistics

[3] J. Jing, W. Christo, X. Wang, P. Huang, W. Sha, Y. Dai, and B. Y. Zhao. Understanding Latent Interactions in Online Social Networks. In Proc. of IMC, 2010.

[4] K. Lai and D. Wang. Towards Understanding the External Links of Video Sharing Sites: Measurement and Analysis. In Proc. of NOSSDAV, 2010.

[5] R. Zhou, S. Khemmarat, and L. Gao. The Impact of YouTube Recommendation System on Video Views. In Proc. of IMC, 2010.

[6] X. Wu, V. Kumar, and et al.. Top 10 Algorithms in Data Minining. Journal of Knowledge and Information Systems, 2007.

[7] P. Gill, M. Arlitt, Z. Li, and A. Mahanti. YouTube Traffic Characterization: a View from the Edge. In Proc. of IMC, 2007.

[8] M. Zink, K. Suhb, Y. Gu, and J. Kurosea. Characteristics of YouTube Network Traffic at a Campus Network - Measurements, Models, and Implications. Computer Networks, 2009.

[9] M. Cha, H. Kwak, P. Rodriguez, Y. Ahn, and S. B. Moon. I Tube, You Tube, Everybody Tubes: Analyzing the Worldąŕs Largest User Generated Content Video System. In Proc. of IMC, 2007.

[10] X. Cheng, C. Dale, and J. Liu. Statistics and Social Network of YouTube Videos. In Proc. of IEEE IWQoS, 2008.

[11] T. Rodrigues, F. Benvenuto, M. Cha, K. P. Gummadi, and V. Almeida. On Word-of-Mouth Based Discovery of the Web. In Proc. of IMC, 2011.

[12] M. Cha, A. Mislove, and K. P. Gummadi. A Measurement-driven Analysis of Information Propagation in the Flickr Social Network. In Proc. of WWW, 2009.

[13] G. Yule, A Mathematical Theory of Evolution Based on the Conclusions of Dr. J. C. Willis. Philosophical Transactions of the Royal Society of London, 1925.

[14] F. Figueiredo, F. Benvenuto, and J. Almeida. The Tube over Time: Characterizing Popularity Growth of YouTube Videos. In Proc. of WSDM, 2011.

[15] M. Newman. Power Laws, Pareto Distributions and Zipfąŕs Law. Contemporary Physics, 2004.

[16] S. Scellato, C. Mascolo, M. Musolesi and J. Crowcroft. Track Globally, Deliver Locally: Improving Content Delivery Networks by Tracking Geographic Social Cascades. In Proc. of WWW, 2011.

Sensor-assisted Camera Motion Analysis and Motion Estimation Improvement for H.264/AVC Video Encoding

Guanfeng Wang, Haiyang Ma, Beomjoo Seo, Roger Zimmermann
School of Computing, National University of Singapore, Singapore 117417
{wanggf,haiyang,seobj,rogerz}@comp.nus.edu.sg

ABSTRACT

Camera motion information is one aspect that helps to infer higher-level semantic descriptions in many video applications, e.g., in video retrieval. However, an efficient methodology for annotating camera motion information is still an elusive goal. Here we propose and present a novel and efficient approach for the task of partitioning a video document into sub-shots and characterizing their camera motion. By leveraging location (GPS) and digital compass data, which are available from most current smartphone handsets, we exploit the geographical sensor information to detect transitions between two sub-shots based on the variations of both the camera location and the shooting direction. The advantage of our method lies in its considerable accuracy. Additionally, the computational efficiency of our scheme enables it to be deployed on mobile devices and to process videos while recording. We utilize this capability to show how the HEX motion estimation algorithm in the H.264/AVC encoder can be simplified with the aid of our camera motion information. Our experimental results show that we can reduce the computation of the HEX algorithm by up to 50% while achieving comparable video quality.

Categories and Subject Descriptors

I.4.2 [**IMAGE PROCESSING AND COMPUTER VISION**]: Approximate methods

General Terms

Algorithms, Design, Experimentation

Keywords

Camera motion analysis, Sensor-aided motion estimation

1. INTRODUCTION

Video cameras have already become an integral component of smartphones and other handheld devices. Due to rapid advances in their quality, wide availability and ease-of-use, it has become increasingly popular to capture, upload and share videos from mobile devices. Because phones are carried by their owners all the time videos are easily collected outdoors, e.g., during vacations and business trips.

Camera motion is a distinct feature that essentially characterizes video content in the context of content-based video analysis. It also provides a very powerful cue for structuring video data and performing similarity-based video retrieval searches. As a consequence it has been selected as one of the motion descriptors in MPEG-7. Almost all existing work relies on a content-based approach at the frame-signal level, which results in high complexity and very time-consuming processing. With the astounding development of sensor technology, we are inspired to classify the camera motion type from auxiliary sensors through light-weight computations. Specifically, we focus on videos from smartphones which are carried by millions of people and are equipped with various sensor receivers in addition to a video camera.

With the pervasiveness of these affordable, portable and networked devices, numerous video clips captured with such cameras have been published on social networking portals such as *YouTube* and benefited amateur journalism such as CNN's *iReport*. Yet, capturing videos on mobile devices is still a compute-intensive and power-hungry process. One of the key compute-intensive modules in a video encoder is the motion estimation (ME). In modern video coding standards such as H.264/AVC, ME predicts the contents of a frame by matching blocks from multiple references and by exploring multiple block sizes. Not surprisingly, the computation and power cost of video encoding pose a significant challenge for video recording on mobile devices such as smartphones.

Our solution for addressing these two challenges is to perform sensor-assisted camera motion analysis and introduce a simplified motion estimation algorithm for H.264/AVC. We employ relatively low-power sensors to classify camera motion types and subsequently apply the motion type information to significantly simplifying motion estimation. Our approach is motivated by two observations. First, modern smartphones include low-power and low-cost sensors, e.g., GPS receivers, digital compasses and accelerometers. These sensors can efficiently provide accurate geographical properties which are generally quite intrinsic to device motion characterization. Second, in many video documents, particularly in those captured by amateurs, a global motion is commonly involved owing to camera movement and shooting direction changes. In outdoor videos, e.g., videos capturing landmarks or attractions, global motion contributes significantly to the motion of objects across frames.

Our method introduces a two-step process which is outlined in Figure 1. First, as a key feature we only use geographic information to detect subshot boundaries and to infer each subshot's camera motion type from the collected sensor data without any video content processing. With generated camera motion information, we modify the HEX motion estimation algorithm used in H.264 to reduce the search window size and block comparison time for different motion categories, respectively. Our experimental evaluations show that our motion characterization method can accurately segment subshots and label their classification, and our simplified motion estimation algorithm can reduce the complexity of the H.264/AVC motion estimation with the HEX algorithm by up to 50% while speeding up the estimation component considerably.

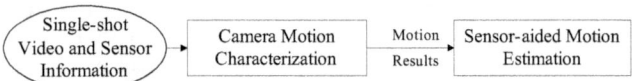

Figure 1: Overview of the proposed two-step framework.

The rest of the paper is structured as follows. Section 2 outlines the related work. In Section 3 we describe our approach to camera motion characterization and explain our method of utilizing motion information in H.264/AVC. We present the experimental results in Section 4. Finally, Section 5 draws conclusions and addresses possible future work.

2. RELATED WORK

Several approaches have been developed to estimate camera motion based on the analysis of the optical flow computed between consecutive images [13, 6, 4]. However, the estimation of the optical flow, which is usually based on gradient or block matching methods, is computationally expensive [12]. Moreover, when the camera moves fast, there will be significant displacement between consecutive frames, which may lead to an inaccurate estimation of the optical flow. Some approaches directly manipulate MPEG-compressed video to extract camera motion using the motion vectors as an alternative to optical flow [19, 16, 1, 14, 8, 17, 10]. Nonparametric motion models have also been proposed in the motion feature space [7]. Nevertheless, the MPEG motion vectors estimated by video encoders are not always consistent with the actual movement of macro-blocks since many of them correspond to the movements of foreground objects. Thus, the effectiveness of these methods relies on their preprocessing stages to reduce the influence of irrelevant motion vectors. When the video contains significant camera or object motions, such irrelevant motion vectors may be prevailing and interfering with the preprocessing stages. Furthermore, accurately detecting camera zoom operations is difficult because of the noise in motion vectors due to independent object motions in a frame or MPEG encoding properties, such as quantization errors, and other artifacts. Hence, these methods usually only work well for videos with special encoding formats. Lertrusdachakul et al. [15] analyzed camera motion by processing the trajectories of Harris interest points that are tracked over an extended time.

However, when the camera moves fast and the background content changes rapidly, interest points in the background may not be tracked for long. Additionally, the Harris interest point detector is not invariant to scale and affine transforms, which may be significant between consecutive frames when the camera moves fast. Battiato et al. [3] used motion vectors of SIFT features to estimate the camera motion in a video, but inaccurate results were prone to be generated with their approach since foreground and background features are treated without discrimination.

In the video encoding part, the key to significant temporal compression is motion estimation, which seeks to identify blocks in a frame that match those in a reference frame at different – but close – locations. To exploit the sensor information to encode videos more efficiently, Hong et al. [11] proposed an accelerometer-assisted model to simplify the motion estimation part in the encoder. However, the authors only considered the horizontal and vertical movements of the camera. Their experimental evaluations is based on MPEG-2, which is no longer a state-of-the-art compression technique. Another sensor assisted motion estimation algorithm proposed by Chen et al. [5] employed additional digital compass information and measurements were obtained with H.264/AVC. Nevertheless, their work is still limited to rotational camera movements. Both the above algorithms cannot handle linear camera movement, which is very common in video clips taken by handheld devices. Furthermore, the sensor information utilized by those algorithms only leveraged accelerometer and compass information, while there are other sensors available, which could also improve the efficiency of video encoding. In addition, the European patent application EP1921867 presents an idea of using vehicle movement information to assist in video compression [18]. However, this method focuses on vehicle motion and a vehicle-mounted camera, and provides no implementation or evaluation.

3. FRAMEWORK DESIGN

We utilize a stream of sensor data which is simultaneously collected with video frames to describe the geographic properties related to the camera view. In Section 3.1 we describe the viewable scene model used and present how we collected videos and their sensor measurements. Section 3.2 describes our sensor data based approach to subshot boundary detection and camera motion characterization. Our simplified motion estimation algorithm that works by reducing the number of candidate blocks is presented in Section 3.3.

3.1 Viewable Scene Model

We adapt the field-of-view (FOV, also called the *viewable scene*) model introduced by Arslan Ay et al. [2]. An FOV describes a scene area captured by a camera positioned at a given location in geo-space. The description of a camera's viewable scene consists of four parameters: the camera location $\mathcal{L}$, the camera orientation α, the viewable angle θ and the maximum visible distance R^{max} (see Equation 1). The camera position $\mathcal{L}$ is composed of latitude and longitude coordinates provided by a positioning device (*e.g.*, GPS receiver) and the camera direction α is obtained based on the orientation angle value from a digital compass. The viewable angle θ is calculated based on the camera and lens properties at the current zoom level [9]. R^{max} represents the maximum visible distance from $\mathcal{L}$ at which a large object within the camera's field-of-view can be recognized.

$$FOV \equiv \langle \mathcal{L}, \alpha, \theta, R^{max} \rangle \quad (1)$$

To acquire sensor-annotated videos we have developed two custom recording apps for Android and iOS smartphones. When users begin to capture a video, GPS and compass sensors are turned on to continuously record location and orientation information of the camera. All collected metadata (*i.e.*, location, direction, the corresponding frame timecode and video ID) are combined into a JSON file and later uploaded to a server.

3.2 Camera Motion Characterization

Our camera motion characterization system works in two steps as illustrated in Figure 2. First, we analyze all the sensor data of the acquired single-shot video to detect subshot boundaries. For each subshot segment we examine the camera location movement states and the shooting direction change states. Then we determine the relationship between the camera trajectories and way the the shooting direction changes. Using the interrelation analysis results, we are able to characterize the camera motion type for every subshot.

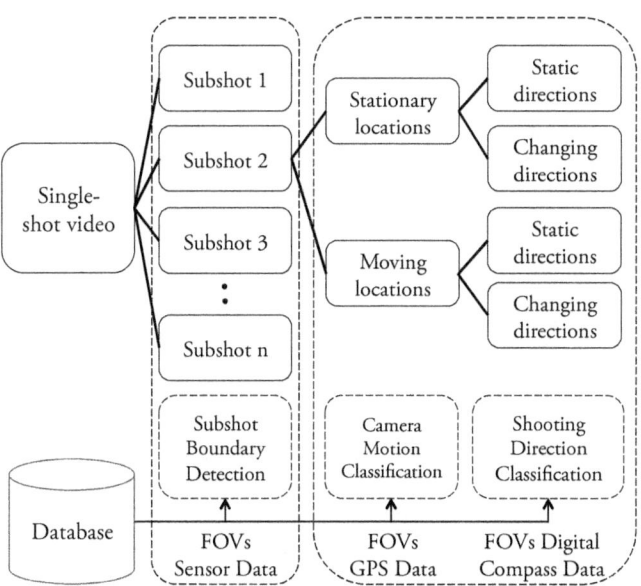

Figure 2: Proposed camera motion characterization framework.

3.2.1 Subshot Boundary Detection

A camera's mobility is characterized as either *moving* or *stationary*. Similarly, during a given period of time, the shooting direction of the camera can also be either *fixed* or *in motion*. A specific camera motion type is a combination of two state components. For example, *Panning* consists of a stationary camera location and a particular change model the of shooting direction.

We first search subshot boundaries based on the camera location mobility. We read the GPS speed value of each FOV sample and binarize them as moving or stationary. We reinforce the results from GPS location signals to achieve more robust judgements. To evaluate the direction state, we read the compass values and compute their smoothed directions as defined in Equation 2 to further seek for the subshot boundaries. The smoothed direction at time index t is a weighted average of the previous w and the next w direction values. If the processed direction exceeds a certain threshold T_d, we consider them as in motion. Next we select the start points of each group of consecutive frames who share the same location movement and direction change status as the boundaries of subshots. Using two different types of boundaries (the boundary between moving and stationary camera location, and the boundary between changing and static shooting direction), we divide the video into subshots and classify each of them by its camera motion category. We further set a threshold T_{temp} as the minimum segment-duration by observing that a camera motion is generally maintained for at least several seconds.

$$a_t = \frac{\sum_{i=-w}^{w} p_i \times a_{t+i}}{2w+1}, \quad (2)$$

Here $2w+1$ is the window size and p_i is the accuracy weight. If $a_t \geq T_d$, t is chosen as one of the subshot boundaries.

3.2.2 Subshot Motion Semantic Classification

After a coarse classification on both location movement and shooting direction change, we assign each subshot's camera motion type further to fine-grained classes. Specifically, we associate the relationship between the moving directions of the camera and its corresponding shooting directions. For each segment we obtained from previous step, we first compute the directions of camera movements. Along the trajectory, we employ the GPS values with a certain sampling rate, and achieve the camera moving direction of every segment by calculating the angle of vectors, which consists of a start location and an end location. Afterwards we are able to compare the relation between the moving directions of camera and their corresponding shooting directions.

If there exists no significant fluctuation in both locations and shooting directions, we categorize it as *Still*. If only the shooting direction changes, a detected subshot can be labelled as *Panning* or *Tilting*. With the help of the accelerometer sensor, we can easily detect a change of the lateral axis (pitch) and consider the shooting behavior as *Tilting*, otherwise, we mark it as *Panning*. If the location moves while the shooting direction is rather quasi-stationary (below a threshold) and the angle between several direction vectors is larger than L but less than $180 - L$ degrees (L is the angle degree border that separates different classifications) we label the shooting behavior at this point as *Tracking*. Otherwise, it will be considered a *Dolly in* (moving forward while shooting in the same direction) or *Dolly out* (moving backward while shooting in the opposite direction), respectively. When a camera's direction and location move simultaneously, it is difficult to clearly identify any useful patterns except possibly *Focusing* (pointing to a specific object). In such cases we term them as *Scanning* (our method does not distinguish those two at present time). In the scope of one segmentation, the majority of shooting behaviors are consolidated into the classification label of this sub-shot. In view of the source of sensor-tagged videos, which are mostly captured by smartphones, functions like zoom-in or zoom-out are currently not available during video recording on those devices.

$\mathcal{L}$ \ α	Quasi-static	Changing
Stationary	*Still*	*Panning, Tilting*
Moving	*Tracking, Dolly in/out*	*Focusing, Scanning*

Table 1: Semantic classification of camera motion patterns based on a stream of location $\mathcal{L}$ and camera direction α data.

After classification, each subshot belongs to one of the camera motion patterns (*Still, Panning, Tilting, Tracking, Dolly in/out*) with the categories listed in Table 1. Since we found the view direction values to be very noisy, we use their exponential moving average during the data analysis, which assigns higher weights to the latest measurement result.

3.3 Sensor-aided Motion Estimation

For video encoding the camera motion information is mostly reflected in the global motion estimation (GME) model. MPEG-4 ASP supports GME with three reference points, although some implementations can only make use of one. GME can perform good estimation for global frame changes and supports different transformation types with very low complexity. However, it does not compensate for some local changes within a frame. Thus, some widely used video encoder implementations do not support GME well, *e.g.*, x264, an open source implementation for encoding video streams into the H.264/MPEG-4 AVC format. Instead, block-based motion estimation (BME) is extensively used in such software. Although BME is capable of achieving a good estimation of the local movement, it also incurs extremely high computational complexity. In order to shorten the processing time of BME, we apply the camera motion information generated in the previous step to simplify the HEX motion estimation, which is the default BME algorithm employed by x264.

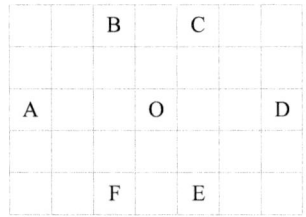

Figure 3: Illustration of the HEX Motion Estimation algorithm. Each grid represents a macroblock in the reference frame.

In H.264, each macroblock is predicted from a block of equal size in the reference frame. The blocks are not transformed in any way apart from being shifted to the position of the predicted block. It is the motion estimation algorithms' responsibility to search and calculate this shift, which is represented by a motion vector. As illustrated in Figure 3, the HEX algorithm starts from the reference macroblock O predicted by the computed motion vector values of the left, top and top-right macroblocks of the prediction macroblock. Afterwards HEX iteratively compares the macroblocks around O with the prediction macroblock following the order from macroblock A to F, located in a hexagonal shape. In one iteration, HEX performs six macroblock comparisons and considers the block with the minimum difference measurement result (*e.g.*, SAD) as the new search center in the next iteration. This search phase ends when the reference macroblock reaches the edge of the search window, or when it encounters a macroblock whose difference value is lower than a configured threshold.

Given the camera motion information computed earlier we reduce the search window size for each motion type. The reduction speeds up the search algorithm which is the most time-consuming part of the motion estimation.

- Class *Panning* and *Tracking*
  Since the shooting direction change and camera location movement both reflect horizontal translation of frames, the reference block stands a high chance of being located at the left or right of the prediction block. Thus, for these two classes, we narrow the search window into a flat rectangle with the same x-axis value as the prediction block, instead of a 16×16 square by default. As a result, in every difference calculation iteration, only block A and block D are compared with block O and used as reference block in the next iteration.

- Class *Tilting*
  In this case, no location movement is involved and the shooting directions include only tilts up and down, which results in a series of frames mostly containing vertical translations. Based on this information, we reduce the search window by ignoring the two blocks with the same x-axis index. Inside the narrow window we select blocks B, C, E and F as comparison blocks for the difference measurements in every iteration.

- Class *Dolly in/out*
  With these two classes, we are concerned about the macroblocks in the left half image and right half image separately. The rationale is that users tend to focus on objects located at the median plane of the FOV. Hence most of the blocks in the left part move towards straight left, top-left or bottom-left corner for a *Dolly in* camera motion. Therefore, when processing the macroblocks with an x-axis index less than half of the frame's width, we only estimate the left part of the search window, namely blocks A, B and F in each iteration. Similarly, prediction blocks located in the right half of the image would be compared with blocks C, D and E during every local search. A *Dolly out* segment looks like a reverse scan of the *Dolly in* motion. Accordingly, we switch the trimmed search window for the left half and right half macroblocks in the *Dolly in* case and apply them to the *Dolly out* pattern directly.

By simplifying the HEX algorithm with our method, most of the important motions of objects can be estimated much more efficiently. From our observation, in most of outdoor videos that capture landmarks or attractions, the local motion does not contribute a lot in the video content. Hence we sacrifice a slight decrease in video quality to accelerate the motion estimation considerably. Since we apply different strategies to different motion patterns, our experimental results show that our compromise is quite reasonable and beneficial.

4. EXPERIMENTS

4.1 Camera Motion Characterization

In our experiments, we apply our algorithms to geo-referenced video dataset from the geovid.org web site and we set parameters w=6 frames, and T_d=0.0054 degrees/sec. We first compare the accuracy of our approach's camera motion classification to the ground-truth of the subshots, which was manually annotated. We report both the accuracy of the subshot boundary detection and the precision of the motion classification.

The first column in Table 2 shows the ground-truth time interval of each subshot and the second column illustrates the boundary times detected automatically by our system. The results match the ground-truth values very well. By comparing the start and end times of each classification's duration, we can see that the inaccuracy of our approach is generally ≤ 1 second. Note that some parts of the 1 second errors are contributed by rounding (because users generally cannot cut the video with an accuracy of less than 1 second, and the results of our approach need to be rounded off before the comparison). The results in the sixth and seventh row are the only boundary errors which are larger than 1 second compared to the ground-truth classification. The second-to-last row in the table represents an over-detection of subshots in our system. We observe that in the original video this part of the time interval does not appear as scanning behavior, rather a strong camera shake occuring when the operator climbs some stairs.

We apply our algorithm to nine sample videos randomly chosen from our video database. A summary of the quality of our classification method is presented in the format of a confusion matrix. As we can see in Table 3, the correctly classified outputs add up to 188 cases in total (the sum of the values across the diagonal) while incorrectly classified cases are 21. Therefore, the classification accuracy our approach can achieve is about 88%. Among the classified results, 40% are evaluated as scanning, which means that we cannot observe any meaningful semantics.

4.2 Sensor-aided Motion Estimation

The smartphones that we employed to record videos and sensor information in our experiments included models from Apple, HTC and Motorola. Videos captured by these mobile phones have a resolution of 720×480 or 1920×1080. The frame rate is either 30 fps or 24 fps. Since smartphones do not support raw video format recording, we converted the captured sequences into the YUV format with the *FFmpeg* tool. To implement our simplified motion estimation algorithm we modified the estimation functions in the source code of the *x264* codec software.

We report the macroblock comparison times in the estimation step and record the real time cost in the reference macroblock search and the block difference computation. Figures 4(a) and (b) show the results from our method and the original HEX algorithm. For every motion type processed differently by our approach, we successfully reduce the block comparison time and the real time cost in the motion estimation. Although we sacrifice some video quality, the results of the PSNR comparison (see Figure 4(c)) show that our method only introduces a relatively small decrease in quality. The reason of this very slight impact is that only minor local motion is involved in most of the outdoor videos that capture landmarks and attractions.

Ground-truth subshots	Subshots detected by our algorithm	Start time difference	End time difference
0:00 - 0:13	0:00 - 0:12	0	-1
0:13 - 0:17	0:12 - 0:17	-1	0
0:17 - 0:22	0:17 - 0:23	0	+1
0:22 - 0:24	0:23 - 0:24	+1	0
0:24 - 0:33	0:24 - 0:35	0	+2
0:33 - 0:51	0:35 - 0:50	+2	-1
0:51 - 0:57	0:50 - 0:57	-1	0
0:57 - 1:04	0:57 - 1:03	0	-1
1:04 - 1:07	1:03 - 1:06	-1	-1
1:07 - 1:12	1:06 - 1:12	-1	0
1:12 - 1:15	1:12 - 1:15	0	0
1:15 - 1:23	1:15 - 1:22	0	-1
1:23 - 1:30	1:22 - 1:29	-1	-1
1:30 - 1:38	1:29 - 1:38	-1	0
1:38 - 1:39	1:38 - 1:39	0	0
1:39 - 1:44	1:39 - 1:44	0	0
1:44 - 1:46	1:44 - 1:46	0	0
1:46 - 2:37	1:46 - 2:22 / 2:22 - 2:26 / 2:26 - 2:38	0	+1
2:37 - 2:41	2:38 - 2:41	+1	0

Table 2: Subshot classification comparison results of a sample video. The first column was obtained from manual observations, while the second column was computed by the proposed system.

5. CONCLUSIONS

We reported on utilizing sensor information to simplify motion estimation in the H.264/AVC codec. With the proposed approach an almost equivalent PSNR performance can be maintained even with a much smaller search window for motion estimation. This leads to significantly reduced computations and therefore diminished hardware requirements and longer battery life for smartphones.

Acknowledgments

This research is supported by the Singapore National Research Foundation under its International Research Centre @ Singapore Funding Initiative and administered by the IDM Programme Office.

6. REFERENCES

[1] E. Ardizzone, M. La Cascia, A. Avanzato, and A. Bruna. Video Indexing Using MPEG Motion Compensation Vectors. In *IEEE Intl. Conference on Multimedia Computing and Systems*, volume 2, pages 725–729, July 1999.

[2] S. Arslan Ay, R. Zimmermann, and S. Kim. Viewable Scene Modeling for Geospatial Video Search. In *16th ACM Intl. Conference on Multimedia*, pages 309–318, 2008.

[3] S. Battiato, G. Gallo, G. Puglisi, and S. Scellato. SIFT Features Tracking for Video Stabilization. In *14th Intl. Conference on Image Analysis and Processing*, pages 825–830, Sept. 2007.

G \ E	Still	Panning	Tracking	D/I	Scanning	D/O
Still	24	0	0	0	0	0
Panning	1	27	0	0	0	0
Tracking	2	0	16	1	2	0
D/I	0	0	1	49	6	1
Scanning	0	0	4	2	70	0
D/O	0	0	1	0	0	2

Table 3: Confusion matrix of our subshot classification method with nine sample videos. G represents the user-defined ground-truth, while E stands for the experimental result from our characterization algorithm. D/I and D/O are short for Dolly in and Dolly out respectively.

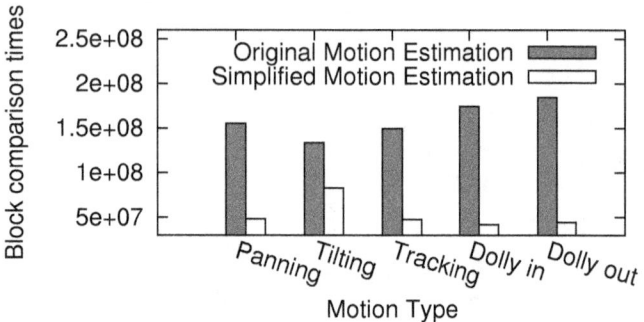

(a) Block comparison time

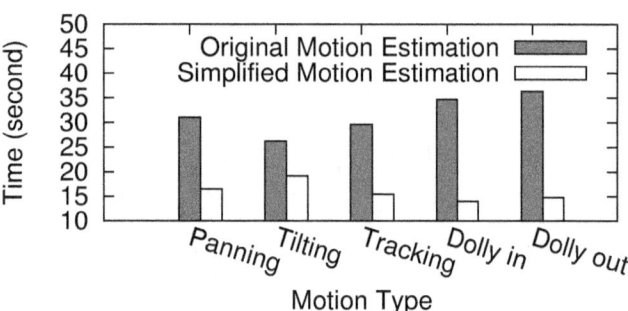

(b) Motion estimation time

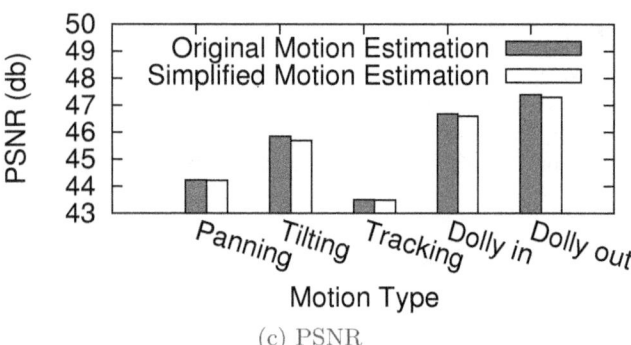

(c) PSNR

Figure 4: Macroblock comparison times, real time cost in the motion estimation algorithm and PSNR results for the original and simplified methods.

[4] P. Bouthemy, M. Gelgon, and F. Ganansia. A Unified Approach to Shot Change Detection and Camera Motion Characterization. *IEEE Trans. on Circuits and Systems for Video Technology*, 9(7):1030–1044, Oct. 1999.

[5] X. Chen, Z. Zhao, A. Rahmati, Y. Wang, and L. Zhong. SaVE: Sensor-assisted Motion Estimation for Efficient H.264/AVC Video Encoding. In *17th ACM Intl. Conference on Multimedia*, pages 381–390, 2009.

[6] J. Denzler, V. Schless, D. Paulus, and H. Niemann. Statistical Approach to Classification of Flow Patterns for Motion Detection. In *Intl. Conference on Image Processing*, pages 517–520, 1996.

[7] L. Duan, J. Jin, Q. Tian, and C. Xu. Nonparametric motion characterization for robust classification of camera motion patterns. *IEEE Trans. on Multimedia*, 8(2):323–340, 2006.

[8] R. Ewerth, M. Schwalb, P. Tessmann, and B. Freisleben. Estimation of Arbitrary Camera Motion in MPEG Videos. In *17th Intl. Conference on Pattern Recognition*, volume 1, pages 512–515, Aug. 2004.

[9] C. Graham, N. Bartlett, J. Brown, Y. Hsia, C. Mueller, and L. Riggs. *Vision and Visual Perception*. 1965.

[10] J. Heuer and A. Kaup. Global Motion Estimation in Image Sequences Using Robust Motion Vector Field Segmentation. In *7th ACM Intl. conference on Multimedia*, pages 261–264, 1999.

[11] G. Hong, A. Rahmati, Y. Wang, and L. Zhong. SenseCoding: Accelerometer-assisted Motion Estimation for Efficient Video Encoding. In *16th ACM Intl. Conference on Multimedia*, pages 749–752, 2008.

[12] R. Jin, Y. Qi, and A. Hauptmann. A Probabilistic Model for Camera Zoom Detection. In *16th Intl. Conference on Pattern Recognition*, volume 3, pages 859–862, 2002.

[13] K. Jinzenji, S. Ishibashi, and H. Kotera. Algorithm for Automatically Producing Layered Sprites by Detecting Camera Movement. In *Intl. Conference on Image Processing*, volume 1, pages 767–770, Oct. 1997.

[14] J. Kim, H. Chang, J. Kim, and H. Kim. Efficient Camera Motion Characterization for MPEG Video Indexing. In *IEEE Intl. Conference on Multimedia and Expo*, pages 1171–1174, 2000.

[15] T. Lertrusdachakul, T. Aoki, and H. Yasuda. Camera Motion Estimation by Image Feature Analysis. *Pattern Recognition and Image Analysis*, pages 618–625, 2005.

[16] J. Park, S. Inoue, and Y. Iwadate. Estimating Camera Parameters from Motion Vectors of Digital Video. In *IEEE Second Workshop on Multimedia Signal Processing*, pages 105–110, Dec. 1998.

[17] F. Tiburzi and J. Bescos. Camera Motion Analysis in On-line MPEG Sequences. In *8th Intl. Workshop on Image Analysis for Multimedia Interactive Services*, page 42, June 2007.

[18] M. Ulrich and S. Martin. Sensor assisted video compression. European Patent Application EP1921867.

[19] R. Wang and T. Huang. Fast Camera Motion Analysis in MPEG Domain. In *Intl. Conference on Image Processing*, volume 3, pages 691–694, 1999.

CAME: Cloud-Assisted Motion Estimation for Mobile Video Compression and Transmission

Yuan Zhao
School of Computing Science
Simon Fraser University
Burnaby, BC, Canada
yza173@sfu.ca

Lei Zhang
School of Computing Science
Simon Fraser University
Burnaby, BC, Canada
lza70@sfu.ca

Xiaoqiang Ma
School of Computing Science
Simon Fraser University
Burnaby, BC, Canada
xma10@sfu.ca

Jiangchuan Liu
School of Computing Science
Simon Fraser University
Burnaby, BC, Canada
jcliu@sfu.ca

Hongbo Jiang
Department of EIE
Huazhong University of
Science and Technology
Wuhan, Hubei, China
hongbojiang@hust.edu.cn

ABSTRACT

Video streaming has become one of the most popular networked applications and, with the increased bandwidth and computation power of mobile devices, anywhere and anytime streaming has become a reality. Unfortunately, it remains a challenging task to compress high-quality video in real-time in such devices given the excessive computation and energy demands of compression. On the other hand, transmitting the raw video is simply unaffordable from both energy and bandwidth perspective.

In this paper, we propose CAME, a novel cloud-assisted video compression method for mobile devices. CAME leverages the abundant cloud server resources for motion estimation, which is known to be the most computation-intensive step in video compression, accounting for over 90% of the computation time. With CAME, a mobile device selects and uploads only the key information of each picture frame to cloud servers for mesh-based motion estimation, eliminating most of the local computation operations. We develop smart algorithms to identify the key mesh nodes, resulting in minimum distortion and data volume for uploading. Our simulation results demonstrate that CAME saves almost 30% energy for video compression and transmission.

Categories and Subject Descriptors

H.5.1 [**Multimedia Information Systems**]: Video; C.2.1 [**Network Architecture and Design**]: Wireless communication

General Terms

Experimentation

Keywords

Mesh-based Motion Estimation, Mobile Video Compression, Cloud-assisted Motion Estimation

1. INTRODUCTION

Video streaming has become one of the most popular networked applications, and it contributes a dominant fraction of internet traffic. Along with the advances in 3G and wireless network, mobile devices become an important end device for Internet video applications. Online statistics [14] shows that YouTube mobile gets over 400M views a day, representing 13% of the overall YouTube daily views. Unfortunately, video compression on mobile devices remains a challenging task due to limited energy. The user has to copy the video to a personal computer, then compress and upload the video. This however is not convenient and discourages people to share mobile videos on Internet.

Another trend of Internet is that Cloud Computing is booming recent years. Cloud Computing provides an illusion of infinite computing resources which include bandwidth, computation and storage. Major cloud providers also provide High Performance Computing (HPC), which suits multimedia processing well.

If mobile devices can leverage Cloud Computing resources to perform video compression, the computation cost on the mobile device itself can be reduced dramatically. However, transferring large video file to cloud server introduces huge energy consumption, which contradicts the benefit. The question then becomes how to leverage cloud server computation resources without transferring the whole video file.

A typical video compression consists of: motion estimation, transformation, quantization, and entropy coding. Among all these steps, the motion estimation is the most computation intensive and time consuming, which accounts for 90% computation time of the whole compression process [4]. Hence it is worthwhile to transfer even part of the motion estimation computation to cloud servers.

This paper proposes Cloud-assisted Motion Estimation (CAME), a novel method to smartly leverage cloud's computation resources for motion estimation. We focus on mesh-based motion estimation, which is known to be highly effec-

Permission to make digital or hard copies of all or part of this work for personal or classroom use is granted without fee provided that copies are not made or distributed for profit or commercial advantage and that copies bear this notice and the full citation on the first page. To copy otherwise, to republish, to post on servers or to redistribute to lists, requires prior specific permission and/or a fee.
NOSSDAV'12, June 7–8, 2012, Toronto, Ontario, Canada.
Copyright 2012 ACM 978-1-4503-1430-5/12/06 ...$10.00.

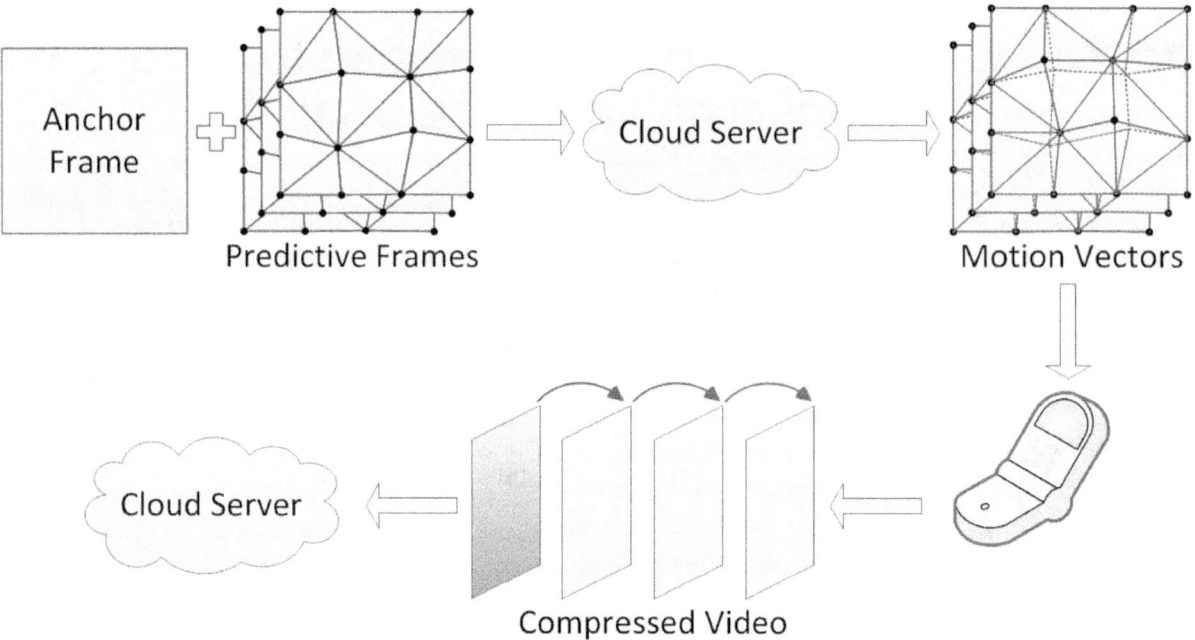

Figure 1: CAME illustration

tive. Our method uploads anchor frames and mesh nodes to cloud server for calculating mesh nodes Motion Vectors (MV). The motion vectors are pushed back to mobile devices for motion estimation of sub blocks and the rest video compression steps. By carefully choosing mesh structure, video compression energy consumption can be largely reduced on mobile devices.

Our simulation result suggests, the proposed method can save up to 30% energy for video compression and transmission compared to All-on-Mobile method which performs the complete video compression on mobile devices.

The rest of this paper is organized as following: We first review the related work in section 2. Then in Section 3, we present CAME system architecture. In Section 4, we introduce the implementation details of CAME. Section 5 evaluates the proposed method using simulated testing system. Finally in Section 6, we draw conclusions and propose the future research work.

2. RELATED WORK

2.1 Cloud-based Video Streaming

With the elastic and on-demand nature of resource provisioning, cloud computing has become a promising platform for diverse applications, many of which are video related [7, 9, 12].

To reduce bandwidth reservation cost and to guarantee the streaming performance, a predictive cloud bandwidth auto-scaling system is proposed in [10] for VoD providers. The predictable anti-correlation between the demands of video channels is exploited in the system for statistical multiplexing and for hedging the risk of under-provision. Built on a peer-to-peer storage cloud, *Novasky* [8] provides on-demanding streaming of cinematic-quality videos over a high-bandwidth network with two novel mechanisms: a coding-aware peer storage and replacement strategy and an adaptive server push strategy with video popularity-redundancy awareness. A cloud-based video proxy system is presented in [5] transcoding the original video in real rime using a scalable codec based on H.264/SVC (Scalable Video Coding), which is aimed at streaming videos of various qualities.

Motivated by these previous studies, our CAME seeks to exploring the resources from cloud as well. Our focus in this paper, however, is to smartly utilize such resource for motion estimation, the most computation-intensive task in video compression, so as to realize realtime highly quality video encoding and streaming from mobile devices.

2.2 Mobile Video Compression

Since mobile devices typically depend on a limited energy supply and video compression is computation-intensive, many existing works have focused on reducing the computational cost for mobile devices [1, 3, 11]. The low complexity video compression system suggested in [6] abandons the ME/MC paradigm and codes the difference between successive frames, making the process significantly less time consuming. A two-step algorithm is introduced in [1], which is further improved in [3] to reduce the computation and memory accesses with variable block size motion estimation. A mobile video communication system is developed [11], in which the transmitter uses a Wyner-Ziv (WZ) encoder while the receiver uses a traditional decoder. An efficient transcoder should be inserted in the network to convert the video stream.

Our work differs from them in that we explores mesh-based motion estimation [13], which is known to be cost-effective and yet has to be examined in the mobile communication context. We demonstrate that, given the small data volume of meshes, they work well with cloud-assisted compression to best balance computation cost, transmission overhead, and compression quality.

3. CAME: CLOUD-ASSISTED MOTION ESTIMATION FOR MOBILE DEVICES

We consider a cloud-assisted mobile video streaming system that consists of mobile devices and cloud servers. A mobile device user captures video in realtime and expects to compress the video and then streaming it to others in realtime as well. Given the high computation overhead of compression and the limited computation power and battery of the device, it is preferable that the compression operation or part of the operation is shifted to the cloud servers. Yet, simply uploading the raw video to the cloud server for compression will consume significant bandwidth and therefore energy for transmission, and is thus not applicable. To this end, our CAME seeks to shift the motion-estimation, the most computation-intensive module in compression to the cloud. Specifically, CAME employs a mesh-based motion estimation, which consists of two parts: mesh node motion estimation and the sub-block motion estimation. As we will show later, the mobile device can upload reference frames and mesh data to the cloud for estimation, which are of much smaller data volume. It then downloads the estimated Motion Vectors (MVs) from the cloud server and completes the remaining video compression steps.

The CAME architecture is illustrated in Figure 1, which includes following four key steps:

1. In the mobile device, the raw video is divided into macro blocks (MBs). For each MB, a reference frame is extracted, together with a mesh for each successive P-frame. The device then uploads the reference frame and meshes to the cloud;

2. The cloud server conducts the mesh motion estimation for the uploaded reference frame and meshes, and pushes the generated mesh MVs back to the CAME client on the mobile device;

3. The mobile devices, upon receiving the MVs for mesh nodes of each P-frame, continues to calculate sub block MVs using block-based motion estimation as well as entry coding;

4. The compressed video is then stored in the device or stream to other devices or servers through the wireless channel.

4. CAME IMPLEMENTATION

While the CAME architecture is intuitive, there are a number of implementation issues to be addressed toward a complete system. In this section, we explain the implementation details of CAME, particulary on mesh node selection strategy for cost minimization.

4.1 Mesh Node Selection

The mesh-based motion estimation is performed by estimating one motion vector (MV) for each mesh node. As shown in Figure 2 and Figure 3, mesh nodes are sampled on the reference frame and MVs are calculated from predictive frames (P-frame).

Generally, two different mesh structures are used: regular triangular or rectangular mesh structures and object-based mesh structure.

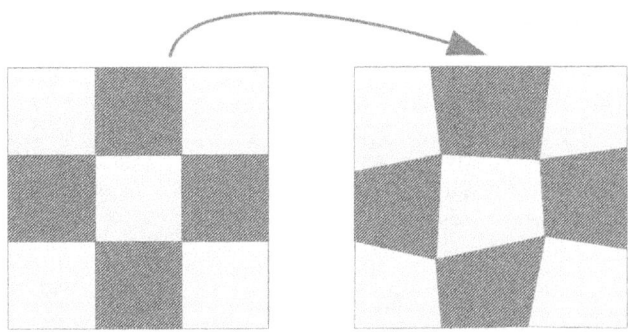

Figure 2: Mesh-based Motion Estimation

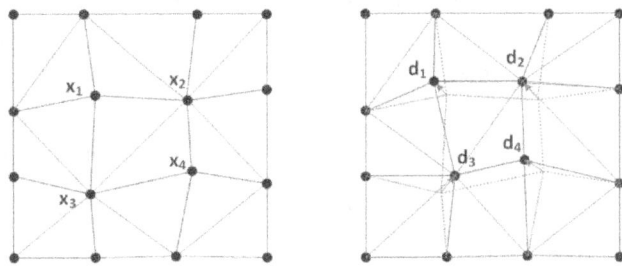

Figure 3: Mesh Nodes in Motion Estimation

Regular Mesh Structures

Triangular and rectangular mesh structures are two commonly used structures in all the mesh structures. Mesh topology is simple and predefined in regular mesh.

Object-based Mesh Structure

The object-based mesh structure is also known as adaptive mesh structure. As in real world videos, usually there are discontinuities at object boundaries, so it would be more accurate to sample mesh nodes along object boundaries. In another word, the mesh selection and sampling should be adapted to the video objects, so that the motion within mesh nodes is smooth. Someone has also proposed algorithms to sample mesh nodes along motion or luminance discontinuities in order to fit the objects boundaries.

Hierarchy Mesh Structures

Hierarchy mesh structure is between regular mesh structure and adaptive mesh structure. It's based on regular mesh, but is adaptive to image objects.

Regular mesh is commonly used since it is simple and predefined. Using regular mesh, both encoder and decoder know the mesh structure, thus there is no overhead to store and send the mesh topology to the decoder. The object-based structure is more accurate because it samples mesh nodes along object boundaries, however it requires extra overhead to analyze objects and mesh topology transmission. Therefore, regular mesh is preferred in CAME method.

Unlike standard mesh-based motion estimation, CAME exploits a smarter algorithm for mesh node selection: CAME applies a reversed mesh node selection and motion estimation algorithm, in which mesh nodes are sampled on P-frames and MVs are calculated from the mesh and the reference frame. Compared to standard mesh-based motion estimation, CAME loses the advantage of tracking the same set of mesh nodes over successive P-frames. However, CAME gains much more benefits by uploading only the reference frame and mesh data of P-frames instead of uploading the whole video frames.

For a single MB, we denote one reference frame as R, one P-frame as P, and the mesh node fraction M_f from P as f. The total transmission cost is

$$C_m = \sum_{i=1}^{m}(C_R + \sum_{i=1}^{n} C_i \cdot f) \qquad (1)$$

where m is the number of MB, and n is number of P-frame in a single MB.

4.2 Cloud Server Motion Estimation for Mesh Nodes

The energy of the cloud server is much more economy than mobile devices, therefore we do not take the cloud side energy consumption into consideration. However, total delay is crucial to the CAME system as CAME is a real-time video compression and uploading system. To reduce total delay of CAME system, we leverage cloud parallel computation resources to compute mesh MVs. The natural separation of frames to MBs provided a great isolation for application level parallelism. CAME server utilize a master-slave paradigm to coordinate the mesh motion estimation for a single video. The CAME server delay can be largely reduced thanks to cloud parallelled computation. The cloud server motion estimation is depicted in Algorithm 1.

Algorithm 1 CloudServer-Motion-Estimation

INPUT: $\{R, M_{fi}\}$, anchor frame R and mesh nodes on P
  $MV_s = \phi$
  for each M_{fj} in $\{R, M_{fi}\}$ **do**
    Full search to calculate MV from R and M_{fj}
    $MV_s = MV_s \cup MV$
  end for
OUTPUT: Push motion vector MV_s back to the mobile device

4.3 Sub-Block Motion Estimation

The mobile device downloads estimated MVs for each P-frame mesh, and we denote the downloading transmission cost as C_d. Then the mobile device uses these MVs to calculate the sub block MVs and finally compose a complete MV for P-frame. The cost to compute all MVs for all sub blocks inside a single P-frame is

$$C_f = \sum_{j=1}^{n}\sum_{i=1}^{m} C_i \cdot f \qquad (2)$$

where n is number of P-frame in a single MB, m is sub block number inside a single P-frame. This step is a local search which is constrained by the mesh node MV, so the computation is also restricted and relatively small energy consumption is consumed. Next, the mobile device regenerates the block pixels based on the motion estimation result. We denote the motion compensation cost as

$$C_c = \sum_{i=1}^{n} C_{comp-i} \qquad (3)$$

where n is the number of P-frames in a single MB. All the other steps are the same as normal video compression process, and we denote their costs as C_o.

4.4 Mobile Device Algorithm

After the whole video compression process is finished, the video is ready for uploading, and only P-frames are uploaded. We denote cost in this step as C_u. The complete algorithm for the mobile device video compression is shown in Algorithm 2.

Algorithm 2 Mobile-Video-Compression

INPUT: Complete raw video V
  Divide V to MacroBlocks(MBs) denoted by $\{MB_i\}$
  for each MB_i in $\{MB_i\}$ **do**
    Calculate $\{R, M_{fi}\}$, anchor frame R and fraction mesh nodes on P
    Upload $\{R, M_{fi}\}$ to server for mesh node motion estimation
  end for
  $MV_{video} = \phi$
  On receiving $\{MV_{mesh}\}$ from server:
  for each MV in $\{MV_{mesh}\}$ **do**
    Local search to calculate sub-block MV_{sub} for current frame
    Interpolate MV_{sub} into MV to get MV_f for frame
    $MV_{video} = MV_{video} \cup MV_f$
    Calculate video compensation for current frame
  end for
  if MV_{video} is complete **then**
    Finish video compression process to get V_{comp}
    Anchor frames are already deducted from V_{comp}
    Upload V_{comp}
  end if

4.5 Total Cost Equation

Finally, the total cost equation is formulated as:

$$C = C_m + C_d + C_f + C_c + C_o + C_u \qquad (4)$$

where C_m is the total cost for uploading all MBs, C_d is MV downloading cost, C_f is the total cost for sub block motion estimation, C_c is the motion compensation cost, C_o is all other costs for video compression on the mobile device after motion estimation, C_u is the final step mobile video uploading cost.

5. EVALUATION

In this section, we evaluate implemented CAME method on a simulated system. Mobile video compression and transmission both require energy consumption. We evaluate CAME method using a two-computer simulation system: one acts as cloud server and the other acts as the mobile device. We use simulated system because it is more generic and the result is not specific to a mobile device.

The transmission energy consumption is measured and calculated from compressed video file size and such CAME system intermediate output as mesh motion vectors. We consider a generic energy model in terms of CPU cycle consumption. Video compression CPU cycles can be directly monitored and measured. However, transmission measurement in CPU cycles is not straightforward, as transmission

Table 1: YUV Video Files Used in Testing

Video Name	Size($W \times H$)	Frame Num	YUV	File Size
Foreman	352×288	300	420	43MB
Mother	352×288	300	420	43MB
Flower	352×288	250	420	36.2MB

consumes energy not only on CPU, but also on wireless. Based on the research work done in [2, 15], we assume the energy conversion between CPU cycle and transmission is: one byte of WiFi transmission consumes roughly the same energy as 132.3251 CPU cycles.

As mentioned previously, mesh node density impacts both transmission and computation. We choose different mesh node fractions f in simulation. CAME are evaluated when mesh node is sampled from 16×16, 8×8, and 4×4 blocks respectively. Our simulation shows that 8×8 mode achieves best energy efficiency. Further, to evaluate how CAME performs over existing mobile video compression and transmission methods, we compare CAME performance with All-on-Mobile and Raw-Upload methods. In the All-on-Mobile method, standard H.264 encoding is performed completed on the mobile device and H.264 encoded video file is uploaded. In the Raw-Upload method, uncompressed video is uploaded in raw format.

In the following sub sections, we first describe the video compression testing data. Then we analyze CAME transmission and computation energy respectively. Finally total energy consumption is evaluated by adding up transmission and computation energy consumption.

5.1 Testing Data

We take three YUV video files in the evaluation which are commonly used in video compression testing. The details of the three videos are illustrated in Table 1. The frame size and frame number are not that important, because the total energy consumption and the total energy saving increase proportionally to them. On the other hand, the video content really matters since the estimated MVs depend on specific video content. Mother and Daughter has low spatial detail, while Foreman has medium spatial detail and Flower has high spatial details.

5.2 Transmission Energy Consumption

We measure and calculate the total transmission consumption in total transmission data size, and convert it to equivalence CPU cycle consumption. There are three transmission phases in CAME: Initial reference frame and mesh node data uploading, mesh node motion vectors downloading, and compressed video data uploading.

The detail measure and calculation result in total transmission data size is illustrated in Figure 4. The total transmission energy consumption in CPU cycles is illustrated in Table 2. Mother and Daughter has the similar result with Foreman. Though Flower's original video size is smallest, the AoM and CAME transmission size is largest, because Flower has higher spatial details. It is obvious that AoM method's data transmission cost is the lowest among all three. The mesh-based motion estimation interpolated to H.264/AVC encoding achieves almost 10:1 compression ratio in our testing. This result is just as expected. Compared to

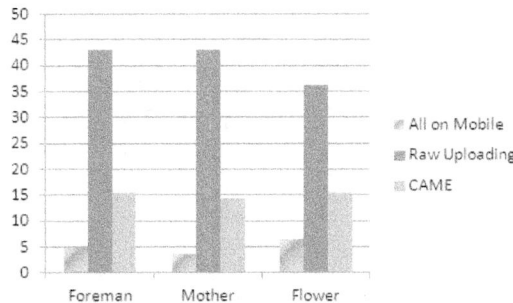

Figure 4: Total Transmission Size (MB)

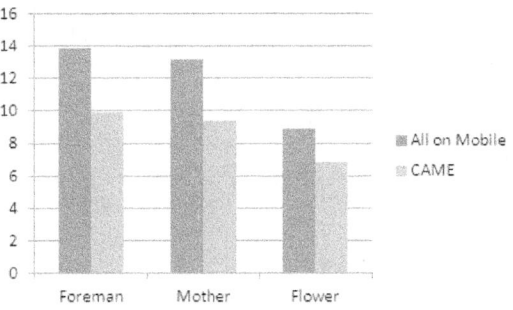

Figure 5: Total Energy Consumption in CPU Cycles (billion cycles)

AoM method, the proposed method introduces more transmission because of the extra data transmission overhead for mesh node uploading and mesh motion vectors downloading. On the other hand, compared to Raw-Upload, the CAME method still saves approximately 60% on total data transmission. This verifies our idea that CAME can leverage cloud server resources for motion estimation and video compression without transferring the whole video data.

5.3 Video Compression Energy Consumption

The measurement of video compression energy consumption in CPU cycles is straightforward. For CAME, the CPU cycles are measured for part of the motion estimation and all the other steps of video compression that performed on the mobile device. For the AoM method, complete video compression is performed solely on the mobile device, the total CPU cycle consumption is measured when video is encoded by the Java H.264 encoder. The measurement result is depicted in detail in Table 3.

In this measurement, we notice that CAME method can save nearly 40% compared to the AoM method, that is exactly what we are expecting. By transferring part of the motion estimation to cloud server, CAME method do save a lot on computation, approximately 50% of the motion esti-

Table 2: Transmission Energy Consumption in CPU Cycles

Video Name	All on Mobile	CAME
Foreman	6.2987×10^8	2.0429×10^9
Mother	4.6843×10^8	1.8814×10^9
Flower	8.4291×10^8	2.0201×10^9

Table 3: Video Compression Energy Consumption in CPU Cycles

Video Name	All on Mobile	CAME
Foreman	1.3225×10^{10}	7.8689×10^9
Mother	1.2650×10^{10}	7.5268×10^9
Flower	8.0500×10^9	4.7898×10^9

mation computation can be reduced on mobile devices. The test result also verifies that motion estimation accounts for 90% of total video compression time.

5.4 Total Energy Consumption

To evaluate the total energy consumption and calculate how much energy we can save using the CAME method, we simply add up energy consumption in transmission and video compression in Table 2 and Table 3, and the results are compared in Figure 5.

As shown in Figure 5, CAME achieves up to 30% total energy saving on video compression and transmission compared to the AoM method. This is a significant improvement towards energy saving on mobile video compression and transmission. Though the total transmission size in CAME is larger than the AoM method, CAME saves considerable energy on video compression, particularly for the motion estimation.

Our experimental result suggests that 8×8 mesh selection mode achieve the best performance compared to 4×4 and 16×16 mesh selection modes. This is because in the 4×4 mesh mode, the mesh nodes uploading and mesh motion vectors downloading data size is too large. In the 16×16 mesh mode, as the mesh node density is not enough, though the mesh uploading and mesh motion vectors downloading data size is small, the mobile device still need to perform a large fraction of the motion estimation.

6. CONCLUSION AND FUTURE WORK

In this paper, we presented Cloud-assisted Motion Estimation (CAME), a novel video compression scheme for mesh-based motion estimation. By taking advantage of computational resource of the cloud server, our proposed method significantly reduces the complexity of video compression on mobile devices, which leads to considerable energy saving. Experimental results showed that CAME is highly energy-efficient. One drawback of this work may be the encoding delay introduced by closed loop design of our scheme, which is mainly due to transmission delay between client and server.

As part of our future work, we will consider some optimization problems in our system, especially the coordination of wireless transmission between the cloud and mobile devices, to achieve even lower transmission overhead and higher energy-efficiency.

7. ACKNOWLEDGMENTS

This research is supported by a Canada NSERC Discovery Grant, an NSERC DAS grant, a Nokia University Relation Fund, and an NSFC Major Program of International Cooperation.

8. REFERENCES

[1] A. Bahari, T. Arslan, and A. Erdogan. Low-power h. 264 video compression architectures for mobile communication. *Circuits and Systems for Video Technology, IEEE Transactions on*, 19(9):1251–1261, 2009.

[2] N. Balasubramanian, A. Balasubramanian, and A. Venkataramani. Energy consumption in mobile phones: a measurement study and implications for network applications. In *Proceedings of the 9th ACM SIGCOMM conference on Internet measurement conference*, pages 280–293. ACM, 2009.

[3] S. Chatterjee and I. Chakrabarti. Power efficient motion estimation algorithm and architecture based on pixel truncation. *Consumer Electronics, IEEE Transactions on*, 57(4):1782–1790, 2011.

[4] M. Dudon, O. Avaro, and C. Roux. Triangular active mesh for motion estimation. *Signal Processing: Image Communication*, 10(1):21–41, 1997.

[5] Z. Huang, C. Mei, L. Li, and T. Woo. Cloudstream: delivering high-quality streaming videos through a cloud-based svc proxy. In *INFOCOM, 2011 Proceedings IEEE*, pages 201–205. IEEE, 2011.

[6] E. Jackson and R. Peplow. Video compression system for mobile devices. *RN*, 2:2, 2003.

[7] Y. Lai, C. Lai, C. Hu, H. Chao, and Y. Huang. A personalized mobile iptv system with seamless video reconstruction algorithm in cloud networks. *International Journal of Communication Systems*, 2011.

[8] F. Liu, S. Shen, B. Li, B. Li, H. Yin, and S. Li. Novasky: Cinematic-quality vod in a p2p storage cloud. In *INFOCOM, 2011 Proceedings IEEE*, pages 936–944. IEEE, 2011.

[9] D. Miao, W. Zhu, C. Luo, and C. Chen. Resource allocation for cloud-based free viewpoint video rendering for mobile phones. In *Proceedings of the 19th ACM international conference on Multimedia*, pages 1237–1240. ACM, 2011.

[10] D. Niu, H. Xu, B. Li, and S. Zhao. Quality-assured cloud bandwidth auto-scaling for video-on-demand applications. In *Proc. of IEEE INFOCOM*, volume 12, 2012.

[11] E. Peixoto, R. de Queiroz, and D. Mukherjee. Mobile video communications using a wyner-ziv transcoder. In *Symposium on Electronic Imaging, Visual Communications and Image Processing (SPIE), San Jose, CA, USA*, 2008.

[12] K. Singh and C. Davids. Flash-based audio and video communication in the cloud. *Arxiv preprint arXiv:1107.0011*, 2011.

[13] Y. Wang, J. Ostermann, and Y. Zhang. *Video processing and communications*, volume 1. Prentice Hall, 2002.

[14] YouTube. Youtube statistics. "http://parsec.cs.princeton.edu/". [Online; accessed 05-Jan-2012].

[15] W. Yuan and K. Nahrstedt. Energy-efficient cpu scheduling for multimedia applications. *ACM Transactions on Computer Systems (TOCS)*, 24(3):292–331, 2006.

Understanding the Impact of Inter-Lens and Temporal Stereoscopic Video Compression

Wu-chi Feng, Feng Liu
Portland State University
Portland, OR 97207
{wuchi, fliu}@cs.pdx.edu

ABSTRACT

As we move toward more ubiquitous stereoscopic video, particularly with multiple (> 2) lenses, the need to understand the efficiency of compression will become increasingly important. In this paper, we explore the impact of spatial (between lenses) and temporal (over time) compression for stereoscopic video images. In particular, because stereoscopic images are taken at the same time, there is expected to be a high correlation between pixels in the horizontal direction due to the fixed nature of the multiple lenses. We propose a vertically reduced search window in order to take advantage of this correlation. Starting with multiple stereoscopic video sequences shot using a production studio 3D camera, we explore the effectiveness of temporal and inter-lens motion compensation for stereoscopic video. Furthermore, the experiments use exhaustive search to remove the effects of heuristic-based motion-compensation techniques.

Categories and Subject Descriptors
H.3.4 [**Information Storage and Retrieval**]: Systems and Software

General Terms
Algorithms, Design, Experimentation,

Keywords
Stereoscopic imaging, stereoscopic compression.

1. INTRODUCTION

One promising area in multimedia systems is stereoscopic imaging, which allows users to capture the feeling of depth in an image by feeding two different images to the left and right eyes. Currently, 3D cameras such as the Fuji FinePix Real 3D Digital and 3D video cameras such as the Panasonic AG-3DA1 3D Camcorder are available. Even smartphones like the LG Optimus 3D and the HTC Evo 3D are equipped with two lenses in order to allow for the capture of 3D video. Furthermore, devices are now emerging that allow for the display of stereoscopic imaging such as the Nintendo 3DS and the LG Thrill 3D without the requirement of shuttered, polarized, or blue/red glasses.

While it might seem that the problem of capture and display of stereoscopic images and video are essentially solved, this is far from the truth. As noted in a recent article, there are problems with such stereoscopic devices [14]. Professor Banks at UC

Permission to make digital or hard copies of all or part of this work for personal or classroom use is granted without fee provided that copies are not made or distributed for profit or commercial advantage and that copies bear this notice and the full citation on the first page. To copy otherwise, or republish, to post on servers or to redistribute to lists, requires prior specific permission and/or a fee.
NOSSDAV'12, June 7-8, 2012, Toronto, Ontario, Canada.
Copyright 2012 ACM 978-1-4503-1430-5/12/06...$10.00.

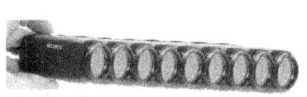 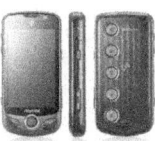

Figure 1. Imaging Devices: This figure shows two mockups of future multi-lens stereoscopic imaging devices

Berkeley has pointed out that viewers can suffer "3D fatigue" from improperly produced sequences. For movies like Avatar, the filmmaker spent particular attention to reducing eye fatigue by drawing viewer focus on just one object at a time.

As described in a previous paper [1], we believe that with more general availability of 3D capture hardware, and without careful consideration of how stereo video is being captured, that more than likely many of the stereoscopic streams captured will end up causing 3D fatigue and viewing issues. Rather than making all users aware of stereoscopic composition and cinematography rules, we envision that a stereoscopic camera may one day be made of many linearly aligned lenses to provide a denser sampling of the viewpoints. With the knowledge of the display size and the viewing distance from the screen, the system can then render a stereoscopic image from a subset of the images taken to maximize viewing experience. As a result, the underlying computing system will need to be able to deal with a large number of streams (one from each camera) during capture and display. An example of such an envisioned system is shown in Figure 1.

As will be described shortly, when greater than two lenses are used for stereoscopic video capture, compression and retrieval become more interesting. First, the greatest compression gains are achieved by removing all redundancy within the streams. For current stereoscopic video systems with two lenses this is not a problem as all the content is required for display. In the multi-lens scenario, the compression may need to take into account the fact that only select sub-streams will be retrieved for display. Second, while multi video codecs have been defined, they are typical standards in that *they specify the format of the compressed stream but not how to get there.*

In this paper, we begin the process of understanding the fundamental trade-off between inter-lens compression and temporal compression for stereoscopic video compression. This paper uses several standard stereoscopic video sequences from a local production studio as input and explores, for a number of parameters, how inter-lens frames and temporal frames impact compression. Our results show that we may be able to take advantage of the motion compensation process to help with feature tracking (required for optimal substream selection) for display, or vice versa.

In the next section, we will briefly review some of the related and background work. This will include further motivation for stereoscopic video versus 3D and multiview video. Section 3 we briefly review our proposed multi-lens video system that we presented at NOSSDAV 2011. Section 4 presents our detailed experimental results followed by a discussion and future work.

2. RELATED WORK
2.1 Stereoscopic Imaging
Stereopsis is the process in visual perception that leads to the perception of depth. Each eye can be thought of as an individual point of view. The brain perceives depth by processing the discrepancy between these views, which is known as retinal disparity. Objects that are far away have a small retinal disparity. As objects are brought closer, we perceive them as being closer because the disparity has increased. What this means is that our perceived depth is inversely proportional to the retinal disparity. The goal of stereoscopic imaging is to recreate depth perception in the brain.

To recreate depth perception, stereoscopic systems try to display the appropriate retinal disparity for the object being viewed. This is accomplished with two images of the same object that each represent the left and right eye point of view. The two images need to be delivered to the eyes separately. This is accomplished by using either red-cyan glasses, polarized light with different polarization for each eye, or shuttered glasses that quickly alternate covering each eye and changing the on screen image.

In a simple model of stereoscopic display, the retinal disparity depends on the interocular distance, the distance between the viewer and the screen and the on-screen disparity between two displayed images. The interocular distance is constant, roughly 2.5" for an adult. The on-screen disparity linearly depends on the raw disparity between two stereoscopic images and the screen size. A stereoscopic image pair designed for a certain viewing scenario (a certain viewing distance and screen size) may not be appropriate for another viewing scenario. The only adjustable parameter with a fixed user distance and display size is the raw disparity in the stereoscopic content. Assuming a fixed viewing distance, as the size of the screen increases, the retinal disparity will usually increase. In order to maintain the same perceived depth, the raw disparity will need to be decreased to maintain the on-screen disparity, thus, maintaining the retinal disparity. Similarly, assuming a fixed screen size, as the distance of the user from the screen increases, the retinal disparity will decrease. In order to maintain the same perceived depth, the raw disparity will need to be adjusted to compensate. The dependence of the retinal disparity on these factors is complicated. Readers interested in a more detailed description are referred to [2].

Unlike 2D content, stereoscopic images need to be adapted to different viewing scenarios for the proper experience [10]. Wang and Sawchuk developed a disparity manipulation system that combines image warping and data-filling techniques for novel view synthesis according to the new disparity map [15]. Lang et al. further discussed the important perceptual aspects of stereo vision and their implications for stereoscopic content creation, and then provided a set of basic disparity mapping operators to enable disparity map editing [6].

2.2 Multi-camera and 3D Video
The use of multiple cameras in multimedia applications and systems has been the subject of research for the last several years. Minimal overlap multi-camera systems have been used for tracking and management in surveillance and traffic monitoring systems. While some inter-camera overlap sometimes occurs, the focus of such systems is typically on the coordination amongst multiple cameras and not necessarily efficient compression.

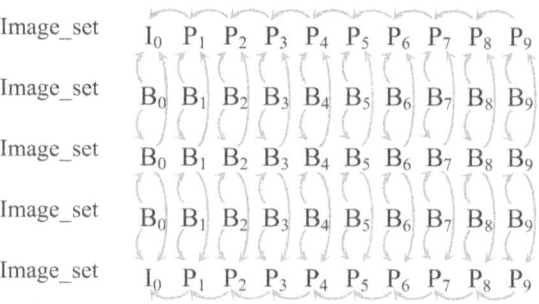

Figure 2. Typical MVC coding example – This figure shows an example compression of multiview images that is typical in the literature. The image sets (horizontal rows) are images that are taken at the same time.

In the multimedia computing and networking community, multi-camera image systems have been used to create better immersion systems. Most notably, efforts from UNC's immersive tele-conferencing system [5] and UIUC's TEEVEE project [16] use multiple cameras pointed towards a small number of object. The purpose of these projects is to capture depth from multiple cameras in order to create 3D geometries of the objects being captured. The main reason for this is that it allows the remote viewer to allow the user to control the view point in the environment being captured. The display in these systems is planar (i.e., displayed to a normal screen).[1]

2.3 Multi-view Video Coding
Several efforts have focused on compression to take advantage of redundancy in multiple camera/video systems. Perhaps the closest work to ours is the recent introduction of 3D stereoscopic Blu-Ray players with content such as Avatar [7]. The underlying standard used for this type of video is the H.264/MPEG-4 AVC standard with amendment for multi-view video coding (MVC) [3]. There are two important points here with respect to our work. First, standards specify the format for a properly formatted stream, not how to get there. Thus, algorithms are still needed to compress the image data into a stream that is useful for the application. Second, current implementations (i.e., 2 channels) use as much compression between frames temporally and between channels as possible. The reason for this is that the entire stream is decompressed when played back so partial access to data is not required. Further details of H.264/MPEG4 AVC and MVC can be found in [9][13].

As an example, a typical compression model found in MVC compression papers typically have a compression structure similar to that found in Figure 2 and in [11]. In this figure, we see that the typical MVC compression approach is to maximize compression. Image_set$_0$ and Image_set$_4$ are key frames (i.e. I-frames of traditional MPEG-1 or MPEG-2 video streams). All frames within the image sets are differentially coded.

---

[1] Capturing 3D depths and texture can, in theory enable stereoscopic display. We, however, focus on systems that are primarily meant for stereoscopic display.

Figure 3 - Stereoscopic Imaging: This figure shows a sequence of images taken using a single DSLR camera with lens spacing of 0.5 inches, similar to what we envision for stereoscopic cameras of the future.

3. A STEREOSCOPIC ARRAY MODEL

Our envisioned system consists of an array of lenses that capture image data in synchrony. Then, depending upon the viewing distance from the screen and screen size, the display system will select or create two images from the array of images that will deliver a pleasant user experience. Our "standard" stereoscopic camera will be an array of 10 image lenses, each 0.5" apart. Given that the standard stereoscopic camera will have the lens 2.5" apart, this configuration will give us, for each eye, two additional images to the left and two additional to the right. Each synchronized and captured frame is referred to as an *image_set*. In Figure 3, we have shown a set of images representing a "multi-lens" stereoscopic array. A standard stereoscopic camera with 2.5" spacing corresponds to the images 2 and 7 in Figure 3.

In the storage and compression of the multi-lens video data we need to do two things. We first need to analyze all the objects within the images to determine the disparity of features. These disparities will then be used in the retrieval process to select the best subset of images for a particular view scenario. Second, we need to compress the data. As previously mentioned, the focus of MVC compression is to typically achieve the highest compression ratio possible, typically sacrificing the ability to retrieve subsets of images.

Our envisioned storage of multi-lens stereoscopic image data will have a *thread* of images that are compressed following a typical video compression algorithm. The thread is chosen based upon the disparity calculations to match the most-likely expected viewing scenario. We note that one of the threads can be predictive coded with respect to the other but that it may affect retrieval times, particularly if the viewing scenario requires images other than from the thread. An example of such compression is shown in Figure 4, where a fixed thread is used.

To accomplish disparity calculations, a method to select important features within an image set, matching them up, and calculating the disparity (horizontal distance) between the corresponding points. Among many local feature descriptors, SIFT [8] is reported to perform best by recent work [12]. We use SIFT points as features for our stereoscopic image sets. The best candidate match for each SIFT point in one image is found by identifying its nearest neighbor in the other image. We do note that the actual best disparity to use is still an open research question, although typically 3-8% disparity is considered to be appropriate working ranges [4].

Because of the large amount of image data expected to be generated from such a system and the need to do both compression and analysis of the image sets, *we need to start understanding the basic trade-offs in terms of inter-lens compression and temporal video compression*. In particular, this paper focuses on the beginning investigations of such compression. We use exhaustive motion compensation for a variety of stereoscopic videos in order to begin understanding this trade-off without bias from heuristic search choices.

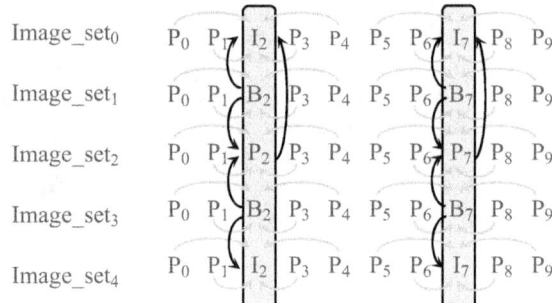

Figure 4 - Stereoscopic Threaded Compression:

4. Experimentation
4.1 Experimental Setup

To study the effect of motion estimation search window size, we have obtained three stereoscopic video sequences from a local production company using a 2-lens Panasonic AG-3DA1 Professional 3D Camera recorder. The first shot was taken from the side of a road using a fixed camera on a tripod. The sequence has two vehicles moving from a far depth towards the screen. The second was taken from a moving vehicle being driven down the road. The sequence contains significant movement as all the scenery is moving past the car. We also note that there was quite a bit of image instability due to the car movement and the camera being hand held. The final sequence is a fixed camera sequence taken at a pier. The movement in the video includes people walking relatively slowly and the ripples from the water surface. Two images from each sequence are shown in Figure 5.

For experimentation, we used the reference MPEG-2 encoder[2]. For all experiments, we chose to use the *exhaustive* search option for all compression. This was to avoid having the heuristics of motion compensation affect the results and to help us establish the upper end for how well the encoder can do for the test sequences. We also note that the popular *ffmpeg* software has long since removed the ability to do exhaustive searches in motion compensation.

Using the software, we encoded each of the three streams at 11 Mbps and 20 Mbps. The former being the average bit-rate of many Blu-ray discs, and the latter being the target bit-rate for HDTV. For each sequence, we encoded each using search ranges of (in width x height), 64 x 64, 64 x 32, 64 x 16, 64 x 8, 64 x 4, 32 x 32, 16 x 16, 8 x 8. Note the software uses these numbers as +/-; hence, 8x8 is actually +/- 8 pixels in width and +/-8 pixels in height.

---

[2] http://www.mpeg.org/MPEG/video

(a) *Cpass* sequence   (b) *Drive* sequence   (c) *Pier* sequence

Figure 5 - Stereoscopic Video Data Set: These figures show two sample left eye images from the stereoscopic video sequence that we used for the experimentation in this paper. They were captured using a Panasonic AG-3DA1 Professional 3D Video recorder.

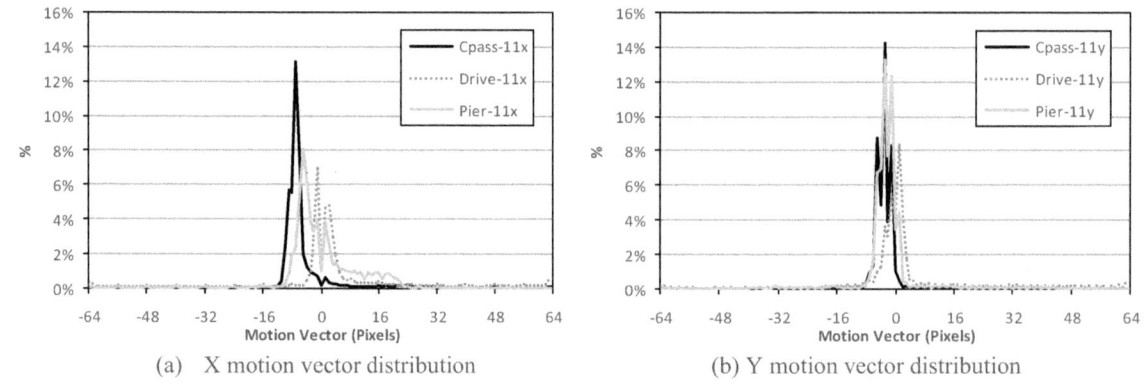

(a) X motion vector distribution   (b) Y motion vector distribution

Figure 6 – Inter-lens Predictive-coded Macroblock Distribution: These figures show the X and Y motion vector distributions for macroblocks where at least one of the components was not zero. That is, predictive coded macroblocks with no motion vector are not in the distributions

4.2 Effect of Inter-Lens Compression

In the first set of experiments, we were interested in understanding the impact of inter-lens compression. To study this, we set up the encoder so that each *left* image served as the reference frame and each *right* image was predicted from the left in the image_set. Thus, each of the left frames was encoded as an I-frame and each of the right images was predictive coded with respect to the left. For these results, we only show the 11 Mbps encodings as the 20 Mbps encoding results were nearly identical.

Table 1 shows the distribution of macroblock encodings for the right images for the 11 Mbps encodings. *Skip* and *Intra* encoding are the skipped and intra-coded macroblocks. *Zero* indicates the percentage of macroblocks with no motion vector but predictive coded coefficients. *Pred* indicates the percentage of macroblocks that were predictive coded. As shown in the table, the Pier sequence is significantly different than the other two sequences. There are many more skipped blocks as a result of the camera being fixed with a static sky, building, and pier. There are also

Movie	Skip	Intra	Zero	Pred.
Cpass	11.5%	0.22%	36.94%	51.33%
Drive	6.73%	0.79%	41.12%	51.36%
Pier	25.34%	2.17%	5.40%	67.10%

Table 1: This table shows the distribution of macroblock encodings for the inter-lens sequences

much fewer zero encoded motion vectors due to the water ripples in the bottom of the image causing residuals to be added to the compressed output stream.

For macroblocks that were encoded with a motion vector (i.e. pred), we have graphed the histogram for the distribution of the motion vector magnitude (in pixels) in Figure 6. Figure 6(a)

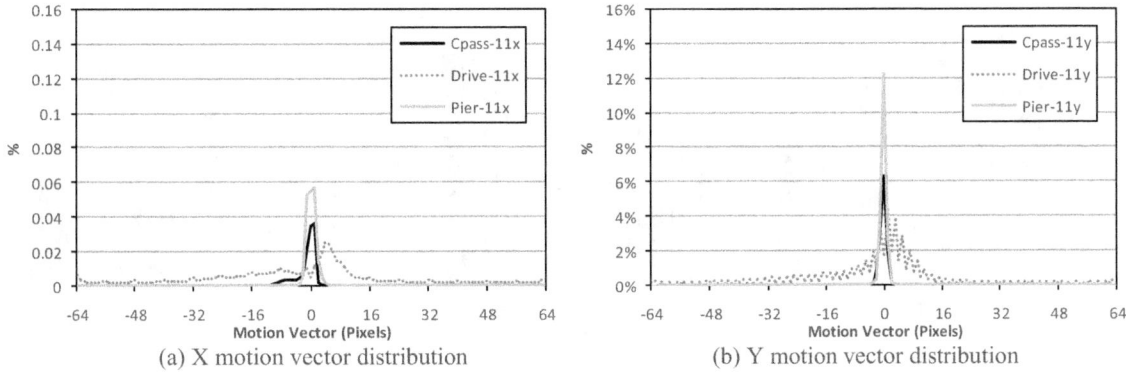

(a) X motion vector distribution (b) Y motion vector distribution

Figure 7 Temporal Predictive-coded Macroblock Distribution: These figures show the X and Y motion vector distributions for macroblocks where at least one of the components was not zero. That is, predictive coded macroblocks with no motion vector are not in the distributions

shows the distribution of the motion vector sizes in the horizontal direction. We note that there are dips around 0 because the macroblocks with no motion vector (i.e., just predictive coded) are not shown. These values are under Zero in Table 1. The *Drive* sequence is fairly evenly centered around 0. The reason for this is that there is significant movement in between frames of the video, thus, motion compensation tends to be more random as the camera shakes more or less randomly. In the *Cpass* and *Pier* sequences, the motion vectors are clearly biased in the negative horizontal direction. This suggests that the motion compensation algorithm may be useful in helping with feature tracking and disparity calculation (or vice versa). In the *y* direction, the *Cpass* and *Pier* sequences show a slight negative bias in motion vectors. We believe that this is due to the sequential search from the top to the bottom of the motion estimation range in the encoder. A candidate motion vector is only replaced if it exceeds the previous best. Thus, ties go to the motion vector that was encountered first. Finally, this suggests that there is the potential to take advantage of inter-frame compression while reducing the search range in the y direction for stereoscopic image sets.

4.3 Effect of Temporal Compression

To understand the difference between inter-lens compression and temporal compression for stereoscopic video, we have also performed temporal compression between frames. In order to make the comparison more useful to the experiments in 4.2, we compressed each of the sequences in the following way: Every frame, *i*, was compressed as an I-frame. Every *i+1* frame was then predictive coded with respect to frame *i*. Thus, every frame (except the first) is compressed as an I-frame as well as predictive coded with respect to the previous frame. For these experiments, we used only the right images to match which frames were being predicted as in the inter-lens study in section 4.2.

Table 2 shows the distribution of macroblock encodings for the predictive coded right images. Here, we see that in the temporal inter-coding case that the number of skipped macroblocks jumps dramatically for the *CPass* and *Pier*. This is somewhat expected as the camera for the reference frame is fixed. We also see that the number of predictive coded macroblocks drops for the Cpass and Pier sequences also because of the shift to zero-motion-vector macroblocks. The *Drive* sequence had similar numbers to the inter-lens compression case. We believe that this is primarily due to the instability of the camera as the car was being driven.

Movie	Skip	Intra	Zero	Pred.
Cpass	52.31%	0%	34.46%	13.22%
Drive	17.80%	2.87%	20.32%	59.01%
Pier	55.44%	0.33%	23.17%	21.07%

Table 2: This table shows the distribution of macroblock encodings for the temporal compression sequences.

Figure 7 shows the distribution of the resultant motion vectors. From Table 2, these represent 13.22%, 59.01%, and 21.07% of the macroblocks in the predictive coded frames. Compared with Figure 6, we a significant decrease in the number of macroblocks encoded. More importantly, we see very little bias in the *x* direction as we saw in the inter-lens compression case. One peculiar issue that arose was in the distribution of the *y* motion vectors for the *Drive* sequence. The distribution was highly jagged. We believe that this might be due to the video stabilization that is built into the video camera.

4.4 Effect of Constrained Search

In this section, we explore the efficacy of reducing the vertical search range in order to improve compression performance. The underlying premise is that given a constant number of compute cycles that it might be more useful to search horizontally rather in the typical unbiased search of today's encoders. For these experiments, we used the same compression encoding as described in Sections 4.2 and 4.3. Instead of using just the 64x64 exhaustive search, we added the search window sizes of 64x2, 64x4, 64x8, 64x16, and 64x32.

In Figure 8, we have grouped the results by sequence and by maximum vertical search range. We note that the actual search range is 2 times the number specified. We have grouped the results by sequence name, bit rate of encoding, and then the search range. As expected in all cases, the 20 Mbps encodings have higher PSNR results than the 11 Mbps encodings.

Surprisingly, there is very little difference in terms of resulting PSNR regardless of the search range used. In all cases using 64x2 results in the lowest PSNR as one might expect. However, the

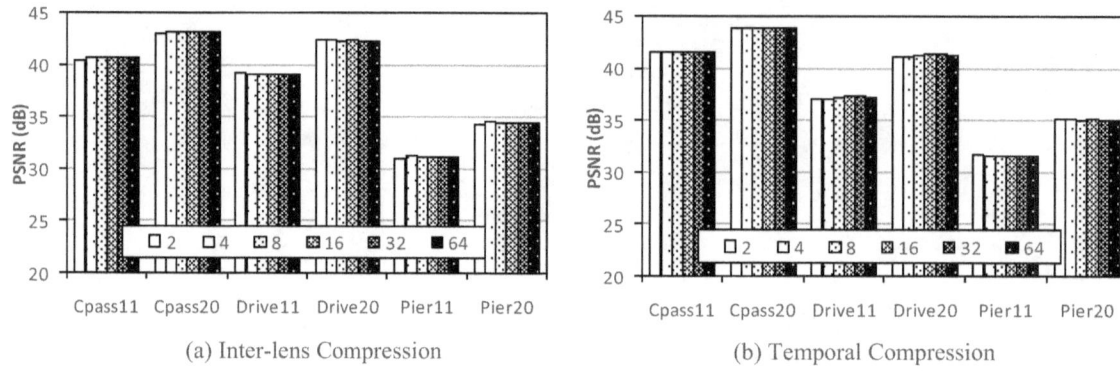

Figure 8 PSNR Results: These figures show PSNR results for the Inter-lens (a) and Temporal (b) compression as described in Section 4.2 and 4.3, respectively. Each column represents a maximum vertical search range of 2, 4, 8, 16, 32, and 64.

difference is not that large. In comparing inter-lens and temporal compression, we see that as the *Cpass* and *Pier* videos all have better compression under temporal compression than inter-lens compression. This suggests that for sequences that are highly unstable in terms of camera motion that having the fixed relation between the stereoscopic lenses provides better reference images.

4.5 Discussion / Future Work / Conclusion

We have shown through exhaustive (+/- 64 pixel) motion compensation for a number of sequences that temporal compression using standard two-lens spacing has higher coherence than the inter-lens coherence, except for highly unstable sequences. We have also found that for the HDTV sequences that we have obtained that the vertical search range for relatively static shots can be greatly reduced without affecting the image quality while improving motion compensation speed.

We are currently in the process of building a multi-lens array from point-of-view cameras. While inter-lens compression, in general, provides less coherence between images than temporal coherence, we will revisit this as lenses are added at finer granularity, which presumably, will increase the inter-lens coherence.

Our results also show a deficiency in the selection of the input sequences. The *Cpass* and *Pier* sequences are very similar in that they have fixed cameras. In the future, we hope to obtain a wider selection of input sequences to provide to the community, including a panning stereoscopic set. We do note, however, that panning shots are somewhat harder to shoot in order to maintain stereoscopic cinematography rules (e.g., not having an object along the edge of the image.

Future work will also entail moving toward H.264 encoding to add quarter pixel search to the half and full pel search in the MPEG-2 encoder.

5. REFERENCES

[1] Wu-chi Feng, Feng Liu, Yuzhen Niu, Scott Price, "Systems Support for Stereoscopic Video Compression", in *Proc. of NOSSDAV 2011*, Vancouver, BC, pp. 99-104, June 2011.

[2] M. Guttmann, L. Wolf, D. Cohen-Or, "Semiautomatic Stereo Extraction from Video Footage", in *Proc. of the IEEE Inter. Conf. on Computer Vision*, pages 136 – 142, 2009.

[3] Y. He, J. Ostermann, M. Tanimoto, A. Smolic, "Introduction to the Special Section on Multiview Video Coding", in *IEEE Transactions on Circuits and Systems for Video Technology*, Vol. 17, No. 11, pp. 1433-1435, Nov. 2007.

[4] http://apophysisrevealed.com/apo3dblog/2009/07/192

[5] San-Uok Kum, K. Mayer-Patel, H. Fuchs, "Real-Time Compression for Dynamic 3D Environments", in *Proceedings of ACM Multimedia*, 2003.

[6] M. Lang, A. Hornung, O.Wang, S. Poulakos, A. Smolic, M. Gross, "Nonlinear Disparity Mapping for Stereoscopic 3D", *ACM Transaction on. Graphics*, 29(4), 2010.

[7] R. Lawler, "Blue-ray 3D Specifications Finalized, Your PS3 is Ready", Dec. 17, 2009, From: http://www.engadget.com/2009/12/17/blu-ray-3d-specifications-finalized-your-ps3-is-ready/

[8] D. Lowe, "Distinctive Image Features from Scale-Invariant Keypoints", International Journal of Computer Vision, Vol. 60, No. 2, pp 91-110, 2004.

[9] D. Marpe, T. Wiegand, G.J. Sullivan, "The H.264/MPEG4 Advanced Video Coding Standard and its Applications", *IEEE Communications*, pp. 134-143, August 2006.

[10] B. Mendiburu, 3D Movie Making: Stereoscopic Digital Cinema from Script to Screen, Focal Press, 2009.

[11] P. Merkle, A. Smolicc, K. Muller, T. Wiegand, "Efficient Prediction Structures for Multi-view Video Coding", *IEEE Transactions on Circuits and Systems for Video Technology*, Vol. 17, No. 11, November, 2007.

[12] K. Mikolajczyk, C. Schmid, "A Performance Evaluation of Local Descriptors", *IEEE Trans. on Pattern Analysis and Machine Intelligence,* Vol. 27, No. 10, pp. 1615-1630, 2005.

[13] MPEG: "Introduction to Multiview Video Coding", ISO/IEC JTC 1/SC 29/WG 11 N9580, Edited by A. Smolic, Jan. 2008.

[14] D. Sanchez, "Are 3D Movies, TV Bad For Your Eyes?", February 24, 2010, Retrieved from KGO News: http://abclocal.go.com/kgo/story?id=7278834

[15] C. Wang, A. A. Sawchuk, "Disparity Manipulation for Stereo Images and Video, in Proc. *SPIE*, Vol. 6803, pages E1– E12, 2008.

[16] Z. Yang, Y. Cui, B. Yu, J. Liang, K. Nahrstedt, S. H. Jung, R. Bajcsy, "TEEVE: The Next Generation Architecture for Tele-Immersive Environments", in *Proceedings of the 7th IEEE International Symposium on* Multimedia *(ISM'05),* Irvine, CA, 2005.

Authors Index

Ahmad, Shakeel 65
Akhshabi, Saamer 9
Al-Arnaout, Zakwan 39
Anantakrishnan, Lakshmi 9
Beck, Andre 21
Begen, Ali C. 1, 9
Benno, Steven A. 21
Biersack, Ernst 27
Brecht, Tim 15
Buyukkaya, Eliya 65
Chen, Fei 51
Dai, Yafei 33
Diot, Christophe 27
Dovrolis, Constantine 9
Eager, Derek 15
Esteban, Jairo 21
Feng, Wu-chi 57, 101
Frean, Marcus 39
Fu, Qiang 39
Guntur, Ravindra 59
Guo, Yang 21
Hamzaoui, Raouf 65
Hilt, Volker 21
Hsu, Cheng-Hsin 71
Huang, Yan 33
Huguenin, Kévin 77
Issaris, Panagiotis 45
Jiang, Hongbo 95
Kermarrec, Anne-Marie 77
Kim, Hyojun 3
Kloudas, Konstantinos 77
Lamotte, Wim 45
Li, Haitao 83
Li, Zhenhua 33
Lin, Ting-An 71
Liu, Feng 101
Liu, Gang 33
Liu, Jiangchuan 51, 83, 95
Liu, Xin 71
Ma, Haiyang 89
Ma, Xiaoqiang 95
Ngai, Edith Cheuk-Han. 51
Nicoara, Angela 71
Ooi, Wei Tsang 59
Quax, Peter 45
Ramachandran, Umakishore 3
Reina, Giuseppe 27
Rimac, Ivica 21
Ryu, Moonkyung 3
Seo, Beomjoo 89
Simon, Gwendal 65
Summers, Jim 15
Taïani, François 77
Vanmontfort, Wouter 45
Wang, Fuchen 33
Wang, Guanfeng 89
Wang, Haiyang 83
Wang, Yichuan 71
Wong, Bernard 15
Xu, Ke 83
Zhang, Lei 95
Zhang, Zhi-Li 33
Zhao, Yuan 51, 95
Zhou, Fen 65
Zimmermann, Roger 89

www.ingramcontent.com/pod-product-compliance
Lightning Source LLC
Chambersburg PA
CBHW082052230426
43670CB00016B/2866